TALES OF THE
CPR

THE WORLD'S GREATEST TRAVEL SYSTEM

Also called the World's Greatest Transportation System as advertised on this van parked in Trafalgar Square, London, England, the CPR did more to promote Canada abroad than the federal government did in the years before the First World War.

A.37246

TALES OF THE
CPR

David Laurence Jones

Cover art by Larry Stilwell
Front cover images: CPR locomotive 209 from "The Race Was On!";
Sir William Van Horne; CPR shipping poster, circa 1906
Back cover photo: Chateau Frontenac, Quebec City, CPR Archives NS.21216
Interior and cover design by John Luckhurst / GDL
Scans by David Hancock, CPR, and St. Solo Computer Graphics

The publisher gratefully acknowledges the support of The Canada Council for the Arts and the Department of Canadian Heritage. We acknowledge the financial support of the Government of Canada through the Book Publishing Industry Development Program for our publishing activities.

Printed in Canada by Friesens.

02 03 04 05 06 / 5 4 3 2 1

First published in the United States in 2003.

National Library of Canada Cataloguing in Publication Data

Jones, David L., 1953-
Tales of the CPR

Includes index.
ISBN 1-894856-10-4 (bound).—ISBN 1-894856-05-8 (pbk.)

1. Canadian Pacific Railway Company—History—Anecdotes. I. Title.
HE2810.C2J66 2002 385'.0971 C2002-910775-X

Fifth House Ltd.
A Fitzhenry & Whiteside Company
1511-1800 4 St. SW
Calgary, Alberta, Canada
T2S 2S5

In the United States:
Fitzhenry & Whiteside
121 Harvard Avenue, Suite 2
Allston, MA
02134

1-800-387-9776
www.fitzhenry.ca

Table of Contents

For Erika and Emma

HAVING A WINNIPEG BEACH PARTY

Clean coveralls and a few dozen Union Jacks were all a good locomotive engineer needed when the annual employee picnic special steamed down to Winnipeg Beach.

A.37250

Foreword

Tales of the CPR is not just another book about CPR history, and believe me, there are lots—more than one hundred that I am aware of, on every conceivable facet of CPR's 120-year existence. In fact, David Laurence Jones (or just Dave, as friends know him) isn't even the only David Jones to write about CPR history. There is another one, coincidentally also in Calgary—the new epicentre of the CPR.

But this is a different type of history book. *Tales of the CPR* is a series of anecdotes covering nearly every aspect of the company that once "spanned the world." The stories are fun, informative, and illustrated, too. No matter how much CPR history you already know, you'll learn something new. I learned plenty and enjoyed myself while I did.

Tales of the CPR is written by a man who knows his stuff. Dave spent the first half of his career in CPR's archives and the second half in internal communications for the company. As a result, not only does he have a lot of stories to tell, but he also tells them well. Dave writes in crisp, interesting, bite-size morsels, so you don't have to pick up this book and read it all at once, although, like eating potato chips, once you start you may not be able to stop.

Dave and I first worked together three decades ago in the vaults of Windsor Station. At that time he still thought of himself as a draftsman in search of a career in architecture. Once when we were still in our teens, I asked Dave if he ever thought of the CPR as a career choice. He scoffed at my suggestion, but here he is thirty years into his "non-career." Dave changed his plans because of his love for history. Shelving his architectural aspirations, he ended up in many of the same Canadian history night courses as I did, at Montreal's Concordia University. Even then, he had a good handle on the subject, and a clear, no-nonsense writing style. On the rare occasion when one of us missed a lecture, the other would be expected to take notes. Mine were long, rambling, run-on scrawls spread over many pages. His were one-page, point-form summaries, with nothing but the facts—and all the facts!

At the end of the summer of 1973, Dave became administrative assistant to CPR archivist (and soon to be nominated historian) Omer Lavallée. Through his mentoring and a great deal of osmosis, Omer gave Dave a growing taste for CPR history. Whereas others in the archives, myself included, had our little specialty niches, Dave savoured it all, although I do recall his special fondness for station and hotel architecture, and a soft spot for those CPR steamships.

I well remember the defining moment in Dave's coming-of-age as a CPR historian. It happened at the end of one of those summers in the late 1970s when I was working in the archives. The story in this book called "Ready-made for Western Settlement" brought it back to me in a flash: the day Dave stumped the great oracle!

At that time staff members handled research in the archives in one of two ways. You could walk up the stairs to the stacks in the small tower, pull out big dusty ledgers, thumb through them, jot down some file numbers, walk down three flights of stairs, take the elevator down four more floors, walk down an additional flight of stairs to the basement, navigate some long hallways, go down a ramp, and walk past the dingy garbage vault and into the air-conditioned confines of archives Vault-17. After you found the files, you then made the long trek in reverse.

You could do that. Or, you could ask the oracle, Omer Lavallée—he who knew all.

Cecil Halsey, who looked after archival images, was looking for a photo of a CPR ready-made farm. Cecil went for research option number two. "Hey, Omer … know anything about ready-made farms?" he called out. Cecil's desk was right outside Omer's office, so he didn't even have to get up.

"Huh? Ready-made farms? Never heard of 'em," came the reply. If the oracle hadn't heard of them, then they probably never existed.

But two cubicles away from Cecil sat David Jones, and Omer's clear, resonant voice easily carried the short distance. Mere moments later, Dave strolled into Omer's office with Hedges' *Building the Canadian West* cracked open to page 240. "Uh, here Omer," he said with surprisingly little trepidation. "Here's the part about CPR's ready-made farms."

In a loud, gruff voice, and ignoring Dave standing right there between them, Omer replied to Cecil, "Well, Jones seems to know all about it. Ask him!" At that moment, even though his lambskin from Concordia University was still a few semesters down the road, David Laurence Jones became a historian.

Now he has gathered, illustrated, re-edited, and re-spun the historical vignettes he's written over the years into one entertaining and informative book. Here it is for all you history buffs, rail enthusiasts, CPR fans, and casual readers alike: *Tales of the CPR.*

Jonathan B. Hanna
Corporate Historian
Canadian Pacific Railway

17 June 2002

Acknowledgements

For the first half of my thirty-year career with the CPR, I was immersed in the details of historical preservation, research, and display that were the mainstay of life in the railway's corporate archives. From silk-screener of vintage posters to assistant archivist of documents, I spent many days in the solitude of the storage vaults beneath the concourse in Montreal's Windsor Station, organizing various records groups and delving ever deeper into the rich heritage of a company whose growth paralleled, intertwined, and more often than not complemented that of Canada and the world.

Like most researchers, I found distractions in every corner—an intriguing piece of executive correspondence, an enigmatic historical reference, an uncaptioned photograph of mysterious goings-on. Hastily photocopying the interesting tidbits before filing away the originals, I slowly acquired a wealth of anecdotal material, some of it merely whimsical, some historically significant, and most of it seeing the light of day for the first time in many decades.

With my move to the communications and public affairs side of the business, I had the opportunity to revisit some of those files and to consider the vast social contributions of "The World's Greatest Travel System," as the CPR once styled itself. Many of the stories in *Tales of the CPR* have appeared before in different guises, from heritage pieces in the company newspaper, to promotional pamphlets and brochures, historical society bulletins, and trade journals. Most are derived solely from primary sources, particularly the executive correspondence of company presidents William Van Horne and Thomas Shaughnessy.

Some of the tales were inspired by published works, but in each case I have discovered new facts or insights from original materials, which I have woven into the telling. Among these are "An Enterprising Life" and "A Taste of the American Wild West," from Pierre Berton's *The National Dream* and *The Last Spike*; "An Elaborate Deception," from Donald B. Smith's *Chief Buffalo Child Long Lance: The Glorious Imposter*; and "Across the Pacific to the Orient," from Ronald A. Keith's wonderful narrative *Bush Pilot with a Briefcase: The Happy-go-lucky Story of Grant McConachie*. The "facts" for "Van Horne's Overcoat" were first related in the *Pembroke Standard* in 1915. Since then the story has been retold and elaborated upon by several writers, and I too have added details gleaned from existing records and spun the tale once again.

Many people—mostly CPR friends and acquaintances—have contributed a fact here, a reference there, and to them I am grateful. I would, however, like to thank three individuals in particular who have been my mentors over the years, and to whom I am most indebted for their guidance and support: the late Omer Lavallée, former corporate archivist and historian, the font of all arcane railway knowledge and an inspiration to all those who worked for him; Ralph Wilson, manager of employee communications, who encouraged me to write about CPR's history, and always took the time to lighten what he likes to call my "Dickensian prose"; and Barb Kuester, current director of internal communications, who is as passionate about her work as she is capable.

For help with the preparation of this edition, I thank the people at Fifth House; the very knowledgeable and helpful folks at CPR Archives—Bob Kennell, Jo-Anne Colby, and David Hancock; my friends and colleagues in CPR's creative services group—artist Larry Stilwell and photographer Rick Robinson; and long-time friend and nitpicker for accuracy, CPR corporate historian Jonathan Hanna, who has graciously reviewed the manuscript and provided a foreword.

All photos are courtesy of Canadian Pacific Railway Archives unless otherwise marked.

Preface

For my sisters and me, the CPR was an integral part of growing up. Our dad was a long-time railway man, one of our aunts worked in a CPR office, and our grandparents on the Jones' side of the family had emigrated from England to Canada in 1912 aboard the SS *Virginian*, a steamship in the Allan Line that merged with the CPR fleet a few years later to form Canadian Pacific Ocean Services. But we didn't think about that much when we were kids. To us, what the CPR represented more than anything were those summer trips from our home in Calgary to our grandmother's farm in Ontario's Glengarry County.

Every detail of those train journeys was magic. From the cozy confines of our bedroom compartment in a stainless steel dome car, we would stroll to the dining car. There the sparking silverware and ultra-white linens found favour with our mum, while we poked each other and laughed at the silly antics of the cartoon beavers that played across the cover of our special children's menus.

As the scenery rolled by, we played cards, explored the lounges, read books, and walked through the coaches, where we would surreptitiously peek through berth curtains and stop to chat with anyone with a friendly face. All our activities took

Royalty Rode the Rails
A royal tour always called for plenty of banners and bunting, and none more so than the 1939 tour of King George VI and Queen Elizabeth.

place under the watchful eyes of the good-natured porters who controlled the onboard schedule with clockwork efficiency. At every station stop, hidden stairs would be folded down and step boxes whisked into place. Soon we would be peering into the cavernous bunkers beneath the railcars, where huge blocks of ice were loaded to provide air conditioning on board. As we weaved our way through the crowds gathered on the platform, we dodged baggage carts with wheels as tall as we were.

At night, the darkness was punctuated by sporadic flashes of light as we passed through small towns along the way, and we would sit up in our bunk beds to lift the window blinds and look out at the eerie stillness of the flat prairie landscape or the stark, jagged rock formations that characterize the route along the north shore of Lake Superior.

It was not until many years later, after I had begun working for the railway, that I heard the story about the poor, unfortunate farmer who blamed all his woes on the institution with the long arms. Burdened by debt, outraged by freight rates, left by his wife, abandoned by his neighbours, and bitten by his dog, he stood in the midst of his hail-damaged crops and, shaking his fist at the sky, muttered "God damn the CPR."

It's a measure of the powerful influence the CPR has had on the lives of Canadians and, indeed, on many abroad, that such myths have arisen. The railway has touched the lives of so many, in so many ways. With the exception of the federal government, CPR has probably done more than any other institution to promote arts and culture in Canada. It played a key role in populating the Canadian west, and its landmark stations and hotels have defined the country throughout the world. For decades, the railway was the only means of accessing remote locations. It shuttled soldiers and supplies to war and ferried the well-to-do around the world on luxury cruises. The railway offered stylish and luxurious accommodation in the midst of some of the world's most spectacular scenic wonders. And for many years, whether news was bad or good, chances are it was delivered by a CPR telegraph messenger, all spit-and-polish and youthful enthusiasm.

Many today think of the railway as an industry on the wane, a thing of the past superseded by automobiles, airplanes, and the ubiquitous trucks that crowd our highways and move the lion's share of freight in North America. In truth, however, railways have as much or more to offer than ever before in terms of the environment, efficiency, and cost-effectiveness. But more than anything else, the railway is about people, and railroaders, on the whole, are wonderful people—friendly, fiercely independent, and as often as not, quirky and eccentric. Colourful people. And every day their ingenuity and perseverance are providing the fodder for new tales, yet to be told. God bless the CPR.

UNTIL WE MEET AGAIN
Stokers like these, deep in the bowels of the *Empress of Ireland*, never made it topside when the liner met its fate in the foggy St. Lawrence Valley.
A.37252

6808

Chapter One

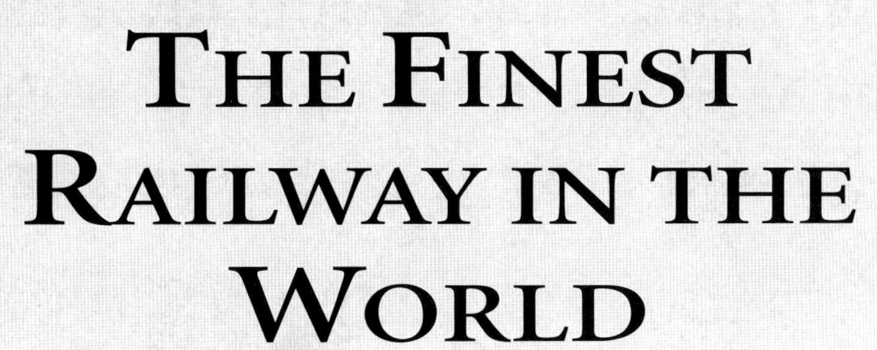

The Finest Railway in the World

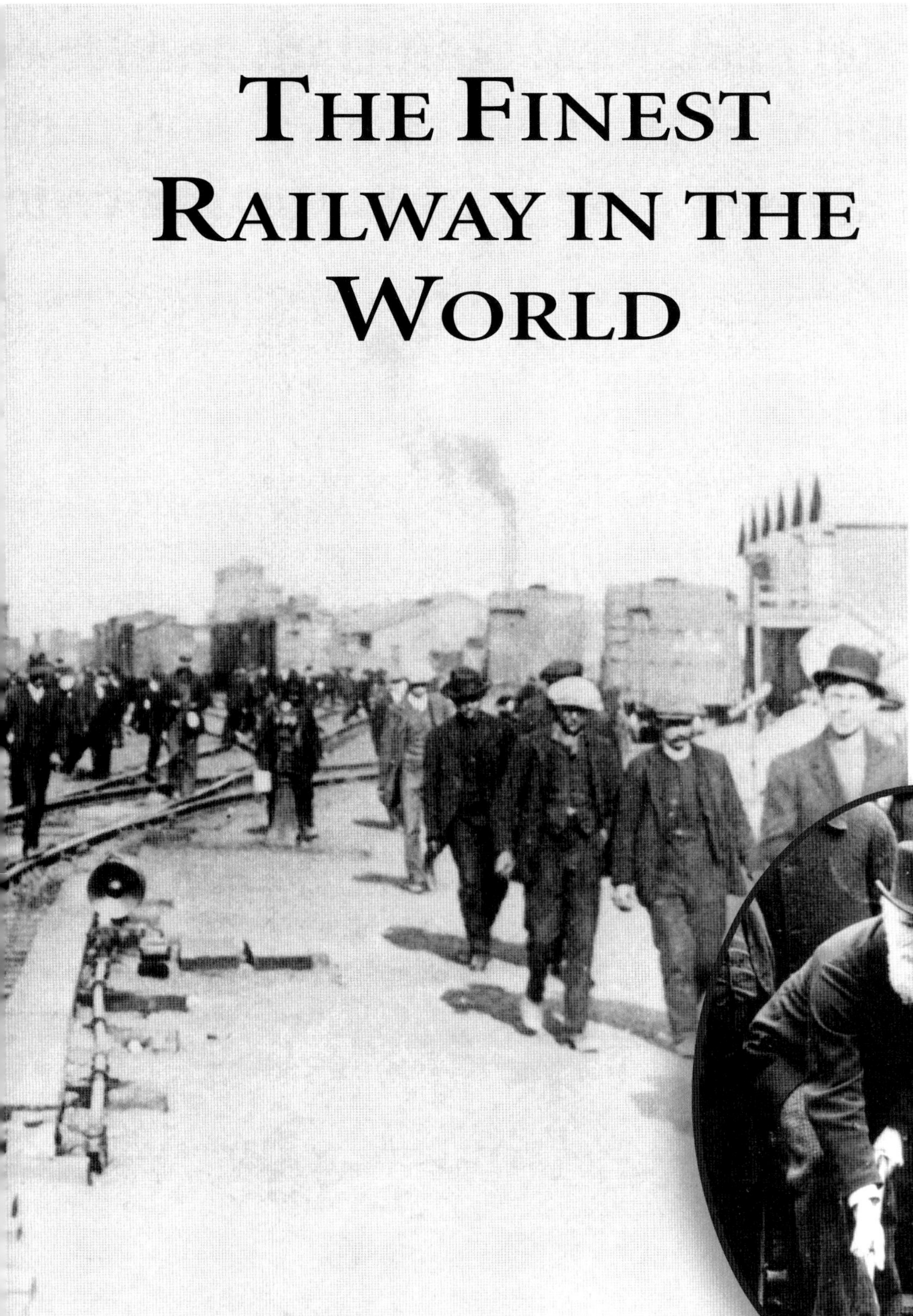

From Cowtown to Now Town
When the Ogden whistle blew to end the day shift, a small army of railway men went home to the neighbouring community.
A.37257

An Enterprising Life
Young Edward Mallandaine hopped a construction train to Craigellachie to witness the driving of the Last Spike.
NS.1960

From Cowtown to Now Town

Stepping down from a varnished coach on CPR's *Imperial Limited* to the platform of the sandstone station, one could hardly recall the bare prairie vistas that had filled the car windows for most of the previous day. It was the summer of 1899 and the frontier community of Calgary had taken on a look of solidity. Where hastily assembled structures had once maintained a tenuous foothold, elegant sandstone edifices now graced the bustling streets.

Not far to the east came the clatter of shunting railcars in the new freight yard dubbed the West Calgary Shop, but known as the Mountain Shop to those who prepared the trains for the assault on the great grey sentinels that dominated the western skyline. And if hungry travellers were to cock their heads just right, they could discern the faint but unmistakable ring of Mrs. Bowden's dinner bell.

When the CPR had arrived in 1883, Calgary was designated as a way station, with nothing more than the most basic railway facilities.

When the CPR had arrived in 1883, Calgary was designated as a way station, with nothing more than the most basic railway facilities. Though the town was on the Calgary Section, the division points at either end of the section, where the railway had constructed more extensive yards, were at Gleichen to the east and Canmore to the west. But all that had changed in 1898, when it became impossible to ignore Calgary's importance as a centre for the western livestock industry and as the junction point between the CPR and the recently completed Calgary & Edmonton Railway.

The railway's Crowfoot Section, named for the respected chief of the Blackfoot, was extended from Medicine Hat to Calgary, relegating Gleichen to secondary status, whereas the Calgary Section continued on to Laggan (now Lake Louise), leaving Canmore to the same fate.

Passengers to Calgary now alit at a thriving divisional point, complete with the extensive freight yards that its new designation called for, along with the sure sign of prosperity: a brand new railway roundhouse and turntable. And right there, alongside the sandstone station, was Mrs. Bowden's dining hall.

At the dawn of the twentieth century, the CPR had much to be thankful for, but there was one burning issue yet to be resolved—land grants. In agreements between the railway and the federal government, land grants had been restricted to areas deemed "fairly fit for settlement," a stipulation that was becoming increasingly difficult to fulfill in the prairie sections of Palliser's Triangle. The Triangle, taking in most of the lands in southern Alberta and extending into Saskatchewan, had been identified in the 1860s by a group of surveyors led by John Palliser as a semi-arid region, with questionable prospects for agricultural exploitation.

Two things saved the day: a large influx of American immigrants, anxious to take advantage of available lands in the Last Best West; and the introduction of irrigation to the area. The centralization of CPR's irrigation efforts in Calgary, in 1903, ensured the continued availability of land suitable for settlement. The prosperity of many southern Alberta towns is a direct result of the decisions that were issued from the railway's irrigation office.

Three blocks of land east of Calgary were divided into the Western, Central, and Eastern irrigation districts, each of which encompassed about 404,860 hectares of land. To irrigate some 161,945 hectares in the Western District, water was diverted from the Bow River at Calgary and carried southeast along a twenty-seven-kilometre canal to a natural reservoir. From there, the reservoir water was fed as required to a system of canals hundreds of kilometres in combined length.

By the end of the decade, with more than two-thirds of the land in the Western District sold, the much more ambitious irrigation plan for the Eastern Section was implemented. It, too, would ultimately bring life-giving water to an enormous area of farmland.

"Ours is neither a land nor a water-selling scheme," said a railway circular. "The CPR is spending millions of dollars on this project purely and simply to build up the most prosperous agricultural community in America. This sounds like philanthropy but it isn't. The railway wants a prosperous community in order to create the greatest possible volume of traffic."

Meanwhile in Calgary, the CPR was able to control townsite development by the imposition of strict guidelines for building in the various neighbourhoods laid out by railway draftsmen. To the southwest were the residential districts of Sunalta and the more exclusive Mount Royal. On the bluffs above the north bank of the Bow River was the working-class suburb of Bridgeland. In the southeast quadrant, a huge industrial complex would soon emerge that would solidify Calgary's position as *the* railway centre west of Winnipeg.

By 1907, the CPR was the largest employer in Calgary. Hundreds of cars were switched every day in the yard.

By 1907, the CPR was the largest employer in Calgary. Hundreds of cars were switched every day in the yard. Traffic was increasing with the new settlers who poured in from the United States and eastern Canada. That same year, in a letter to second vice-president William Whyte, CPR president Thomas Shaughnessy approved yet another new station to reflect Calgary's rising prospects: "There can be little doubt that Calgary itself will continue to grow and that a building which at this time would appear almost extravagant will in the not so remote future be quite warranted by the traffic." Thus, Shaughnessy brought in the company's own architect, Walter S. Painter, to design the four-storey building, with two wings half that height, that would serve as the railway's Calgary headquarters until 1966 when it was torn down to make way for the Husky Tower and Palliser Square complex.

By this time, it was clear that a major new investment in yard facilities and repair shops would be required between Vancouver and Winnipeg. Several communities in southern Alberta vied for the honour and the considerable revenue that such a development would inevitably bring. For many reasons Calgary was the obvious choice, but Medicine Hat held one key advantage: the presence, in large quantities, of inexpensive, easily extracted natural gas. By 1910, however, with the completion of the Calgary Power Company's massive Horseshoe Falls project, power was no longer an issue and Calgary was chosen.

At the eleventh hour, the town of Bassano tried one last gambit. In a letter to

Shaughnessy, the secretary of the town's board of trade was willing to offer "freedom of taxation for 25 years, together with any other reasonable concession." He went on to say, in his best marketing appeal, that: "We guarantee this location will be the best in the west by a dam site." While it was true that Bassano had the "dam site" (it was at the centre of the CPR's Eastern District irrigation project), the decision to locate in Calgary was, nevertheless, final.

In 1911, work began on a new yard and engine terminal at Alyth in southeastern Calgary, on land now occupied by the Alyth Diesel Shop. When a new thirty-six-stall roundhouse was completed, the older facilities at the West Calgary Shop and the Calgary & Edmonton Shop were dismantled.

The following spring, ground was broken for the 5.25-hectare Ogden Shops, named for the railway's vice-president of finance and accounting, and the oldest living officer of the company at the time. The firm of Westinghouse, Church, Kerr Company of New York and Montreal was retained to build the vast industrial complex, under the supervision of CPR civil engineers J. G. Sullivan and N. E. Brooks. A mere eleven and one-half months were required to erect the estimated 2,041,200 kilograms of steel that went into the original construction.

The shops brought a new source of employment to the city, along with skilled labourers from as far away as Montreal's Angus Shops, a trend that has continued into the 1990s. On 31 December 1912, the Calgary Municipal Railway inaugurated its new street railway line to Ogden, offering free rides to the construction site and allowing workers to scout out the subdivisions that would soon see an incredible boom in housing construction. Calgary's population soon surpassed fifty thousand.

The new shops alone were enough to expand both the prestige of the CPR and its power to shape Calgary's future, but more plans were in the works. The CPR's Department of Natural Resources was set up in Calgary in 1912, primarily to develop coal mines on railway lands near Banff and Lethbridge in Alberta and in the Kootenay district of British Columbia. And just west of the CPR station and gardens, a new hotel was rising that would, in Shaughnessy's words, "be almost an essential link in our mountain hotel system, if we are to avoid difficulties about accommodation in the hotels and on the trains that we experienced last season."

The Palliser Hotel, built to the drawing specifications of architect William Maxwell, was opened in May 1914. The hotel was an immediate success, due in part to the decorative scheme created by Kate Reed, wife of CPR's manager-in-chief of hotels, Hayter Reed, whose treatments of the public rooms were said to render the place quite "homey."

In a wildly effusive letter to Shaughnessy from a group of prominent Calgary businessmen, among them the cattle and meat processing baron Pat Burns, the prevailing mood was put to words: "We can hardly realize we are in a Calgary hotel," the message gushed. "The magnificence and splendor of the Palliser is beyond the wildest dreams of the ever-optimists who came here thirty years ago."

Indeed, it had been thirty years of growth and, for the most part, prosperity for both Calgary and the CPR. It was just the beginning.

A Potent Symbol of National Pride

The introduction of the streamlined, all stainless-steel, dieselized transcontinental train *The Canadian*, on 24 April 1955, gave the CPR the world's longest dome-car operation over the world's longest diesel-haul route—Montreal and Toronto to Vancouver. The company had invested forty million dollars in a dramatic attempt to lure back some of the travelling public that had forsaken rail for the speed of the airplane and the convenience of the family car.

The 173 new railway passenger cars were not only attractive, they incorporated every modern convenience that the manufacturer, the Budd Company of Philadelphia, could provide. The latest in wheel assemblies, couplers, disc brakes, and mechanical air conditioning allowed the CPR to cut sixteen hours from the transcontinental train schedule. *The Canadian* could make the trip between Montreal and Vancouver in seventy-one hours and ten minutes, so a round trip was only a few hours longer than a one-way trip on the first transcontinental *Pacific Express*, in 1886.

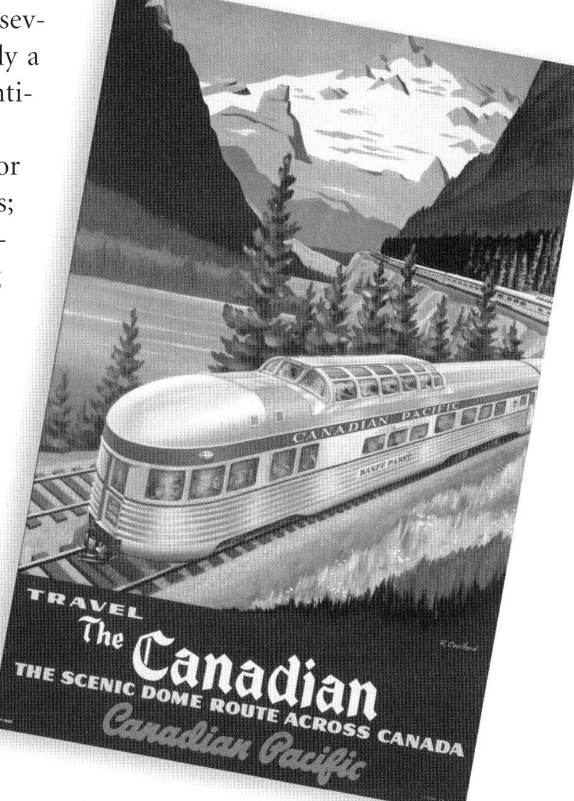

A Potent Symbol of National Pride
In the twilight years of passenger service, CPR offered the finest accommodation on the world's most scenic rail route. A.6118

The Canadian provided the finest in accommodation for the discriminating traveller: tourist cars; deluxe coaches; coffee shops for meals or snacks; modern "electrically-kitchened" dining cars; spacious new sleeping cars offering open sections, roomettes, double bedrooms, compartments, and drawing rooms; and the newest thing on Canadian rails—"scenic-dome" cars.

From the introduction of the new service, dome cars figured prominently in the company's advertising and were immediately, and from then on, identified in the public mind with the CPR's passenger operations. Similar cars had been introduced in the United States throughout the 1940s. General Motors introduced what it called the *Train of Tomorrow*, with "Astra Domes," built by the Pullman-Standard Car Manufacturing Company, of Chicago. The Missouri Pacific had "Planetarium-Dome" coaches on its famed *Eagle* trains, operating in the American west and southwest. The B&O's (Baltimore & Ohio Railroad) *Columbian* featured "Strata-Domes"; the Milwaukee Road's *Olympian Hiawatha* ran "Skytop Lounges"; and the Burlington, Rio Grande and Western Pacific Railroads offered their "Vista-Domes" on the *California Zephyr* between Chicago, Denver, Salt Lake City, and San Francisco.

To draw attention to the thoroughly modern appearance of the ribbed stainless-steel cars and the bright, new diesel locomotives, Gyrolites were installed on top of the lead engines. As *The Canadian* moved along the track, these specially designed spotlights traced figure eights in the night sky with concentrated laserlike beams.

The Canadian operated daily, westward from Montreal and Toronto, with the two sections linking up in Sudbury, Ontario, for the remainder of the journey to Vancouver. For the inaugural run, the three terminals were festooned with decorations, in a manner normally reserved for royal tours. Stations along the route hung out welcome signs, and arrangements were made for the stereotypical red-coated Mountie to be on hand at Montreal, Winnipeg, Calgary, Banff, Revelstoke, and Vancouver, for those who wished to be photographed with new and old national icons. Ottawa was the only station where no fuss was made. Canadian National was celebrating the inauguration of its own new transcontinental, *The Supercontinental*, in the nation's capital that same day.

Along for the ride with reporters from virtually all the Canadian dailies came representatives from *Railway Age*, *British United Press*, *Financial Times*, *Canadian Business*, *Wall Street Journal*, *New York Times*, *Chicago Tribune*, Federal News Photos, and *Canadian Transportation*. Shelley Films, representing Fox Movietone, had a cameraman on board, as did the CBC. And some CPR publicity man, obviously intent on pleasing the public, made sure that Hockey Night in Canada's Danny Gallivan was around to call the shots.

Quebec premier Maurice Duplessis had been invited to launch *The Canadian* in Montreal, but in his unavoidable absence, city mayor Jean Drapeau was more than willing to don an engineer's cap and mug for the photographers with N. R. "Buck" Crump, then a CPR vice-president and the driving force behind the new passenger service.

More than one hundred department stores across North America participated in an international promotion organized by *Vogue* magazine, featuring styles inspired by the continent's newest train. Windows in such Montreal stores as Eatons, Simpsons, Morgans, and Holt Renfrew featured the "Canadian look," along with photographs and glowing write-ups spotlighting the CPR's newest equipment.

Travelling on *The Canadian* meant luxury, relaxation, and most of all, spectacular scenery, and the slogans devised for the inaugural run reflected this ideal. The brochures said: "Canadian Pacific for top views and stopovers," "Sight-see Canada on Canadian Pacific trains," "Let yourself go—see big, beautiful Canada in armchair ease," and "Canada passes your train window." But my personal favourite, and one that you gotta love, still does it for me: "Glide by Canadian Pacific train through glorious Canada—land of vacations unlimited."

A Link to the Far East

For the first fifteen years of passenger operations on the Canadian Pacific Railway, the westbound and eastbound transcontinental trains were known simply as the *Pacific Express* and the *Atlantic Express.* Whereas the *Pacific Express* was appropriately named—the terminus being at Vancouver on Burrard Inlet—the *Atlantic Express* was somewhat of a misnomer, as it came only as far east as Montreal, where the railway's head office was located. Although lacking in colour, the names clearly indicated the scope of the service and remained in use until the summer of 1911.

However, during the summer of 1899, the names were temporarily shelved in favour of the more glamorous designation *Imperial Limited* on transcontinental passenger trains operating in both directions. Now *there* was a name that properly reflected the status of the Canadian Pacific Railway, a vital link in the British Empire's route to the Far East, and one that prompted enthusiasts to refer to the iron road as the "Imperial Highway."

A Link to the Far East
The *Imperial Limited* was the first CPR "name-train" to be luxurious throughout.
NS.88

During its first few seasons, the *Imperial Limited* substituted for the *Pacific Express* and *Atlantic Express* during the summer months only, operating on a daily basis. But in 1902, it began to run as an independent service, three times a week, in addition to the regular transcontinental trains. The first run that summer was treated as a special occasion, not only to showcase the specially appointed equipment, but also because the *Imperial* was operating for the first time over the "short line" between Montreal and Ottawa.

To celebrate the event, invitations were issued to a party of journalists to travel in the company of the railway's chief of advertising, George Henry Ham. The rolling stock, which consisted of a baggage car, a tourist car, three sleepers, and the dining car *Sandringham* (which company pamphlets extolled for its "excellent service as part of the second section of the Royal Train, during the recent visit of Their Royal Highnesses the Duke and Duchess of Cornwall and York"), were said to "approach nearer perfection in railway equipment than anything previously reached."

Whereas the exteriors were uniformly finished in mahogany, the interiors reflected the various means of the railway's clientele. The "Palace" sleeping cars were elaborate creations of dark woods, ivory, and gold, with velour upholstery in the style of Louis XV. The tourist sleeping cars were only slightly less luxurious, finished in light woods and upholstered in leather and corduroy. In addition, they were equipped with kitchen compartments, complete with cooking ranges for those who desired to prepare their own meals.

The dining cars were always inviting, with their red mahogany walls, embossed-metal ceilings painted in "old gold," and floors carpeted in green. Passengers were assured the kitchen and pantry were fitted with "every modern convenience that will ensure the choicest viands and service." Special dishes were offered when in season, and the menu was changed on a daily basis.

As an inspired piece of advertising, the CPR designated the westbound and eastbound trains as numbers 97 and 98, respectively, to reflect the hours required to complete the transcontinental trip in each direction.

Asked to comment on the new service, George Ham drew a comparison with the first transcontinental, which pulled out of Montreal's Dalhousie Square Station on 28 June 1886: "At that time there were more people living who believed the C.P.R. wouldn't pay for the grease on its axles than there are now, and there were few who anticipated that in sixteen years the daily transcontinental service would have to be supplemented by a train of the elegance and speed of the Imperial Limited."

In 1932, still operating alongside CPR name-trains *Dominion*, *Soo-Dominion*, and *Mountaineer*, the west and eastbound *Imperials* were renumbered One and Two. With the waning of Britain's imperial power and the increasingly independent stance adopted by Canada as a maturing nation, the name was dropped at that time and never revived.

Royalty Rode the Rails

Amid the tumultuous events of 1939, Canada was treated to what was then a rare and festive occasion: a royal visit from reigning British monarchs. For the entire westbound leg of the tour, King George VI and Queen Elizabeth were in the hands of the agents and officers of the CPR's transportation network. And capable hands they proved to be, as the monarchs glided from Portsmouth, England, to Victoria, British Columbia, all under the management of the company that—as its slogan used to say—spanned the world. Not even the three idle days on the North Atlantic, brought on by extremely foggy conditions, could upset the arrangements, although the delay did send staff throughout the company's railway and hotel system scurrying to reschedule every detail.

Royalty Rode the Rails
Whereas King George VI was somewhat reticent, Queen Elizabeth chatted freely with the sailors and railwaymen assigned to the Royal Tour.
R.164

On board the stately *Empress of Australia*, the King and Queen took advantage of the setback to walk the promenade deck, visit the bridge, and attend nightly showings of movies to which the Queen insisted the entire off-duty crew of several hundred men be invited. The King also found time for a daily swim in one or another of the ship's three pools and was often seen on deck or in the public rooms indulging his passion for candid photography.

Landing at Wolfe's Cove in Quebec City, their majesties were whisked to the Chateau Frontenac, up the bluff and through the hotel archway, which was illuminated by a huge glowing crown. There the food, the décor, and the accommodations were truly fit for a king.

Since the CPR was to have the honour of running the first train in the British Empire outside Great Britain to carry reigning monarchs, every minute consideration received special attention. An exterior paint scheme of royal blue, silver, gold, and stainless steel was applied to CPR Hudson locomotive 2850 and twelve selected railcars. The coach interiors were completely refurbished to provide the royal couple with every possible convenience, and more than two hundred of the company's finest locomotive engineers, firemen, conductors, and trainmen were readied for duty on their respective railway divisions.

Permission was sought and granted to apply royal crown castings to the running boards of the locomotive, a feature that was afterwards a trademark of all the CPR locomotives of the same class and led to their popular designation as "Royal Hudsons." In addition, a twelve-car pilot train was assembled to accommodate members of the royal entourage, as well as the legion of newspaper correspondents, photographers, and commentators who made the cross-Canada trek with King George VI and Queen Elizabeth.

Major receptions were organized at Montreal, North Toronto, Winnipeg, and Vancouver, where the stations were festooned with banners, bunting, flags, and shields. Thousands of spectators vied for the best vantage points. Security efforts were coordinated by the company's own investigation department in co-operation with the RCMP, city and provincial police, and the members of Scotland Yard assigned to the tour.

Additional stops were made at several of the CPR divisional points, where impromptu greetings and gifts from the crowds got a friendly response from the King and Queen, who often stayed longer than had been scheduled to shake hands and chat. At White River, Ontario, the Queen decided to get a good look at the locomotive by strolling along the platform to the front of the train, a notion that was heartily endorsed by her husband. The nervousness of the train crew in its desire to have everything in perfect operating order and appearance must surely have been eased when the Queen, upon completing her front-end inspection, exclaimed: "It is a lovely engine."

Other highlights of the excursion included a locomotive cab ride through the Rocky Mountains, from Beavermouth to Stoney Creek; rest stops at the CPR's Banff Springs, Chateau Lake Louise, and Empress hotels; and a crossing from Vancouver to Victoria aboard the company's British Columbia coastal vessel *Princess Marguerite.*

Most of the eastbound portion of the tour wasn't handled by Canadian Pacific, but King George VI and Queen Elizabeth were back with the CPR for two short segments of the rail trip in the east and were ferried home from Canada aboard the pride of the company's steamship fleet, the *Empress of Britain II.*

Locomotive 2850 went on to stardom at the 1939 New York World's Fair, in the "Railroads on Parade" pageant. It is preserved at the Canadian Railway Museum in Delson/Saint Constant, Quebec, just south of Montreal.

Smooth as Silk

So much has been written about the silk trains that sped across the continent from the 1880s to the mid-1930s that their fame has taken on a mythology of its own. There's a certain romance associated with that particular product, a commodity so valuable that all other traffic, including the most prestigious passenger trains, were forced to take a siding to make way for the silk trains. A single bale of silk could bring eight hundred dollars in the 1920s, and rail shipments often represented enormous sums, sometimes as high as ten million dollars or more.

Those who manned the silk trains recall hair-raising journeys to markets in

New York at speeds that sometimes bordered on folly, while trackside observers remember trains of a dozen or more "Tuscan red" baggage cars, specially mounted on passenger wheel sets for their better operating capabilities. But what is often overlooked amid the nostalgia for the elite trains is the equally important role the CPR's steamships played in securing contracts.

Although several railroads in the United States ran special silk trains, as did the Canadian National in Canada, it was the CPR's integrated railway and steamship service that gave it the competitive edge. The first trains from Vancouver to Montreal included bales of silk among their cargoes of tea, rice, china, and curios, transported from the Orient in chartered ships.

By 1913, when the CPR's *Empress of Asia* was setting new speed records on her run across the Pacific, shipments of silk could reach New York City from Japan in just seventeen days—an admirable schedule, but one that was surpassed in 1924 when the company's new Pacific greyhound, the *Empress of Canada*, sped across the ocean in eight days, ten hours, and nine minutes. Quickly shuttled onto a waiting train, her silk cargo reached New York only thirteen days after leaving Yokohama harbour. For a commodity with insurance rates sometimes charged by the hour, the speedy delivery was a magnificent performance.

While tug boats manoeuvred the *Empresses* up against their berths at Vancouver's Pier B-C, the ships' captains bawled out instructions through megaphones to agents and stevedores waiting on the dock. Well before the passengers disembarked, long electric conveyor belts were run through open hatches into the ships' specially protected silk holds. Steady streams of ninety-kilogram bales, wrapped in strong brown paper, began their procession under canvas awnings, down to the warehouses, where they were checked and sorted according to

SMOOTH AS SILK
With its speedy trans-Pacific steamships, the CPR had the upper hand in getting silk to market.
A.37245

destination. Despite the chaotic appearance presented by stevedores, railway officials, and customs officers all in simultaneous motion, there was an underlying clockwork efficiency that enabled the waiting trains to be loaded in an average fifteen minutes per car, or less.

An interesting outcome of the silk trade was that the *Empress of Russia* and the *Empress of Asia* both remained as coal-fired steamships long after most passenger liners had converted to oil. When the CPR was considering their modification, Japanese mine owners feared the loss of the more than 45,000 metric tons a year in coal business for which the *Empresses* were responsible, and the depressing effect such a loss would have on the local economy. The mine owners convinced the Japanese government to give CPR preferential treatment in the awarding of silk shipments from Kobe and Yokohama. In return, CPR agreed to continue burning Nagasaki coal, which was, after all, a good, cheap, and relatively clean fuel, which gave off very little dust in handling. With the aid of hard-working stokers, the *Empress of Asia* and *Empress of Russia* could maintain a steady speed of nineteen knots in moderate weather, and they remained coal-burners to the end of their days.

The Race Was On!

Since the advent of passenger railway timetables, there has been fierce competition between rival lines to better each other's schedules. But perhaps no competition was more intense than the battle between the Canada Atlantic Railway (CAR) and the CPR to provide express passenger service between Montreal and Ottawa.

As early as the winter of 1882, CPR assistant superintendent C. W. Spencer was in touch with D. C. Linsley, a manager with the CAR, to discuss what he felt to be foolishly short scheduled times between the two cities. Apparently no agreement was reached, for when CAR advertisements ran the next summer in local papers, they showcased "four lightning express trains daily; the fastest of which cover the approximately 111-mile distance from Montreal to Ottawa in three hours flat."

Not to be outdone, CPR announced their summer arrangement as: "The old line—always ahead—Ottawa to Montreal in two hours and fifty-five minutes." To further titillate the travelling public, the larger railway with the deeper pockets pointed out that it operated the "finest equipped passenger trains in the world" and had the "grandest drawing room cars in America."

Thus began a two-decade contest to provide the fastest and most luxurious service possible along the popular corridor, which reached its apex at the turn of the century after both lines had acquired brand new Atlantic-type steam locomotives. The three CPR engines, numbered 209, 210, and 211, were specially equipped with oversized two-metre driving wheels, the largest ever on the company's locomotives, to get all possible speed from them. The locomotive cabs had attractive

The Race Was On! The locomotives sported oversized driving wheels for maximum speed to keep the CPR minutes ahead of the rival Canada Atlantic Railway. NS.108

lines, rounded at the corners, with no rivet heads or bolts to spoil the finish, and were lined on the interior with hardwood. The tenders were of a new design, built to provide the exceptionally large capacity of 20,450 litres of water, an amount sufficient to complete the Montreal to Ottawa run without a stop. Their capacity for 7.25 metric tons of coal was enough for the round trip.

The CPR express trains were marshalled into various combinations of baggage, smoking, second-class, and first-class coaches and invariably included a parlour car. All of the cars were lit by electricity, with incandescent globes hung on the walls of the passenger coaches and from the ceiling in the baggage car. The exteriors were finished in polished mahogany. Inside, passengers were surrounded by satinwood panels and richly carved and ornamented columns. The observation windows were hung with damask silk, and the chairs were upholstered in terra cotta plush.

By 1904 the CPR scheduled run between the port city and the nation's capital had been reduced to two hours and fifteen minutes, but most locomotive engineers were still only interested in putting as much distance as possible between their tail-end marker lamps and the headlamps of their rivals at the opposing railway. Around that time, CPR president Thomas Shaughnessy is said to have called one of his locomotive engineers to his office for a dressing down. "They tell me you've been racing with the Canada Atlantic," the president said gruffly, subjecting the man to the full weight of his authority.

"Yes sir," gulped the chastised engineer, fixing his gaze on the floor at his feet.

"Well I won't stand for it," Shaughnessy barked. "There'll be no speeding on this railway," he said, dismissing the man with a wave of his hand. "But," he called out, as the engineer rushed to exit the room, "don't let the other guy win, either."

A Rolling Art Gallery

When CPR introduced its elegant new passenger train, *The Canadian*, in 1955, people were impressed by the attractive stainless-steel contours and thoroughly modern appearance it presented. Few would have guessed that some of the train's interior panels would end up on museum walls.

Throughout the early 1950s, Ernie Scroggie, design supervisor with the CPR's graphics department, was responsible for interior details on the train that rekindled the public's fascination with luxury train travel. In the proud tradition of earlier CPR name-trains like the *Imperial Limited* and the *Trans-Canada Limited*, *The Canadian* was meant to be first class in every way.

Most popular with railway fanciers were the eighteen scenic dome cars that graced the rear of each of the daily trains to leave both Montreal and Vancouver, criss-crossing the country. Named for Canadian national and provincial parks, they became widely known as "Park" cars, and were favoured not only for their

A Rolling Art Gallery
Original artwork by A. Y. Jackson graces the bulkhead and sidewall of this "mural lounge" in the railcar *Kokanee Park.*
M.6412

domes—a revolution in rail travel itself—but also for the beverage rooms and adjoining lounges in their rear quarter.

It was in the cars' beverage rooms that Scroggie employed a unique concept that he adapted from similar installations aboard trains in the United States. Each of the eighteen rooms received a distinctly Canadian treatment, replete with original murals executed by members of the Royal Canadian Academy of Arts. The paintings were originally installed on the end wall in each of the beverage rooms, thereafter referred to as "mural lounges." As the Park cars were removed from service, beginning in the early 1970s, three of the murals were carefully removed by members of the company's archives department and were preserved with other pieces in the CPR's art collection. A fourth car sustained extensive damage in an unfortunate accident, and its Lawren Harris mural was destroyed.

The remaining Park cars were sold to publicly owned Via Rail, the passenger service operated by the Canadian government, mostly over the tracks of the country's two Class-I railways. Faced with the task of refurbishing the twenty-year-old cars, and in light of the now enhanced status of many of the mural artists, the decision was made to remove the original artworks for cleaning and restoration. Although they no longer roll around the country on rails, they are periodically back on the road with one art exhibition or another.

Built to CPR Standards

It was June 1943, and the Second World War was raging in Europe, North Africa, the Pacific theatre, and in many of the far-flung corners of the world. In British India, on the Burmese frontier, Louis Mountbatten's jungle guerillas were bogged down in a struggle that was as much a battle of logistics and supply lines as it was a firefight.

Railway motive power was urgently required to ferry much-needed supplies to the Allied soldiers in Mountbatten's command, and a contract for 145 locomotives had recently been awarded to the Montreal Locomotive Works and the Canadian Locomotive Company in Kingston, Ontario. There was one important proviso: the contract stipulated that the locomotives were to be "built to CPR standards," and the inspection of all components, as well as their packing and shipment to India, was to be conducted by CPR engineers. It was an unprecedented arrangement, and one that reflected the enormous respect in which the railway's workforce was held for its abilities and expertise.

The CPR was itself engulfed in a maelstrom of logistical problems brought on by the global conflict. Merchant ships were in short supply on both the Atlantic and the Pacific, and the effects of the Japanese bombing of Pearl Harbor on gasoline and rubber supplies, coupled with the lack of building starts for highway vehicles, soon reduced the effectiveness of trucking services in Canada.

Built to CPR Standards
The locomotives were dismantled and packed into crates for shipment to the jungles of Burma.
NS.4926

Railway freight tonnage climbed steadily. The twenty-seven million metric tons handled in 1938 rose to nearly forty-one million by 1941, and fifty million in 1944. Over the same period, average shipment distances jumped precipitously, as the production of war *matériel* spread farther and farther inland. As the country's industrial capacity rose, so too did the CPR's ability to squeeze efficiencies from its existing infrastructure. Thus, when the Indian State Railways requested that the CPR supervise its locomotive purchase in Canada, two teams of engineers were dispatched to the builders' shops to inspect every aspect of the construction and shipping.

The CPR was operating about six hundred fewer locomotives than it had in service at the height of the First World War, in 1917. But now the company was getting an average of 54 percent more productivity from them. One CPR Hudson locomotive was said to have steamed more than 14,000 kilometres in a month, or more than 480 kilometres a day. The locomotives for the Indian State Railways would also be expected to perform yeoman's service, under the most adverse conditions of weather and war.

Along with supervising the machining of parts, construction of boilers and tenders, erecting of the locomotives, and testing of components, the CPR also took charge of stripping down and packing the iron horses, each of which required seventeen crates loaded on five flatcars to get it dockside. The crates were packed to facilitate a quick rebuild upon arrival in India, where finishing coats of paint and the logo of the Indian State Railways would be applied on top of the locomotives' grey primer.

By year's end, the first of the locomotives were ready for shipment, and the CPR selected locomotive erection engineer J. Marshall Watson to travel to India and oversee their reassembly and testing. Watson had been with the railway's mechanical and motive power departments since 1909, rising through the ranks from machinist to general locomotive foreman. He had put in thousands of hours in the

CPR's Weston Shops, in Winnipeg, and its Alyth and Ogden Shops, in Calgary. Though his assignment was vital to the war effort, the CPR was not about to let one of its people go all the way to India without having a good look at how railways operated there. Accordingly, Watson was instructed to "study the set-up of the state railway and report on its methods," along with carrying out his inspection duties.

Before leaving the more temperate shores of Canada for the steamy climes of India, Watson was subjected to his own physical tune-up, which may have helped him to empathize with the poor devils fighting and dying in the jungles of Burma. He was inoculated for smallpox, typhus, tetanus, cholera, and yellow fever.

Montreal's Greystone Castle

In 1909, the CPR was in the midst of its golden years. The company's steamships were operating on the Atlantic and Pacific Oceans, the hotel system was on the verge of its greatest period of expansion, and the railway was adding hundreds of kilometres of branch lines in the prairies, while effecting significant grade reductions in the mountains, notably through the construction of the famous Spiral Tunnels through the Rockies.

Accordingly, the most ambitious expansion of the company's Montreal headquarters at Windsor Station, extending the building's eastern façade to St. Antoine Street, was assigned to architect Walter S. Painter. The Foundation Company of New York, Chicago, and New Orleans, and the Bishop Construction Company of Montreal and Toronto, were awarded contracts for the massive new structure, breaking ground in December 1909.

Initially there were two challenges to overcome: one of architecture, the other of engineering. The façade had to blend harmoniously with the existing building, and the massive proposed tower that would anchor the south end had to be built on a foundation solid enough to support the fifteen floors that would make the station the tallest building in Montreal at the time. Though Painter used a steel framework for the extension, he was careful to emulate the style of Bruce Price, the architect of the original station building, with very satisfactory results. Inside the cathedral-like vestibule on the corner of St. Antoine and Peel, two large staircases ascended to the passenger concourse at the level of Osborne (now La Gauchetière) Street.

Through 1910 and the first six months of 1911, the steel girders rose fifteen storeys high for the tower block, dwarfing everything in the surrounding neighbourhood. Hundreds of riveters and steel erectors swarmed over the structure. Many of them were from the Caughnawaga (now Kahnawake) Mohawk Indian Reserve, as was usual on most high-level construction jobs in Quebec and in the

MONTREAL'S GREYSTONE CASTLE
Montreal's Windsor Station was the very essence of clockwork efficiency.
NS.8168

New England states. By mid-summer, more than twenty-two hundred metric tons of steel provided by the Dominion Bridge Company of Lachine, Quebec, were in place, and excavation work began on the boiler house.

Hard on the heels of the steelworkers were the stonemasons, most of whom were French Canadians whose task was to sheath the reinforced concrete shell with a fine stone veneer of Quebec limestone. The job was accomplished in a remarkably short time, and by the end of the year, the exterior was all but complete.

Large quantities of marble for use in the principal halls and corridors were brought in from Italy and France, as well as from closer sources in Indiana and Tennessee. Although a portion of the building was opened for business early in 1913, construction work on the concourse and train shed continued well into the next year.

The station's new configuration required the use of thirteen elevators: eight for passengers, four for freight, and one for the exclusive use of the kitchen and restaurant facilities. All were operated by hydraulic pressure from pumps located in the station's engine room. The main waiting room, running parallel to and opening onto the concourse, was finished in marble. Its seven hundred square metres of space featured an elaborately decorated ceiling and an imposing bronze statue of CPR founding president George Stephen. At either end were the men's and women's waiting rooms, and a nursery. The baggage and express rooms were located at the Osborne end of the concourse. A dining room and lunch counter were close to the elevators leading from St. Antoine to the concourse.

The dining room operated for more than fifty years as the Alouette Room. It soon became one of the most popular places to eat in Montreal. Every modern innovation was employed, including the "Victor dishwashing machine," the "Curtis egg boiler," the "Blakeslee concrete potato peeler," the "Smith's Buffalo meat chopper," and the "Reinhold ice cuber." The double range, the broilers, and all the other kitchen equipment were supplied by the George R. Prowse Company of Montreal. The extensive refrigeration system was capable of churning out more than twenty metric tons of ice a day, for use in the dining room and lunchroom, and on the railway's dining cars.

Such was the popularity of the Alouette dining room that, by 1920, an extension was required to boost its seating capacity from 170 to 320. The extra space was found by putting in a stairway to the floor below, where an additional 160 square metres was available. At noon, a special table d'hôte meal was served for seventy-five cents, and in the evening, meals were priced at a dollar and a half. An orchestra set the appropriate mood.

Work on the concourse and train shed continued through the winter of 1913–14 and involved the systematic organization of immigrant waiting rooms and vault space below. During the planning stages, CPR special engineer G. G. Ommanney was dispatched to the United States to examine the railway facilities for handling baggage and immigrant traffic in major American centres. The final design for Windsor Station was influenced, in part, by what he saw in the Chicago & North Western's terminal, in Chicago.

Stairways from the train shed platforms were connected directly to the passenger quarters, providing for orderly handling of large crowds. An area of nearly seventeen hundred square metres of space was available beneath the concourse and track level for passengers, whereas an additional six thousand square metres was devoted to the storage of records and various supplies.

A baggage checking system, similar to the one adopted by the New York Central and Pennsylvania Railroads, was established in rooms adjacent to the ticket office. Electric baggage trucks were used to shuttle to and from the station platforms. The train shed was of the "Bush" type, constructed of a series of short-span arches and supported by rows of steel columns. Whereas most sheds of this design allowed for two tracks, side by side under each arch, in this case, the tracks were separated by intervening three-metre platforms for baggage handling, leaving clear the five-metre platforms under the columns for the exclusive use of passengers.

Skylights extended the entire length of the train shed and provided an airy and pleasant atmosphere. The framework consisted of formed lattice girders, but the roof proper was encased in reinforced concrete, protecting the steel from the corrosive effect of locomotive exhaust fumes. The train shed covered an area large enough to house 120 passenger coaches on eleven tracks. The massive glass-domed, open concourse ran the width of the shed and integrated the various components of the old and new station structures. Its roof consisted of riveted arch trusses, covered by an enormous, continuous skylight, reputed to be the largest in Canada. The glass panels, strengthened with encased wire mesh, were engineered to withstand the extreme expansion and contraction caused by Montreal's climate, which could range from forty-three degrees Celsius to minus thirty or forty degrees in any given year.

More than fifteen hundred employees worked in the 160 offices in the new castle-like structure. Although one would have been hard pressed to list all of the station's features, the company's staff bulletin summarized: "What is especially striking is that everything goes like clockwork. Everything has its place. Every person knows his duty. There is no confusion. Every clock is identical with every other clock. Every bit of work is allotted to a nicety. The eleven platforms are so clean that you could eat off the concrete. That is the great and insistent feature all through, neatness and order." This is a glowing tribute, to be sure, but a fitting one for the largest railway terminal in Canada, and one of the busiest on the North American continent.

Who's the Artist?

With buildings as old as Montreal's Windsor Station, renovations are more like archaeological digs, and although it may not have rivalled the discovery of King Tut's tomb, workers were treated to quite a surprise when they broke through the ceiling in the second floor premises of what was CPR's communications and public affairs department in the 1980s.

Exposed to light for the first time in many years, the beautiful mosaic ceiling of the original 1889 station waiting room was discovered, evoking an era of craftsmanship and artistry long forgotten in our postmodern age. The ceiling was uncovered while workers were building a studio for the railway's outstanding photography department, one of the finest in Canada at the time.

The cavernous waiting room, originally two storeys high before alterations cut it in half, was then occupied on the concourse and train shed level, in part, by a barbershop and CPR's employment bureau and administration offices. The railway's graphic arts and marketing communications services of the department of communications and public affairs were above.

Though the original wing of Windsor Station was the creation of New York

architect Bruce Price, the interior decorations in the waiting room were the work of Edward Colonna, a practitioner of what was then the avant-garde Art Nouveau school of design. Establishing a pattern that would haunt Colonna's career in Canada, a Montreal journal gave much of the credit for the work to the legendary builder of the CPR, William Van Horne: "The idea of the decorated ceiling and the mosaic pavement for the large waiting room at the Windsor Station belongs to Mr. Van Horne, and Mr. Colonna, the designer for the CPR, is carrying it out. The

WHO'S THE ARTIST? With its beautiful mosaic ceiling and imported tile floor, the Windsor Station waiting room was deemed to be "aesthetic in a high degree." NS.26279 whole design is aesthetic in a high degree. Mr. Van Horne has a soul for the beautiful. There are brown, and terracotta, and gold combinations which are very sweet. The pavement is to be a joy. The tiles have not yet arrived from England, and the floor is not to be touched till they are here. When the ceiling and floor are finished, this waiting room will be the finest in America."

Death Highballs through Windsor Station

Railway men from the days of steam were quick to point out the hardships they endured to keep the fires stoked and the axles greased, as locomotive crews coaxed their snorting and wheezing charges through the rigours of everyday service. Man and machine functioned as one. But occasionally the same forces that animated the great iron beasts could explode forth with grave consequences, as happened on the morning of 17 March 1909.

The *Boston Express* was keeping good time on its run to Windsor Station, just east of Montreal West, when a spring on the engineer's side broke, causing the locomotive boiler to lean against one of the powerful driving wheels, which in turn sheared the head from a washout plug. Superheated steam and boiling water gushed forth into the locomotive cab.

Fireman Louis Craig dove out the window, while engineer Mark Cunningham strove to gain control of the speeding locomotive. After sticking to his post for an excruciating half kilometre and seriously scalding both hands, Cunningham was blown from the cab. Neither crewman had been able to apply the emergency brakes. The train was now completely out of control, with nobody at the throttle, and the train's conductor and trainman realized there was trouble when the express barrelled through Westmount without stopping. The slight downward grade gave the train added momentum, propelling it at an estimated eighty kilometres per hour toward Windsor Station.

The brakeman, acting quickly and instinctively, was able to release the brake valve on one of the cars, reducing the train's speed to about forty kilometres per hour; but he could do nothing to prevent the inevitable. The force of the impact demolished the stopblock at the end of the southernmost track, as the train plowed through the station wall. In the midst of falling rubble, the locomotive came to rest in the waiting room, sinking part way through the floor into the barbershop below. The passenger cars telescoped, forcing the baggage car through the south wall of the train shed, where it hung precariously.

Miraculously none of the 150 people on board was seriously injured, but a man, a woman, and three children who had been awaiting the arrival of the train were killed, and twenty-three others were injured. One man, getting off the train, had

DEATH HIGHBALLS THROUGH WINDSOR STATION
The aftermath of the accident was captured by a sketch artist on a souvenir card.
A.16039

been told there were no casualties. Shortly after arriving home, he received the horrifying news that his wife and two children had perished in the wreckage.

The death toll might have been even higher had it not been for the heroic efforts of two men on duty at the station that day. The stationmaster, Thomas Whelan, had realized as the train came into view that it was going much too fast. Rushing onto the platform, he shouted and pushed back the crowd that had gathered there. Constable Richards of the railway police force had just watched another train depart, when he became aware of the impending disaster. Although he was able to clear many people from the waiting room, he was knocked senseless by falling debris as he tried to reach a small girl who stood petrified in the path of the oncoming train.

Both the fireman and the engineer from the runaway locomotive were picked up by the crew on the following train from Pointe Fortune, Quebec, and rushed to Notre-Dame Hospital. Sadly the engineer, suffering from multiple injuries including a fractured skull, did not survive.

The locomotive, number 902, had just been in for an overhaul, and was only on its second run after being out-shopped when the accident occurred. Following the tragedy, it was repaired and continued in service until August 1938, when it was scrapped.

Sixteen Years to a Landmark Station

Railways have been a prominent feature on Toronto's waterfront ever since the Grand Trunk arrived in the mid-1850s. When the Great Western Railway came on the scene around the same time, the Grand Trunk Railway depot became the first union station, or jointly operated terminal. Since then, there have been three more union stations in Toronto: an enlargement of the first structure at Front and Bay Streets; a second depot one block west, which served the Toronto, Grey & Bruce (later absorbed by the CPR) and four other railways, all of which became components of Canadian National; and the current, familiar terminal, which stretches along Front Street, between Bay and York.

In terms of the number of trains, passengers, and pieces of baggage that have passed through its cavernous passages, this landmark is one of the most successful terminal stations in North America. However, it was sixteen years from the time

the first spade broke ground until the station was fully operational. Of course, the timing left something to be desired. The First World War broke out the same year construction began, and the subsequent slowdown due to shortages of manpower, material, and equipment caused work on the exterior to drag on.

Indiana limestone was imported in twenty-seven-metric-ton blocks for the exterior walls. Special lathes were used by George Oakley & Son of Toronto to turn the massive columns for the Front Street façade. At the time, the stone-cutting contract was the largest in the British Empire.

The CPR and the Grand Trunk incorporated a separate company called the Toronto Terminals Railway to operate the huge depot, but, even as construction was well underway, there were a couple of important issues that the two railways and the City of Toronto had not resolved.

The Grand Trunk favoured a through-track arrangement for the station, which would eliminate the need to turn locomotives and rolling stock operating in and out of the city. It also proposed that the approach tracks be elevated on a viaduct from the waterfront freight yards to a train shed level with Front Street. The CPR

SIXTEEN YEARS TO A LANDMARK STATION
The newly constructed Union Station presented a magnificent façade on Toronto's Front Street. NS.11305

argued for a more conventional stub-end track arrangement and a low-level train shed that would shave five or six million dollars from the final cost of the project.

The City of Toronto sided with the Grand Trunk and agreed to absorb one-third of the cost of the more elaborate viaduct and track plan, which continued to expand and cause further delays. By mid-1920, the offices in the station were occupied by the two railway companies, but the vast public areas remained unused, awaiting the completion of the viaduct.

An impending royal visit in 1927 provided the impetus to apply the finishing touches to the concourse, waiting rooms, and ticket counters. All was in readiness as the Prince of Wales (later King Edward VIII) and his brother, Prince George (later King George VI), arrived by train at the wooden platform on the south side of the station on 6 August. The princes were accompanied by British Prime Minister Stanley Baldwin and Mrs. Baldwin, and Dominion Prime Minister William Lyon Mackenzie King. They were greeted upon arrival by a welcoming party consisting of Ontario's Lieutenant-Governor Ross and Mrs. Ross, and numerous representatives of the federal and provincial governments. Acting as master of ceremonies was U. E. Gillem, general manager of Toronto Terminals Railway.

Amid enthusiastic cheers from the assembled guests, Mr. Gillem handed a pair of gold scissors to the Prince of Wales who cut a ribbon stretched across the entrance to the concourse. After a rousing chorus of "God Save The King," performed by a sixty-voice choir, the prince was escorted to the Canadian National and CPR ticket counters, where he was issued the first tickets from the new terminal. Tickets were also issued to Prince George and Mr. and Mrs. Baldwin, as the choir let loose with a lively rendition of "Land of Hope and Glory." The party then proceeded to the front entrance of the ticket lobby, where the Prince of Wales unlocked the door with a ceremonial gold key and threw the doors open to the travelling public.

The station had been thirteen years in the making, but the opening ceremonies were over in a mere eleven minutes. It was another three years before the elaborate viaduct was fully operational.

Ever since, the station has been an integral hub in the overall Toronto transportation network. Stairways at either end of the concourse lead down to the level where GO trains arrive and depart, used by tens of thousands of commuters daily. There is also access to the Toronto Transit Commission subway, the Royal York Hotel, and the Royal Bank Plaza.

In 1986, to coincide with the 150th anniversary of passenger rail service in Canada, Union Station underwent a $3.5-million renovation to restore it to its 1920s appearance. Unlike many railway stations, it is as vital today as it was those many years ago, when the royal party breezed through its pristine corridors.

THE IMPOSSIBLE MADE POSSIBLE

"Two hundred miles of engineering impossibilities." That's how Van Horne described the Canadian Pacific Railway line along the north shore of Lake Superior. But there was no choice—the railway had to go that way. The only alternative would have been to pass through the northern United States, and that would have been political suicide for a fledgling Canadian enterprise, dependent on the goodwill of the Canadian government. So, impossible or not, it had to be done. Though the work was tough, the line was completed between Montreal and Winnipeg on 6 May 1885—six months before the Last Spike was driven in Eagle Pass.

The unyielding rock of the Canadian Shield had to be blasted or bored. Vast areas of muskeg swallowed whole sections of ballast, ties, rails, and occasionally, an ill-fated locomotive. Again and again, wooden trestles were needed to span the numerous rivers and creeks that empty into Lake Superior and to shore up the often treacherous banks of the greatest of the Great Lakes. All of those labour-intensive activities required not only men, but also literally tons of equipment and stores, the acquisition of which often proved as much of a barrier to construction as the physical constraints.

One inspecting engineer complained: "If the railway were almost completed,

THE IMPOSSIBLE MADE POSSIBLE Because much of the north shore of Lake Superior was not accessible by land, supplies were ferried to the construction camps by a large and somewhat motley flotilla.
A.4390

reluctance to supply new horses and plant might be explicable, but at this stage it would certainly be much better to have some reserve plant on the work than pay hundreds of men full wages for half work on account of the want of a few wheelbarrows, worth a dollar a piece."

Because much of the north shore was inaccessible by land, supplies were ferried to the construction camps by a large and somewhat motley flotilla of steamboats, barges, and sailing craft. The camps sprang up wherever there was a sheltered bay. McKay's, McKellar's, Peninsula, Jackfish, and Gravel Bay Harbours were the main camps, but there were several others where small docks were constructed.

However, even the largest piers in the most protected bays suffered from the pounding of the tumultuous and temperamental Lake Superior waters. Solid walls of masonry, constructed at great pains to support the unstable ground upon which the roadbed was laid, disappeared overnight. Giant trestles, pieced together from millions of board feet of lumber, crumbled like matchsticks during a storm. On one occasion, the dock at Gravel Bay sank below the surface shortly after taking on a fresh load of rails, fishplates, and ties. Another time, a large chunk of land at McKay's Harbour went under, along with the dock, buildings, and construction supplies.

The railway "navvies," or tracklayers, were constantly rotated on and off duty, causing one steamboat captain to note there were really three construction gangs: one coming, one going, and one on the job.

Sault Ste. Marie and Port Arthur (which together with Fort William now forms Thunder Bay) were the most common ports of call for the construction fleet, but there were also forays into American waters, notably to Duluth. One of the Port Arthur firms, Smith & Mitchell, organized a service with its two steamboats, *Butcher's Boy* and *Butcher's Maid.* Known jointly as the Butcher's Mail Line, the two modest but sturdy vessels were employed in the conveyance of track gangs and, as their names suggested, cattle and other fresh meat on the hoof. The most efficient means of delivering large quantities of meat to the construction workers was to load the live cattle on board, sail for the destination camps, and do the slaughtering upon arrival.

The urgent need for this service—and no doubt the considerable profits to be made—led to some trouble for the captain of the *Butcher's Maid* on one trip. En route from Duluth, he neglected to call in at Canadian customs in Port Arthur, a legal requirement to help combat the lucrative smuggling trade. A heavy fine was the result.

For the most part, however, the ragtag fleet performed well under the circumstances, and the impossible became possible. There are no tonnage figures for the amount of supplies delivered, but over the course of the four-year period of intensive construction activity, upwards of twelve thousand men and fifteen hundred horses were on the job.

A Cryptic Game of Wordplay

Often railway depots were the first structures to break ground in small North American communities. But, whereas CPR stations were more often than not built to standard specifications, there was nothing standard about their names.

Railway officials were certainly recognized in the nomenclature sweepstakes. Creelman, Drinkwater, Ernfold, Flintoft, Griffin, Kelstern, Neville, Tisdale, Vogel, Wallace—literally hundreds of CPR executives, contractors, surveyors, and in the case of McMahon, Saskatchewan, a brakeman from Smiths Falls, saw their monikers painted in bold block letters on station name boards.

In some cases, the connections were more obscure. Gouverneur, Saskatchewan, took the middle name of Isaac G. Ogden of Calgary railway shops fame; Kerrobert, Saskatchewan, was a variation on the name of CPR general passenger agent Robert

A Cryptic Game of Wordplay
Sometimes pejorative town names were jettisoned by a rebellious citizenry for more genteel monikers.
A.37253

Kerr; and Estevan, Saskatchewan—also a code name that was used on telegraph cable messages by first CPR president Lord Mount Stephen—was said to be composed of the "e" from his first name "George," the "ste" from Stephen, and the "van" from CPR general manager William Van Horne.

Two or more names could be strung together. According to some historical accounts, Blairmore, Alberta, owes a debt to two CPR conductors or contractors named, not surprisingly, Blair and More or Moore; however, other sources claim that the town was named after Minister of Railways Andrew George Blair. Enlaugra, Quebec, celebrated the daughters of CPR general manager Alfred Price—Enid, Laura, and Grace. Sometimes, as was the case with general superintendent William Whyte at Fort Whyte and Whytewold, both in Manitoba, people were commemorated at two locations.

This name game even extended to mixing provinces, as evidenced by Altario, Alberta.

Railway company connections also appear. Delson, Quebec, is a contraction of the Delaware & Hudson Railway, now a component of CPR. And did you know that Milate, Ontario, means mileage eight, when reckoned from Sudbury, Ontario? Or that Ioco, British Columbia, is short for sometime-railway-client Imperial Oil Company?

What about royal connections? Regina and Prince Albert, both in Saskatchewan, as well as Port Arthur (now part of Thunder Bay) in Ontario and Lake Louise in Alberta, were named for Queen Victoria and her relatives. Balmoral, Manitoba, was named for the royal castle in Scotland.

Early settlers also fared well, singly and in pairs. Milden, Saskatchewan, was derived from settlers Miles and Bryden; Medstead, Saskatchewan, did the Medford and Hamstead families proud; and Andross, Alberta, would have been nothing if not for lumber dealers Anthony and Ross. This name game even extended to mixing provinces, as evidenced by Altario, Alberta.

Some of my personal favourites have literary origins. Shelley, Manitoba, needs no explanation and Swinburne, Saskatchewan, will be familiar to fans of that turn of the twentieth century English poet. Hugo, Manitoba, comes from Victor Hugo; Rudyard, Manitoba, from Rudyard Kipling; and Elstow was reputedly named for the birthplace of *Pilgrim's Progress* author John Bunyan, by an engineer who happened to be reading the book during construction of the line through Saskatchewan on which it is located. Clemens, a brother of Samuel Clemens, better known by his *nom de plume* Mark Twain, gave his name to Clemens, Saskatchewan, by virtue of being an early settler there. And what traveller and Shakespeare fancier would not be intrigued by Iago, Juliet, Jessica, Lear, Othello, Portia, and Romeo, all stops on CPR's former Kettle Valley route through British Columbia.

Other countries were also tapped for ideas. Altona, in Manitoba, can also be found in Germany, and Orthez, Manitoba, was but a smaller version of Orthez, France. British Columbia is particularly rich with these borrowings: Tokay and Sirdar are places in Hungary and Egypt, respectively, while Natal, Kimberley, and Ladysmith all come to us from South Africa.

Sometimes foreign place names fell out of favour, as was the case with Berlin, Ontario, during the First World War, when it was rechristened Kitchener, after Lord Kitchener of Boer War fame. Sometimes pejorative names like Rat Portage, Ontario, were jettisoned by an indignant citizenry for more neutral handles like Kenora.

Other languages? Bruderheim, Alberta, means "brethren's home" in German; Wolstock, Alberta, is Russian for "east" (which may seem strange in the Canadian west); and returning once again to the Boer War, all good Afrikaners know that Veldt, Alberta, is just another way of saying "plain," as in "prairie," not as in "unattractive."

Canada's Native peoples could always be counted on to provide some interesting and even poetic names. Pasqua, Saskatchewan, Kaministiquia and Manotick, both in Ontario, simply mean "prairie," "twisting waters," and "log land." Even more descriptive are Maniwaki, Quebec, and Oshawa and Komoka, both in Ontario, which say "land of the Virgin Mary," "where a trail crosses a stream," and "quiet resting place of the dead." (I think I'll wait awhile before heading for Komoka.) Saskatoon, Saskatchewan, means "many berries."

Canada's Native peoples could always be counted on to provide some interesting and even poetic names.

Mythology? We named Vulcan, Alberta, not for Mr. Spock's home planet, but for the Roman god of fire; Diana, Saskatchewan, for the goddess of the hunt; and Gimli, Manitoba, for the Norse word for "paradise."

If all else failed, place names could always be spelled backwards, as in Dranoel, Ontario, after a CPR officer named Leonard; Dramis, Quebec, after a Mr. Simard of Ville Marie in that province; or Adanac, Saskatchewan, after—now you're getting the hang of it—Canada.

Alberta Bound

Locomotive 87 lurched to a halt. As locomotive engineer Jim O'Hagan and fireman John "Scotty" Ormiston swung down from the cab, they marvelled at the burgeoning tent city lying on the east bank of the Elbow River. O'Hagan was piloting the "front train" of the CPR's construction forces led by contractors Langdon and Shepard. The river had temporarily put a halt to their relentless advancement. End-of-track had reached Calgary.

Ten days earlier, John Egan, the railway's western superintendent, had advised William Van Horne, then CPR general manager, "At Calgary on section 15, there is a very good location for a townsite. No squatters are on this section, as the mounted police have kept them off there. Mr. Hamilton has arranged to lay out a town, and I have no doubt that when you see the place it will please you." The message has been called Calgary's birth certificate.

As a direct result of Egan's assessment, the site would soon become the main agricultural and retail distribution point between Winnipeg and Vancouver, and—more than one hundred years later—headquarters of the Canadian Pacific Railway.

Shortly after the CPR was incorporated in 1881 to fulfill the federal government's obligation to build a transcontinental link with British Columbia, it entered into a contract with Langdon, Shepard & Co., of St. Paul, Minnesota, to construct the section of track from Flat Creek, Manitoba (near Brandon), to Fort Calgary, the site of a North West Mounted Police (NWMP) post established in 1875. With the crossing of the Bow River on 10 August 1883, the terms of the contract were all but met, and the contractors discharged most of their men amid the tents and ramshackle wood frame structures of the fledgling Calgary community.

George Murdoch, who was elected Calgary's first mayor in 1884, would say in later years, "When (the) railroad arrived, our town was a newly discovered inhabited island on a landless oasis, on a desolate desert, all towns along the line having

ALBERTA BOUND
A boxcar body served as a makeshift depot in Calgary when end-of-track reached the frontier settlement.
ALBERTA PROVINCIAL ARCHIVES A.3955

been made by the railroad with this exception." In a manner of speaking, that was true. But the CPR was determined to control land sales in townsites along the line to partly offset its enormous construction costs. Calgary was no exception.

Land speculation had been rampant along the proposed transcontinental route, and lots in section 14 on the east bank of the Elbow River were selling briskly. But the CPR had already decided to locate its station in section 15 on the west bank of the river, an area granted to the NWMP as grazing land. Fort Calgary and a few trading posts, among them I. G. Baker's, were the only man-made structures between end-of-track and the Rocky Mountains looming on the horizon.

While the bridge was constructed across the Elbow, many of the itinerant railway workers—with time on their hands and some with bellies full of rotgut whisky—engaged in boisterous foot and horse races, letting off more steam than the idle locomotives that languished in the hot prairie sun. Assuming that their services would no longer be required by the railway after their discharge by the prairie contractors, a large contingent of workers clambered aboard flatcars headed back east. Strong threats by a gun-toting NWMP officer were necessary to persuade them that this was not in their best interest. Many signed on anew for the push that would take the end-of-steel as far as Laggan (now Lake Louise), until the construction season ground to a halt in the heavy snowfalls of the Rocky Mountains, just short of the summit.

When the bridge over the Elbow River was completed on 15 August, the front train crossed over to the site now occupied by Palliser Square and began to put down sidings. As was a common practice when time and materials were in short supply, a surplus boxcar body was unloaded beside the main line and quickly converted to meet the requirements of a frontier railway depot. The makeshift station put in a year of service while a more permanent two-storey structure was built.

Less than two weeks later, on 28 August 1883, the first official train arrived from Montreal with senior railway officials and directors on board. Among them were CPR President George Stephen (later Lord Mount Stephen) and the railway's irrepressible general manager, William Cornelius Van Horne, widely recognized as the "world's ablest railway general."

It was on this inspection tour that Van Horne hosted a dinner on his business car for Father Albert Lacombe, an Oblate missionary. Van Horne admired Lacombe for his courage and tenacity in winning the respect of the Plains Indians. On a more official level, he owed the priest a debt of gratitude for mediating a dispute between the CPR and Chief Crowfoot when the transcontinental line was approaching the Blackfoot Indian reserve near Gleichen, in what was then part of the Northwest Territories (now Alberta). Included on the guest list were Stephen and CPR directors R. B. Angus and Donald A. Smith, along with their guests Baron Pascoe du Pré Grenfell, one of the railway's European backers, and His Royal Highness, Prince Hohenlohe of Germany, who was scouting out the country's potential for prospective German emigrants.

For the duration of the meal, Angus moved that Stephen vacate his position as president of the CPR in favour of Father Lacombe—a move that was quickly reciprocated when the priest installed Stephen as rector of his nearby mission of St. Mary's. "Poor souls of Calgary," Stephen is reputed to have said, looking out at the frontier community, "I pity you."

The CPR, holding land grants in the odd-numbered sections along the railway right-of-way, was able to secure control of section 15 from the NWMP by way of an Order-in-Council from the federal government. Prospective land buyers submitted their names to the local CPR agent, and names were picked from a hat to determine who would get first choice of the best lots.

Whereas some would dig deep for the $450 necessary to buy a corner lot, others needed a more modest $100, roughly two months' pay for an unskilled labourer, to acquire any one of the other lots. In addition, the CPR offered a 50 percent rebate to buyers who erected buildings on their lots before April 1884.

The first name to be drawn, appropriately enough, was John Glenn, one of the oldest and most respected settlers in the area. More than one hundred lots were grabbed up on the first day alone. With the onset of winter, the town had begun to take shape upon a grid of streets named for the most part after CPR officers and directors.

As for the motley band of squatters and speculators who had settled on the east bank of the Elbow, many took a pragmatic approach to their situation, loading their flimsy buildings onto sleds and pulling them across the frozen river to new lots in the chosen townsite.

First to move was James Bannerman, postmaster and owner of the local feed and flour store. When the government was slow to move the post office closer to the railway station, the CPR offered two free lots and one hundred dollars cash as an incentive. As for logistics, CPR chief engineer Herbert Holt, who would be one of the country's richest men and most influential industrialists fifty years later, took matters into his own hands. Taking a team of bulls to the building, he dragged the post office to a site more pleasing to the local citizenry and, by happy coincidence, to the CPR as well.

By December 1883, the railway was operating a regular service between Winnipeg and Calgary. The town had been officially incorporated that year. The following summer, sleeping cars were added to the trains, allowing well-heeled easterners to make the westbound trip in fine style. Already underway was a massive advertising program touting the merits of the "Golden Northwest" to lure settlers from eastern Canada, the United States, and Europe.

In three years, the population of the little town nestled in the foothills of the Rocky Mountains had grown from less than one hundred to one thousand. Business was booming and trade with eastern Canada had grown apace. The future belonged to Calgary.

Town Central

While rail gangs were speeding the construction of the Canadian Pacific Railway across the west, another group of men were hard at work on their heels at an equally arduous and, ultimately, no less important task: station building.

The railway was divided into two-hundred-kilometre sections (later referred to as subdivisions), a section being the effective distance for steam locomotive operations, after which time they required fuel and water, and normally a change of crew. At intervals of eight to sixteen kilometres, sidings were needed to allow faster traffic to pass, or to unblock a meeting of trains travelling in opposite directions. In many cases, this meant the establishment of stations, no matter how rudimentary, to house the company's agents.

At first, these shelters were often nothing more than aging freight car bodies, unceremoniously dumped alongside the tracks at chosen sites. There they remained until a decision was made by headquarters about which of the various standard stations would be appropriate to the predicted future status of the

Town Central
The station agent was at the nerve centre of small-town prairie life.
NS.17598

location. Although the CPR went through several sets of these so-called standards over the years, ranging from the truly utilitarian to the uniquely picturesque, the formula remained basically the same: small depots for small towns; larger stations for areas where natural resources or other advantages might be exploited; and Class A structures for locations deemed to have the potential for greatness.

The first stations were constructed with amazing dispatch. Specialized gangs would move down the line from building to building so that several were always under construction at any given time. The first gang threw up the framing, joists, and rafters, followed by the sheeting, flooring, and roofing men, and finally the plasterers, joiners, and painters.

Railway agents often played a variety of roles in the community, such as cab driver, insurance broker, travel agent, club organizer, or even mayor.

In addition to the necessary waiting rooms, ticket offices, and freight sheds, station layouts often included an apartment for the station agent and his family, consisting of a dining room, living room, and kitchen on the ground floor, and a couple of bedrooms on the level above. But they were modest structures and lacked almost any sort of comfort, including insulation, storm windows, or basements, not to mention luxuries such as central heating, running water, electricity, and plumbing.

Although most of these drawbacks were remedied in the decades that followed, it took a strong-willed and closely knit family to cope with the rigours of life in the railway station. Often nearby rivers and creeks were the only source of water, but enterprising agents looked to the skies to fill strategically placed barrels or cisterns with rainwater. Although electricity was introduced in Canada in the 1880s, it was not a feature of station life at most locations until well into the 1920s and 1930s, and was often installed only after the repeated urgings and at the expense of the station agent. The most important fixture, of course, was the small shed with the half-moon on the door, a short distance from the station itself. Some were not replaced by modern facilities until after the Second World War.

The effect of trains passing in the night was something one soon grew accustomed to, but nature also conspired against the station dwellers, sending dust storms so pervasive that not even damp cloths in the cracks around windows and doors could prevent a thin film of dust from forming on every interior surface. The legendary ferocity of prairie snowstorms sometimes caused temperatures to plummet to such depths that frost could be seen on nailheads flush with the interior walls.

But for all the faults of the railway stations, most families who grew up in these local landmarks have only good memories to relate. The drawbacks to life in the depot were usually characteristic of life on the prairies in general, and in fact, as often as not, the station agent's family was as comfortably housed as anyone else in the community.

Railway agents often played a variety of roles in the community, such as cab driver, insurance broker, travel agent, club organizer, or even mayor, and the station was invariably the hub of activity around which the entire community revolved. The waiting room was an inviting place to gather around the pot-bellied stove, whether to hold a local meeting of the Boy Scouts, the Masonic Lodge, or a fledgling church organization, or simply to shoot the breeze on a quiet afternoon.

The edges of the wooden station platforms were soon rounded by the women pushing their strollers, the children playing at their games, and even the marching feet of local militia units, all in an attempt to escape the ubiquitous mud that was so much a part of early prairie life.

Harvesters Were a Wild Bunch

By the time the dust had settled, the wagons were empty, many of the horses were missing, the platform was deserted, and nary an arrest had been made.

It wasn't the usual welcoming committee on the Winnipeg station platform—a half-dozen horse-drawn paddy wagons, or Black Marias, lined up ominously. In the late summer of 1906, the local constabulary was waiting in apprehension as a trainload of harvest workers steamed into the depot from eastern Canada.

For a few brief moments, all hell broke loose. As the first wave of men descended from the colonist cars, they were quickly hustled by the police into the waiting paddy wagons, only to be just as quickly liberated by their fellow labourers whose numbers soon overwhelmed the earnest, but rather naïve, law officers. By the time the dust had settled, the wagons were empty, many of the horses were missing, the platform was deserted, and nary an arrest had been made. Harvest hijinks had struck again.

Every year since 1891, it had been the same. Combines had yet to revolutionize farming and for each section of wheat planted by one man, ten were required to bring in the harvest. For the western farmer, this seasonal need for many able hands was problematic, as time was the chief enemy. The wheat had to be cut, stooked, and loaded into boxcars as soon as possible. If left too long in the fields, the crop could be ruined by an overabundance of rain, or even snow. Late crops were vulnerable to price fluctuations, and worse, could miss the deadline for the close of shipping on the Great Lakes.

As manpower was scarce on the prairies, the call went out across the country for able-bodied men willing to put in sixteen hours a day of back-breaking work for a fair day's wage—$1.50 in 1891. The annual tide rose from an initial five thousand men that first year, to crest at about forty-five thousand in the peak years of the 1920s.

Those policemen on the platform at Winnipeg really should have known better. The harvest excursions were nothing if not rowdy, and the advance telegram from back down the line had given specific warning. Eight hundred unemployed Nova Scotia miners had descended on the quiet community of Ignace, on the north shore of Lake Superior, like a swarm of hungry locusts—or should we say thirsty locusts. According to the frantic message, they had consumed all of the hard liquor in the Ignace station restaurant, and then—you couldn't fault those boys for lack

Harvesters Were a Wild Bunch
You could expect the unexpected when the harvesters rolled into town to help bring in the bountiful produce of the Golden Northwest.
NS.1159

of initiative—they commandeered the water coolers from the CPR passenger coaches in which they were travelling and filled them with draft beer from the restaurant's supply, without so much as a by-your-leave.

During those rolling stag parties, CPR trains suffered more than a little wear and tear. One was reported to have had all its windows smashed within a few minutes of departing for the west. It must have been a mighty cold ride to Winnipeg after that.

However, the mayhem was not specifically aimed at the railway, given that

harvest-excursion rates were really quite reasonable, all things considered. From any point on the CPR in New Brunswick, Quebec, or Ontario, an intrepid harvester could pick up a ticket to Winnipeg for fifteen bucks in the early years. The travelling passenger agents—all that the railway could muster—set up makeshift booths to handle the arduous task of getting sufficient numbers of the men to all points on the prairies. A half cent per mile was the going rate from Winnipeg to all Manitoba destinations.

A retired CPR agent recalled that he and six of his associates once worked a solid thirty-six-hour stretch to disperse the eager workforce among the anxiously waiting homesteaders. Usually tickets included a stub for return passage that would be honoured upon presentation of a written confirmation of employment in the fields and a further hard-earned thirteen dollars.

At times, farmers bypassed the labour distribution process. Standing on the platform at any little whistle stop along the route to Winnipeg, they were only too happy to make a direct appeal to the partying masses in transit. Though a few farmers were successful in recruiting instant labour, others ran the risk of being shanghaied by the onboard pranksters and finding themselves unceremoniously dumped onto a railway platform somewhere down the line—the same fate visited upon more than one station agent.

Most of the harvest excursionists were unemployed labourers from cities in the east. Nearly all were men. But there were also teenage boys and the occasional adventurous, and probably regretful, woman. After the recruitment campaign had spread to the British Isles, a contemporary London newspaper offered the useful insight that some of the men "are going more for a holiday, than for the sake of the wages they will earn." The sixteen-hour workdays must have come as quite a shock when they arrived at the work sites.

To be fair, though, many of the men did put in an honest season's work. Some liked the prairie lifestyle so much that they settled in the west and kept their return ticket stubs as souvenirs. Maybe the best known of these was the Right Honourable James Garfield Gardiner, who was twice premier of Saskatchewan and also served as minister of agriculture in the Mackenzie King federal government.

One of the CPR's last excursions, in 1942, was joined by five hundred students from McGill University and Macdonald College in Montreal, along with a few from Bishop's University in Lennoxville, Quebec, and Queen's University in Kingston, Ontario. However, by that late date the job seekers made the journey to the west under the watchful eyes of four RCMP constables who were regularly assigned to the harvest trains.

Those Little Packets of Seeds

For winter-weary railway workers in the first half of the twentieth century, spring was heralded not only by the budding of local flora, but also by the annual arrival of flower seeds sent out by the horticulture section of CPR's department of natural resources.

Unofficially there had always been a scattering of gardening enthusiasts among the hundreds of station agents, section foremen, and railway constables across the system who took the initiative, whether for recreational or aesthetic purposes, to till the soil when things were quiet on the job. In Europe and the United States, it was common practice to landscape railway grounds where construction of lines

Those Little Packets of Seeds Gardens that could be viewed from passing trains received special attention, like these manicured grounds at Kenora, Ontario, in 1928. NS.13001

and buildings had scarred the countryside. In Canada, there was the added incentive to demonstrate the fertility of the land, particularly in the west, in a bid to entice prospective settlers. Accordingly, the efforts of CPR's green-thumbed volunteers were often rewarded by the divisional superintendents with modest cash prizes—or with those welcome little packets of seeds.

As early as 1908, the company established nurseries at Wolseley, Saskatchewan, under the direction of Dr. Gustaf A. Bosson-Krook of Sweden, who held degrees in the science of horticulture. What had begun as a spontaneous response to the arrival of spring had grown to an institutionalized effort to turn railway properties into community showpieces.

Until his death in 1927, Dr. Krook criss-crossed the CPR system, racking up between forty-eight and sixty-four thousand kilometres of travel annually, to inspect more than two thousand stations and provide expert gardening advice and guidance. In some communities—notably along the north shore of Lake Superior—carloads of topsoil were delivered by rail to cover bedrock that was inhospitable to plant life. In places like Schreiber, Ontario, temporary tracks were laid to bring in the tons of earth required.

Trees and shrubs were another consideration and, again most particularly in the west, necessary to provide shelter from the wind and snow. Cedar, spruce, Scotch pine, and red pine were common choices, and still stand prominently in many a prairie town.

Vegetable gardens were also encouraged, partly for the benefit of local railway workers and partly for the agricultural experimentation and research opportunities they afforded. During the First World War, all of the planting beds on CPR property were converted to war gardens for food production, one-third of which grew potatoes.

To succeed Krook, the railway hired Bob Almey as chief horticulturist, at the same time that responsibility for the gardens was transferred to Winnipeg under the operating department. Almey, a graduate of the Ontario Agriculture College in

Guelph, Ontario, had been employed as provincial horticulturist for the Manitoba government before being recruited by CPR. In the thirty years he spent with the railway, Almey built quite a reputation in his field, becoming an expert in the cultivation of gladiolas. In the mid-1940s he was honoured by having a new crabapple, developed by the Dominion experimental station at Morden, Manitoba, named for him.

Almey dealt with two kinds of railway gardeners: the casual enthusiast who made up the bulk of the beautification workforce, and the hired hand, assigned the more onerous task of keeping the gardens at major stations in immaculate condition. Between 110 and 125 varieties and kinds of flowers were grown. By the 1940s, more than eleven thousand packets of seeds were distributed annually; moreover, CPR greenhouses at Fort William, Kenora, Weston Shops, Moose Jaw, Ogden, Revelstoke, Kamloops, and Vancouver were growing six hundred thousand bedding plants every year, supplemented by more than forty thousand purchases from Winnipeg suppliers. Marigolds, poppies, nasturtiums, petunias, geraniums, asters, pansies, roses, zinnias, and snapdragons were all familiar choices, but more exotic plants such as Tatarian honeysuckles, nemesia, cyclamen, portulaca, and candytuft were also available.

Almey was said to be so familiar with the gardens along the right-of-way that he could "recite from memory their layouts, the variety of flowers they grew and the amounts needed." In addition to perennials, grass, shrubs, trees, bulbs, and bedding plants, the horticultural department would provide fertilizers, insecticides, and in some cases, even lawn mowers.

Each year, gardens were judged in a number of categories: Best District Garden, Best Visible New Garden, Best Invisible New Garden, Best Visible Old Garden, and Best Invisible Old Garden. The "visible" and "invisible" designations referred to whether or not they could be viewed by passing trains.

Among all of the station gardens, perhaps the most talked about and photographed was a unique creation at Harvey, New Brunswick. Where once coal cinders, tin cans, bottles, and automobile tires formed useless and unsightly piles, an "animal park" was created from carefully clipped bushes and trees. Populated by a leafy man in a top hat sitting on a bench, a dog sitting up and begging, and a pair of deer, the station grounds were a major attraction. "After watching passengers sitting in the cars, slumped in their seats, travel weary, with bored expressions, suddenly sit bolt upright and stare in open-eyed wonder, call to people across the aisle and point out the windows; after seeing troop trains during summer months when the windows were open, fairly bristle with guns pointing at the little Animal Park, I knew we had something," said U. V. Caulfield, the agent who created the trackside curiosity.

Most of the gardeners, though, were quite content to heed the advice of the horticulture department: "Do not start too large a garden, do not scatter plants around indiscriminately, avoid fancy designs and, most of all—keep your eyes open for those little packets of seeds."

Winter Woes

How cold was it? The storm began on the last day of January. As winds of more than sixty kilometres per hour whipped the snow into a white froth, a mass of frigid arctic air sent temperatures plunging from the Rocky Mountains to Ontario. In the Yukon, in the little town of Snag, thermometers cracked as the mercury dropped to a bone-chilling minus sixty-one degrees Celsius, a North American record for which nobody cheered. Across the CPR system, travellers huddled around stoves, while those in transit rubbed frost from windows, hoping to catch a glimpse of any landmark that would signal the proximity of hearth and home.

Throughout the week, the snow continued to fall. Saskatchewan was hit the hardest. City buses ceased operations, milk and bread companies cancelled deliveries, schools closed, and airlines grounded all flights. All freight and mixed trains were held at division points. Snowplows and double-headed locomotives, pulling the CPR's priority transcontinental trains, burrowed through the solid walls of snow that drifted across the tracks until they, too, invariably ground to a halt.

By noon on 8 February, seventeen CPR locomotives and five snowplows were struggling to clear the main line between Moose Jaw and Regina. Virtually no trains had moved for two days. A plow making its way from Indian Head to Regina

WINTER WOES
From the beginning of operations in the 1880s, CPR faced an annual war with winter, as this early shot of the roundhouse at Rogers Pass, British Columbia, clearly illustrates.
M.1282

struck a deep drift near Balgonie, Saskatchewan, and derailed across both eastbound and westbound tracks, adding to the woes faced by the large army of shovellers and sweepers sent out by the CPR.

Winter on the prairies had always been a time of blizzards and drifting snow, of delays and missed schedules, but few could remember hardships of this magnitude. All activity ground to a halt. Hundreds of isolated communities hungered for supplies and foodstuffs. Cattle and horses died by the score.

By 9 February, the CPR main line had been cleared and railway operations slowly returned to normal. Plows barged their way through deep drifts to open branch lines that had been closed to traffic for several days. Life went on—that's the way it was in 1947.

Under Rogers Pass

When Alice Macredie attended the opening ceremonies for the CPR's line through Rogers Pass with the completion of the Macdonald Tunnel in 1989, she was on hand to honour the contribution her father had made to enhancing the same route more than seventy years earlier. John Macredie was one of the builders of CPR's Connaught Tunnel. During the years from 1915 to 1917, Alice lived with him on the project site and witnessed one of the most amazing engineering achievements of the time.

From the beginning of railway operations through Rogers Pass in the 1880s, it was apparent that the problems of excessive grades and relentless snowfall would eventually have to be addressed. By 1913, traffic on the main line through the Selkirks had reached a critical point. Something had to be done.

For the engineers, the solution was simple. If Mount Macdonald stood in the way of achieving an easy route to the west coast, they would bore straight through it, thereby reducing the grade of this section of track from 2.2 percent to 1 percent and eliminating nearly six kilometres of snowsheds. The work itself, however, was far from simple, involving the removal of 170,000 cubic metres of muck and rock from the eight-kilometre hole.

To facilitate the project, an innovative tunnelling method was used, whereby a smaller "pioneer shaft" was bored alongside the route of the main tunnel so that work could be carried out from many places simultaneously. Although this approach was unique in North America, it had been successfully employed in tunnelling projects in Europe, including the Simplon Tunnel frequented by the renowned *Orient Express.* The more common practice in Canada and the United States was to dig one or more vertical shafts to the depth of the proposed tunnel, and then work outward in both directions. This method had been proven effective when the Canadian Northern Railway drove its line through Montreal's Mount

Under Rogers Pass
Three model villages housed the construction forces boring the Connaught Tunnel through Mount Macdonald, one at each portal and a third at nearby Bear Creek.
NS.3679

Royal a few years earlier, but that project had only ninety-one metres of mountain above the roadbed, whereas the Rogers Pass line was one thousand metres below the summit of the Selkirks. As a result of using this method, tunnelling progressed at twice the rate of previous North American projects and required nearly six hundred workers at the peak of activity.

Three model villages were designed by CPR architect Walter S. Painter to house the construction forces, one at each portal and a third at nearby Bear Creek. Alice could still recall the elevated walkways that connected one building to another, an absolute necessity in an area that often recorded snowfalls in metres rather than centimetres.

The work was contracted to the firm of Foley, Welch & Stewart, and conducted under the watchful eye of the CPR's A. C. Dennis. The men were supervised by J. G. Sullivan, chief engineer of Western Lines, and aided by assistant superintendents Joseph Murphy and Joseph Fowler. Tailings were removed from the tunnel in narrow-gauge railway cars, initially pulled by a team of sturdy mules. A small locomotive powered by compressed air was used after the work had advanced under the mountain.

The original intent was to electrify the line through the tunnel, but studies deemed it prohibitively expensive to operate such a small section of track with special locomotives and technologies. Ventilation was also a major challenge. A system of enormous exhaust fans driven by diesel engines was eventually decided upon to blow fresh air against approaching trains.

The initial breakthrough occurred in December 1915. A small party of CPR officers, accompanied by a number of British Columbia and Winnipeg businessmen and public figures, passed through the tunnel the morning of 19 December, on a flatcar outfitted with several rows of benches.

On 18 July 1916, Grant Hall, CPR vice-president and general manager of Western Lines, was there to escort the Duke of Connaught, governor general of Canada, through the tunnel on a special car, in the company of the Duchess of Connaught and Princess Patricia. Upon reaching the west portal, the Duke officially named the tunnel "The Selkirk." It would be several weeks before the decision was taken to honour the governor general and rename the CPR's newest engineering wonder the "Connaught Tunnel."

Terminal Rivalry

While the CPR line was being pushed through the mountains of Alberta and British Columbia and around the north shore of Lake Superior, there was a great deal of speculation about which west coast community would be the line's Pacific terminus and reap the inevitable economic benefits.

At the time, the two frontrunners were Victoria, on Vancouver Island, and Port Moody, at the eastern tip of Burrard Inlet. Port Moody had been specified by the Canadian government in the railway's charter, but there were some obvious drawbacks to the site. It was twenty-two kilometres from the entrance of the first narrows at English Bay, a long distance for ships to navigate inland in an area subject to fog; there was a steep incline running up from the waterfront and leaving little room for townsite development; and the tide could vary by as much as four or five metres.

In the spring of 1884, CPR general manager William Van Horne made the trip to the coast to assess the situation. Arriving at Elgin House, a pioneer hotel in the neighbourhood of the proposed terminus, the railway boss was soon holding court with prominent members of the local citizenry, many of whom defended the suitability of Port Moody. Not wishing to show his hand too early, Van Horne was noncommittal. Ever wary of the CPR's increasingly tight financial position, though, he did make the proclamation that no railway extensions or branch lines would extend farther west than Port Moody without a considerable land grant from the federal government to cover construction costs. Certainly the company's

Terminal Rivalry
When the CPR main line was extended to Coal Harbour, Port Moody's fate was sealed.
A.12534

own over-extended resources did not leave any possibility for the CPR to finance such a line, a situation that was confirmed by the board of directors upon Van Horne's return to company headquarters in Montreal.

Equally, however, there was a clear understanding that Port Moody could not hold its favoured status forever. "The matter has been carefully considered by our directors," Van Horne announced, "and they have concluded that there is not sufficient available room at Port Moody for their requirements, as it is estimated that not less than 400 acres of level ground will be required for railway purposes alone, and it would cost from two to four million dollars to reclaim this amount of land from the tide flats at Port Moody."

The citizens of Port Moody, of course, were determined to defend their interests in the matter and continued to tout the merits of their townsite while heaping scorn upon all potential rivals.

Because of the enormous costs that would have been incurred to ferry trains across the Strait of Georgia to Vancouver Island, had the railway chosen to locate its Pacific terminus there, Victoria never really received serious consideration—it was in the running for political reasons more than anything else, being the settlement where the most voters resided. Instead, the principal contenders were sites along Coal Harbour and English Bay on the mainland, where the depth of the water was more than adequate, and where there was plenty of flat land adjacent to where the docks would be situated.

But initially Port Moody had to suffice, and dock facilities and storage sheds were soon under construction in anticipation of the opening of the transcontinental line and the arrival of the first trains from the east. In keeping with the plan to ultimately extend the line, the wharf pilings were constructed of wood rather than iron, and the station and freight facilities were modest.

Despite its tentative status as anchor of the westernmost point of the CPR, the good people of Port Moody were determined to make the most of the occasion when the first scheduled passenger train lurched to a halt there on 4 July 1886. A letter sent to Van Horne read, in part: "We heartily congratulate you and the other members of the Directory of the CPR, on this the arrival of the first through daily train, at Port Moody, the western terminus of the Canadian Pacific line." Within days, the first chartered ship, the *W. B. Flint*, arrived from the Orient with a cargo of 17,430 half chests of tea headed for markets in the east. Seven chartered vessels delivered freight from Japan during the next six months, and passenger trains left Port Moody on a daily basis, except Monday.

Alas, Port Moody's heady days as the busy Pacific terminus of the CPR could not and did not last. The following year, with federal assistance, the line was extended and officially opened at Coal Harbour, the new townsite of Vancouver. The Port Moody facilities were disassembled and the docks abandoned, leaving the town to its destiny as a residential suburb of Vancouver, the bustling new metropolis and western terminus of the CPR.

Destined to Be Great

"Hamilton! Hamilton! This is destined to be a great city, perhaps the greatest in Canada, and we must see to it that it has a name commensurate with its dignity and importance, and Vancouver it shall be, if I have the ultimate decision." Thus spoke CPR vice-president William Van Horne to CPR land commissioner L. A. Hamilton, in 1884, as they stood in the midst of the woods along Burrard Inlet that would soon give way to the new railway terminus townsite.

The first survey of the area was conducted the following year by Hamilton on the peninsula between the waterfront and False Creek. By 1886, much of the site was covered by logs, stumps, branches, and leaves—an ideal setting for a fire. The inevitable occurred on 13 June that year. The beginnings of the city were completely wiped out in a giant conflagration. Fortunately for the CPR, construction of the terminal facilities had just barely begun and damage was negligible. The city made a remarkably fast recovery.

On 23 May 1887, locomotive 374, pulling five cars with passengers from the east,

DESTINED TO BE GREAT
The CPR's strained financial resources resulted initially in a very utilitarian station and wharf complex at Vancouver's Coal Harbour.
A.1880

was the first to pull to a stop at the CPR station and steamship docks at the end of the extension from Port Moody to Vancouver. The engine, tarted up for the occasion, had been decorated at Kamloops, British Columbia, by CPR master mechanic L. R. Johnson, before being sent down to North Bend to fill its ceremonial role. Painted with the slogans "From Ocean to Ocean," "Our National Highway," and "Montreal Greets the Terminal City," its headlight sported a portrait of Queen Victoria, surmounted by a crown.

The journey along the Vancouver extension was described by the press in the most glowing terms: "The trip from Port Moody to Vancouver is delightful in the extreme, and a pleasant ending to the finest scenic route on the continent. Skirting the pleasant waters of Burrard Inlet the entire distance, the laughing waters seemed to smile a kindly welcome, while the ever-lasting hills, snow-crowned towering above, seemed to realize their majesty and sublimity."

The *Victoria Daily Colonist* described the arrival of the *Pacific Express* amid the countless flags and streamers: "It seemed as if all Vancouver congregated, and a mighty shout went up as the train thundered into the station between the handsome double arch of fir. As the engine rolled on, it was greeted with the following mottoes: 'Occident greets the Orient' and 'Confederation Accomplished,' while facing the city "Labour Omnia Vincet and 'Vancouver' surrounded the arch."

The Vancouver city band delivered a spirited rendition of "See the Conquering Hero Comes," and speeches were heard from the mayor and CPR general superintendent Harry Abbott. Everyone agreed the railway had ensured Vancouver's future prosperity, and three cheers for the Queen brought the proceedings to a close.

Less than a month later, the steamship *Abyssinia* tied up at the CPR wharf, inaugurating a regular service on the Pacific, along with fellow former Cunard ships *Parthia* and *Batavia*. These three ships were chartered by the company to handle the Pacific leg of the "All-Red Route" to the Orient, and supplemented occasionally by other steamships, landed more than one hundred thousand metric tons of cargo at Vancouver during their three years of operation for CPR.

As a result of the increased economic activity, Vancouver's population flourished, approaching ten thousand by 1890. The CPR's Hotel Vancouver opened its doors to guests in May 1888. A modest structure, it was eventually replaced by a more substantial building in 1917. Land sales in Vancouver were sufficient to cover the cost of the terminal facilities, as well as the hotel.

Over the ensuing years, the railway's investments have kept pace with the growth of the city. In 1891, the first three *Empress* steamships arrived on the west coast to begin Canadian Pacific's own service to Asia, one that would last until the Second World War. A new passenger terminal was opened in 1899 on the corner of Granville and Cordova. It was completely rebuilt in 1914 to accommodate increased traffic. The waterfront was totally revamped, culminating in the construction of Pier B-C in 1927, while a tunnel was excavated to connect the rail yards at False Creek with the harbour.

For years, Pier B-C served the company's ocean-going *Empresses* and the beloved *Princess* vessels of the British Columbia coastal fleet. Today it's the site of Canada Place, one of Vancouver's most spectacular structures and, of course, the former Canada Pavilion at Expo '86. The beautifully restored passenger station has been refurbished by the city as a terminal for Vancouver's Skytrain and Seabus services.

And old locomotive 374 Well, it hasn't been forgotten, either. You can find the refurbished iron horse down by False Creek at the CPR roundhouse, which was restored and converted into a pavilion for the world's fair and is the focal point of a large residential redevelopment. The locomotive is one of Vancouver's most historically interesting artifacts.

Van Horne's Overcoat

William Van Horne was pleased with himself as he strode toward the CPR station in Toronto one Christmas Eve. The crisp night air was no match for the warm, comforting embrace of the CPR president's new fur-lined overcoat, a Christmas gift to himself. Sir William was heading to his home in Montreal for the holidays.

Boarding the train with a flourish and pausing only momentarily to toss his coat onto a chair in the day coach, the burly railway president headed down the corridor, anxious to lean back and enjoy his half-finished cigar in the quiet elegance of the smoking car.

Before too long, the train was gliding to a stop to board passengers and luggage in Brady Junction, where the now refreshed Van Horne hopped down to visit and chat with the station agent. Returning to his coach seat a few minutes later, the winter chill from the platform bringing back pleasant memories of his luxurious new overcoat, he was astonished to discover the prized garment had vanished. Cussing under his breath and looking quickly from side to side, he shook a fellow passenger awake and coaxed from him a sketchy picture of a suspicious looking character who had been seen lurking about the car at Burketon Falls.

A now fuming Van Horne sent a telegraph to alert the police in Burketon and headed for the baggage car to retrieve an old overcoat from his trunk. Storming through the third-class coach, he saw from the corner of his eye a man huddled in a seat with an overcoat around his shoulders—an overcoat remarkably similar to the one that had just gone missing. As Van Horne attempted to establish eye contact with the lone passenger, the man looked away nervously, sinking even farther into his seat. "Guilty," the angry rail boss concluded, hissing at the suspected rogue to follow him to the baggage car if he wished to avoid a fuss in front of the other passengers.

Together with the conductor, they ducked into the cluttered confines of the baggage car, where Van Horne pulled a handkerchief from the top pocket of the overcoat with a deft flick. "Do you know to whom this coat belongs?" asked the railway president.

"No," came the reply from the visibly alarmed man.

"Well I'll tell you whose it is, it's mine," said Van Horne, waving the handkerchief in the man's face to back up his claim. "And I've a mind to turn you over to the police as soon as we get to the next stop."

"Oh please sir, don't do that," the man stammered. "I didn't mean to steal the coat."

"In that case, why didn't you hand it to the conductor," roared Van Horne. "What's your name?"

"Kennedy," came the weak response.

"And where are you from?" demanded Van Horne.

"Peterborough," the man replied.

"Well, Kennedy, there's too much thievin' going on around here, and I for one won't have it on this railway. I'll have you in the hands of the police if I have to deliver you myself."

"No please sir, don't do it," wailed the man. "My poor wife and children are waiting for me to arrive for Christmas and I've been working in the bush for the last six months."

VAN HORNE'S OVERCOAT
Van Horne found warmth in his new fur-lined overcoat and, ultimately, in his heart as well.
A.75

"Stop your snivelling, you thieving coward," Van Horne shot back, now shaking with anger. "You thieves are all alike; as soon as you're caught at your games, you start to snivel about your wife and kids back home. No, my mind's made up, it's off to jail with you."

As the train pulled to a stop in Dranoel, Van Horne ordered the conductor to fetch the police, and the man was cuffed and led off into the night.

Back in the baggage car, resting on a packing case and now beginning to calm down, the president noticed a baby carriage in the corner. "Must have been a man who bought that," he muttered to the conductor. "A woman would have had the good sense to outfit the thing with runners for the winter."

The conductor casually turned over the baggage tag hanging from the handle of the buggy and dropped it as if he had seen a ghost. "What is it man?" Van Horne queried.

"The baggage tag, sir. It says Kennedy, Peterborough."

"Good God, that's the man I just had arrested," Van Horne blurted out, thoughts moving through his mind in rapid succession. He could picture a woman standing on the platform in Peterborough, children at her side, anxiously awaiting her husband's return for Christmas. Maybe the man had acted innocently enough. Maybe he thought the coat had been abandoned and would end up in some railway lost and found somewhere.

Van Horne was off the train before it came to a full stop at the next station.

"Give me the key, man," he called out to the telegraph operator as he strode into the agent's office, the president himself being a skilled telegraph sender and receiver. Quickly a message was fired off to the agent in Dranoel: "Great mistake has been made. Get police to release Kennedy immediately. Get engine and car and run special to Peterborough. Kennedy must get there tonight."

"By whose order," came back the reply.

"The president of the CPR," was the terse response.

Before long, the president's train was easing into Peterborough. A light snow blanketed the station platform. Sure enough, as Van Horne descended from the coach vestibule, he could make out the silhouette of a woman with a baby in her arms and three other children flocking around her legs.

"Excuse me, ma'am," said Sir William, "are you Mrs. Kennedy?"

"Yes, sir, I am," came the reply.

"Well, your husband will be along before too long; he has had a slight delay," the president said, as he extended his hand in greeting. "May I wish you and your loved ones a very Merry Christmas," he said, pumping the woman's arm with great vigour.

As he turned and swung himself back up on the train, Mrs. Kennedy looked down at her hand, somewhat mystified by the rapid exchange. There in her open palm was a twenty-dollar bill.

An Enterprising Life

On the morning of 7 November 1885, as photographer Alexander Ross prepared to record the driving of the Last Spike on the CPR, a young boy pushed his way to the front of the assembled train workers and company officers, positioning himself just behind Lord Strathcona. As the shutter clicked on that historic moment, the two would become inextricably linked for all time, front and centre in one of Canada's most famous photographs.

It was not by chance that the young lad, Edward Mallandaine, was on hand for the occasion. The boy was rather enterprising for his age, having established a small courier service out of Farwell, British Columbia (later renamed Revelstoke) that same year. The son of an architect and civil engineer who emigrated from England in 1860, Mallandaine lived and was schooled in Victoria, British Columbia.

While Mallandaine was in school, his teacher had once made the mistake of commenting within his earshot that "you can't set fire to water." Taking up the challenge, the boy soaked wood shavings and paper in oil, dumped them into Victoria harbour, and set them alight. Fortunately no harm came from the prank, but it was an early indication of the lad's impetuous nature.

At the age of seventeen, Mallandaine set off eastward to fight Indians during the

An Enterprising Life
Over the shoulder of Lord Strathcona, the young boy Edward Mallandaine has stared at generations of school children from the centre of Canada's most famous photograph.
NS.1960

Northwest Rebellion. He had only reached Golden, in the British Columbia interior, when the hostilities came to an end. Returning west to Farwell, Mallandaine started a freight service, catering to railway contractors, newspapermen, and those operating small businesses. On average, he earned ten cents per letter delivered.

Farwell was a wild town in those days, as were many of the fledgling communities along the rail line. In later years, Mallandaine would comment: "Life was exciting, for there were numerous accidents, fights, rows and thrills every day, and all day on the road and in the camp and town. Drinking! Yes, the medical men were kept busy." When he heard that the railway party from the east was en route to Craigellachie to witness the completion of the line, he was determined to be there. Hopping a construction train, Mallandaine headed east on 6 November, arriving in time to ensure his place in history.

Fifty years later, as stipendiary magistrate and reeve of Creston, British Columbia, a town he helped found, Mallandaine could still remember the excitement of the moment. "Everyone cheered," he recalled. "The locomotive whistle shrieked, several short speeches were made, and hands were shaken. Major Rogers, the discoverer of the pass named after him, became so gleeful that he up-ended a huge tie and tried to mark the spot by the side of the track by sticking it in the ground."

Mallandaine kept up his association with the CPR, serving as land agent for the company in Cranbrook for several years under Colonel Dennis, the department head in Calgary. Enterprising throughout his life, he worked as an architect, engineer, land surveyor, tie and lumber agent, irrigation engineer, townsite commissioner, magistrate, councillor, and reeve, as well as serving as a colonel in Canada's First World War Forestry Corps.

The last surviving figure in the Last Spike photograph, Mallandaine died in Creston in August 1949, at the age of eighty-two.

Lady Macdonald and the Lure of the Buffer Beam

When the first transcontinental passenger train pulled out of Montreal's Dalhousie Square Station on 28 June 1886, no senior railway officials were on board, and stranger yet, no politicians were either. As a long-time proponent of the Pacific Railway, Prime Minister John A. Macdonald had hoped to make the trip, but was unavoidably detained in Ottawa. By 10 July, however, his trip westward had been arranged, and a special train was placed at the disposal of Sir John and Lady Macdonald.

The CPR had decided to avoid transporting the prime minister on board the regular *Atlantic Express*, wishing to allow as many stops along the route as were necessary or desirable. Along with the locomotive and baggage car came the sumptuous official car *Jamaica*, acquired by the CPR from the Quebec, Montreal, Ottawa & Occidental Railway, and the sleeping car *Ignace*. The *Jamaica* was made available for the exclusive use of the Macdonalds and their servants, whereas the *Ignace* was provided to accommodate the assortment of railway officials and aides-de-camp accompanying the special train. In Winnipeg, CPR general superintendent John Egan's official car number 77 was added to the train, as that gentleman was heading for Donald, British Columbia, in the normal performance of his duties.

At Gleichen, Alberta, a group of Indian chiefs, including the legendary Crowfoot, requested an audience with Sir John, arriving trackside in full Blackfoot regalia. Among the problems discussed were prairie fires started by the railway's "fire wagons," described as a great "vexation" to the Indians.

As their train left Calgary, Lady Macdonald decided to avail herself of the superb view from the locomotive, riding in the engine cab to Banff, where a short spur had been put in to allow the party to spend the night. Proceeding the next day to Laggan, Alberta (now Lake Louise), superintendent Egan took Lady Macdonald forward to see the larger Consolidation locomotive being coupled to the front of the train to negotiate the steep grades through the mountain passes.

At that moment, Lady Macdonald made a decision that would fill Egan with horror. As she recorded in her diary, "From the instant my eyes rested on the broad

LADY MACDONALD AND THE LURE OF THE BUFFER BEAM
At one point in the trip, Lady Macdonald managed to coax her husband from the relative safety of the back platform of the *Jamaica* to join her at the extreme opposite end of the train.
A.18965

shining surface of its buffer beam and cowcatcher, over which a bright little flag waved from a glossy brass pole, I decided to travel there and nowhere else for the remaining six hundred miles of my journey!"

Try as he might, Egan was unable to dissuade the lady from her purpose, so a cushioned box was fastened to the front of the locomotive where Lady Macdonald intended to sit. Although Sir John pronounced the idea "rather ridiculous," he agreed to her quixotic request, and Egan, succumbing to the inevitable, seated himself beside the prime minister's wife, so she would not be alone in such a dangerous position.

Fortunately all went well down the big hill at Field, British Columbia, and along the Kicking Horse River. At the station platform in Palliser, British Columbia, when Sir John walked forward to check on her, Lady Macdonald was even able to convince *him* to climb aboard for the forty-five-kilometre ride to Donald, along the Columbia River. At Donald, Egan's car was removed from the train, and the party was joined by Harry Abbott, general superintendent of the CPR's Pacific Division. Again, Lady Macdonald returned to her perch on the buffer beam and the train proceeded.

Spring water leaked from the roofs of the tunnels through which they passed; however, prepared for any contingency, Lady Macdonald had worn a raincoat and was equipped with an umbrella as well. As the train emerged from one such bore, a group of English sportsmen with guns in hand were startled at the sight. "I am sorely afraid I laughed outright at the blank amazement of their rosy faces," Lady Macdonald later said, "and longed to tell them what fun it was; but not being introduced, you know, I contented myself with acknowledging their presence by a solemn bow—which was quite irresistible under the circumstances."

Stops were made for meals, and at tea time, a cup of tea and slice of buttered bread were served to Lady Macdonald on the buffer beam. A number of stops were made for the magnificent views they afforded. When the ninety-one-metre Stoney Creek Bridge was reached, several of the party, including the Macdonalds, elected to walk across and be picked up on the other side.

Most of the remainder of the trip was uneventful, with the exception of a close call while Mrs. Macdonald was being accompanied by Joseph Pope, the prime minister's personal secretary. As she related to CPR vice-president Van Horne, "I felt perfectly secure and the only damage we did from Ottawa to the sea, was to kill a lovely little fat Pig, whom an error in judgment led under the engine near Nicomen, yesterday morning. I shut my eyes while he flew up and past, striking Mr. Pope who was sitting at my feet."

The prime minister's special train arrived at the Pacific terminus of Port Moody, British Columbia, on 24 July, where a steamer waited to ferry the party over to Victoria. Sir John was on hand two weeks later, on 13 August, to drive the last spike on Vancouver Island's Esquimalt & Nanaimo Railway at Cliffside, a silver mallet and golden spike having been prepared for the event.

A Gallant Gentleman, Great of Heart

Just inside the La Gauchetière Street entrance to CPR's Windsor Station, at the corner of Peel Street in Montreal, there's a plaque that honours the memory of Colonel George Henry Ham, head of the railway's publicity department in the 1890s. Installed by the Canadian Women's Press Club after his death in 1926, it pays tribute to the man who founded their club and was, as was engraved on the plaque, "a gallant gentleman and great of heart."

Ham was that and much more, judging from the many accolades lavished upon him during his successful career as a newspaperman and publicist. Variously described as "a great national asset" and "the Mark Twain of Canada," Ham was called "the greatest unprinted wit in Canada" by *Colliers* magazine.

Born in Trenton, Ontario, on 23 August 1847, Ham began newspaper work as a reporter for the Whitney (Ontario) *Chronicle*, in 1865, and subsequently was employed by other Ontario newspapers in Uxbridge, Guelph, and Toronto. He enlisted in the Canadian Militia and served during the 1866 and 1870 Fenian raids, making him a perfect candidate for newspaper field correspondent during the second Northwest Rebellion of 1885.

Ham had a long and varied career in Manitoba, joining the *Manitoba Free Press* in 1875 and working his way up to city editor. He also published the *Winnipeg Tribune*, sat as a member of the Winnipeg Board of Education, and served as a city alderman for a number of years.

His association with the CPR began in 1891 when he was appointed travelling passenger agent in charge of the railway's publicity department. For the next thirty-five years, Ham was invaluable to the company, acting not only as publicist and tour guide for visiting journalists, but as the CPR's lobbyist and ambassador-at-large. As a result of his efforts, Ham was said to have "the unchallenged reputation of being able to call more individuals by their front name than any

A Gallant Gentleman, Great of Heart
A Christmas card received by Ham in 1924 takes a good-natured poke at the colonel's peccadillos.
NS.12547

other man on the continent of North America." In 1914, he achieved the rank of colonel as an honorary appointment from Sir Sam Hughes, the Canadian minister of militia and defense, for acting as spokesman for Canadian patriotism and for his ardent support of the war effort.

Anecdotes abound of the colonel's public relations abilities and quick wit. Normally a very willing and able speaker, Ham was asked to make an impromptu speech one night at a particularly boring function. In no mood for speaking, and being quite unprepared, he replied to the master of ceremonies: "I am unable to make a speech tonight, as I have a bad headache, am suffering from rheumatism in my legs, have Asiatic cholera, adenoids, gastritis, ingrown toenails, premature baldness and housemaid's knee. And anything I haven't got, I'm going out right now to get it."

When the seventy-nine-year-old colonel fell ill and died on 16 April 1926, a special funeral train was organized and a number of CPR officials and personal friends rode aboard it from Toronto to Whitby, where he was buried. The man who had joked about having the distinction of being the only male member of the Women's Press Club was honoured by the club with the construction of a beautiful memorial porch before the door of St. John's Church in Whitby, as well as with a bronze plaque on the wall at Windsor Station.

Major Rogers' Famous Pass

The decision to change the route of the Canadian Pacific Railway from the northern course mapped out by Canadian government engineer Sandford Fleming to the more southerly and direct line through the Kicking Horse Pass remains controversial to this day. When the railway enterprise was turned over to a private consortium of investors, they opted for a route that would discourage American railways from building branch lines north of the border into the resource-rich interior of British Columbia. It was a move that was deemed prudent from both economic and military points of view. The more direct route still afforded a measure of speed over the competition, particularly in the movement of goods between Pacific Rim countries and marketplaces in Canada and the northeastern United States; however, the more physically demanding terrain has required enormous capital expenditures to maintain that edge.

For better or worse, the die was cast in August 1882 when Major A. B. Rogers, a rough-and-tumble American engineer working for the CPR, announced the discovery of the pass through the Selkirks that now bears his name. Born in Orleans, Massachusetts, in 1829, Major Rogers came to Canada at the request of CPR syndicate member James J. Hill. Rogers had a fine background in engineering. In addition to receiving an education as an apprentice ship's carpenter and an engineering degree from Yale, Rogers also worked as an engineer on the Erie Canal and with several railroads in the United States, culminating with the Chicago, Milwaukee & St. Paul. Rogers served with the United States Cavalry during the American Civil War and received a major's commission in 1862.

Hill's purpose in sending Rogers west in 1881 was to examine the more southerly passes through the Rocky and Selkirk Mountains, and to prove their viability for the railway. At the end of his first season in the mountains, where he was aided in his surveying work by his nephew Albert and a party of ten Indians recruited at Kamloops, British Columbia, Rogers joined CPR general manager William Van Horne in announcing the practicability of a route through the Kicking Horse Pass, even though he was not absolutely sure a corresponding pass existed through the Selkirks. But Rogers was able to confirm the existence of the now-famous Selkirks pass the following year, and the railway's destiny was sealed.

The cost of keeping the route open has been high, both in dollars and labour. Many kilometres of snowsheds have been built and enormous tunnels excavated. The bridges along the line are among the most impressive engineering features on the CPR system, and the locomotives required to move traffic over the summit are the most powerful. The snowfall in Rogers Pass is measured in hundreds of centimetres, and the war against snow slides and avalanches is never-ending.

Yet the southern route has yielded many benefits as well, not least of which was enabling the CPR to speed freight to the Pacific in sufficient time to secure the mail contract from the British government, at a time when such agreements meant the difference between success or failure for the enterprise. It is also fortunate that the line runs through some of the best farming, ranching, and mining areas in the country, and the scenic attractions are among the world's finest. Clearly, the original directors of the CPR board were pleased with the accomplishments of "Hell's Bells" Rogers, as he was awarded a cheque for five thousand dollars and a gold watch for his discovery of the pass through the Selkirks.

Certainly the "short, sharp, snappy little chap with the Dundreary whiskers" was one of the most colourful characters in the company's history. Although honest and hardworking, Rogers was known for his eccentricities. James Secretan, a British engineer who worked closely with Rogers, described him as "a master of picturesque profanity, who continually chewed tobacco and was an artist in expectoration." Sadly, Rogers fell ill with cancer in 1889, and while, in his own words, "awaiting the muffled oar," died in the month of May.

Major Rogers' Famous Pass
A crusty and frugal man, Rogers never cashed his five-thousand-dollar cheque for discovering the pass that bears his name. Instead he framed it and hung it on the wall, as an inspiration to his nephews.
NS.3997

The Duke of BC Could Spin a Tale

The tall tales of veteran railroaders rival the best of those spun by any sailor or fisherman. But when the CPR's "Duke of British Columbia" got to reminiscing about his early days on the line, he needed few embellishments to his real-life stories to leave jaws agape.

Duke McKenzie apprenticed with the Grand Trunk Railway as a fireman, but his career—and a boxcar full of adventures—took off when he grabbed the throttle of a CPR locomotive in May 1883, at the front line of railway construction across the prairies.

McKenzie was in the cab when the last load of rails arrived in Craigellachie, British Columbia, to complete the transcontinental link. In later years, he even claimed to have the only original print of the first of the two famous photos of the "Driving of the Last Spike." He liked to relate, "After the photographer gave it to

THE DUKE OF BC COULD SPIN A TALE When the Duke piloted the first train over the spectacular wooden trestle at Stoney Creek, more than ninety metres above the water, the bridge creaked and groaned ominously. A.1928

me, he broke the plate while making the next print, so that any photos now in existence are copies of the original in my possession."

After the brief ceremony at Craigellachie, McKenzie was one of the locomotive engineers piloting the five iron workhorses required to haul the train full of officials through the heavy snows already accumulating that November. In the absence of snow-clearing equipment, no attempt was made to keep the main line open through the mountains in the winter of 1885.

When regularly scheduled service began the following year, the Duke was at the controls of the daily *Atlantic Express* and *Pacific Express* trains running between Kamloops and Port Moody, and to Vancouver, once the line was extended in 1887. "From Kamloops west, in 1887, it was one continuous string of slides," McKenzie recounted. "Every night, something came down, and there was scarcely a night that I didn't break a pilot [cowcatcher] on my engine."

When the CPR's famed Stoney Creek Bridge opened to traffic, McKenzie's locomotive was the first to cross the mammoth trestle. "It made me feel rather creepy," he said, not surprisingly, as those early wooden structures creaked and groaned at the best of times, and in this case, not even a flimsy guardrail stood between precariously perched rolling stock and a nearly ninety-one-metre plunge to the river below.

The Duke earned a reputation for luck. On one occasion, warned only by a distant cloud of dust and an uneasy feeling that something was wrong, McKenzie brought his train to a sudden, if undignified stop. The curses and pointed remarks of the somewhat-ruffled dining car patrons turned to praise when it was discovered that McKenzie's instincts had averted a headlong rush into a huge chunk of mountain that had slid onto the right-of-way.

Then there was the time when the sudden onset of thick fog caused McKenzie to run his locomotive right through the caboose and seven refrigerator cars of the train just in front of him. Fortunately, locomotive and engineer came through unscathed, as did McKenzie's career when the cause of the accident was determined to be the leading crew's failure to set signal flags far enough back to prevent a collision.

But when it came to piloting royalty across the CPR system, luck never entered the picture. The Duke's solid record as a sure and steady hand on the throttle won him a spot in the company of kings, queens, princes, and princesses, as they viewed the Canadian landscape from McKenzie's cab or, in one instance, from the front end of McKenzie's locomotive where a platform was rigged to seat the adventurous Duke of York (later King George V) and his party.

During his thirty-eight-year career, McKenzie was said to have been at the controls of more royal trains than any two other locomotive engineers combined. It was, no doubt, a great source of fodder for spinning yarns, and a fitting tribute to an experienced and accomplished railroader known to his co-workers as the Duke of BC.

EDWARD COLONNA AND L'ART NOUVEAU When Van Horne's Sherbrooke Street mansion in Montreal was razed, more was lost than a greystone façade. NS.8040

EDWARD COLONNA AND L'ART NOUVEAU

When William Van Horne's mansion on Montreal's fashionable Sherbrooke Street was razed in 1973, there were those who believed the house, once described by its owner as "fat and bulgy, like myself," had no particular architectural merit. However, architectural, historical, and sentimental considerations aside, the destruction of the solid greystone building did constitute a significant loss, of which few were aware.

Van Horne was a discerning collector of paintings, fossils, ship models, and oriental bric-a-brac. However, only the chosen few ushered into the great railway-man's presence ever caught a glimpse of the magnificent setting in which they were displayed.

Van Horne bought the house in the early 1890s. The interior design was supervised by Edward Colonna who, in the end, created a good deal of the embellishment himself. The result was so impressive that Van Horne's biographer described the home as "a depository for art that was itself a work of art".

Colonna was relatively unknown outside the art community. He was a leading advocate of the Art Nouveau school of design and, from a Canadian perspective, an important contributor to the development of the railway-chateau style of architecture.

Born in Germany in 1862, Colonna imigrated to New York when he was twenty. There he worked for the likes of lamp- and window-maker Louis C. Tiffany and the architect Bruce Price. His association with railways began in 1885, when he became chief designer for Barney & Smith Manufacturing Company of Dayton, Ohio, the second largest railway car maker in the United States after the Pullman Company.

Three years later, he came to Canada and set up shop in Montreal. At this time Van Horne made his acquaintance, and the CPR soon became his major employer. Once again, he found himself designing cars for Barney & Smith, as the CPR was one of the firm's most important clients, and Van Horne took a very hands-on approach to interior design. His work was so well received by the railway's management that Colonna was chosen to design the elaborate coaches, sleeping cars, and dining cars exhibited by the CPR at the Chicago World's Fair in 1893.

In a five-year period, Colonna also drew up plans for the railway's stations at Banff and Calgary, in Alberta; Trois-Rivieres, in Quebec; Windsor and Fort William, in Ontario; Brandon and Portage la Prairie, in Manitoba; and Vancouver, in British Columbia. All but the Vancouver structure were built.

Through the recommendations of Van Horne and J. M. Niblock, CPR superintendent at Medicine Hat, Alberta, Colonna was chosen to design leaded windows for the new hospital in Medicine Hat. He showed his versatility in another CPR contract, creating the coat-of-arms, stationery, dinnerware, and linen pattern for the Chateau Frontenac in Quebec City.

For the Van Horne house—one of several on which he worked in Montreal—Colonna developed magnificent friezes, mosaic ceilings, leaded windows, mantles, and fireplaces. Similar works by Colonna could be viewed by the public in the waiting room of the Windsor Street Station, headquarters of the CPR for several decades.

Despite Colonna's many talents, his inability to build sufficient business drove him back to Europe. There he finally achieved a measure of recognition, executing some of his best work while employed by Siegfried Bing in his famous Parisian store, L'Art Nouveau, from which the name of the design style is derived.

A Master of Engineering Marvels

The sudden death of John Edward Schwitzer in 1911 deprived the CPR of an enormously gifted engineer and relegated the architect of such marvels as the Lethbridge Viaduct and the world-famous Spiral Tunnels to an obscure corner of Canadian history.

Schwitzer was born in Ottawa, in April of 1870. An overachiever from an early age, he excelled at lacrosse, football, and hockey, games that he pursued enthusiastically with his boyhood friends. Noted for his inquisitive nature, he was nicknamed the "Sandy Hill detective," after the Ottawa neighbourhood in which he grew up.

A MASTER OF ENGINEERING MARVELS
Enabling the CPR main line in the Rockies to loop over itself twice, the Spiral Tunnels lowered the railway grade from a disastrous 4.5 percent to a more manageable 2.2 percent.
M.1266

At age twenty-one, Schwitzer graduated from Montreal's McGill University with a degree in engineering. He never looked back. In 1888, he signed on in a junior capacity with the Lake Temiscamingue Colonization Railway, followed by senior positions in the engineering departments of the Ottawa & Gatineau Railway, the Parry Sound Colonization Railway, and the Canada Atlantic Railway. By 1899, Schwitzer had established his own practice in Rat Portage, Ontario, later renamed Kenora. It was there that the CPR hired him to overhaul its terminal facilities. Rising swiftly through the company's engineering ranks, he was intimately involved with efforts to transform the pioneer transcontinental railway into an efficient, no-nonsense enterprise.

Among his achievements was the double-tracking and grade revision on the CPR main line between Winnipeg and Fort William (now Thunder Bay), allowing for a more efficient flow of grain from the Canadian west to the thriving port at the head of Lake Superior. But it was two engineering wonders, both completed in 1909, that earned Schwitzer an honoured place in the pantheon of Canadian notables.

The Lethbridge Viaduct, also known as the High Level Bridge, eliminated twenty wooden-decked bridges over the Belly and Oldman Rivers with a spectacular 1,624-metre span, more than 91 metres above the valley floor. Canada's longest and highest railway trestle of its kind, it required more than 900 railcars of material for its construction, 645 carrying steel alone. Two coats of paint were applied to the bridge, requiring 34,550 litres of paint.

The Spiral Tunnels involved the excavation of 572,520 cubic metres of solid rock from the 2.4 kilometres of tunnel through Mount Ogden and Cathedral Mountain. It took seventy-five railcars to bring in the 682 metric tons of dynamite required. The result was a reduction in grade from 4.5 percent to 2.2 percent, meaning that two locomotives rather than four were needed to pull most trains up the "Big Hill."

Tragically Schwitzer's career was cut short at its apex, a mere three weeks after his appointment to the position of CPR's chief engineer. While Schwitzer was hospitalized at Montreal's Royal Victoria Hospital, the CPR sent oxygen cylinders by express train from the Toronto General Hospital to support attempts to save his life. The effort was in vain. Schwitzer died of pneumonia on 23 January 1911, at age forty.

The chairman of the CPR, Sir William Van Horne, ordered flags to be flown at half-mast on all company properties across the railway system. A railway junction eight kilometres southwest of Souris, Manitoba, was named in his memory—scant recognition for the prime mover behind two of the engineering wonders of the world, but perhaps suitably modest for a man remembered fondly by his colleagues as "Jack." His legacy speaks for itself.

The Reluctant Saboteur

There are many spectacular structures on the CPR, not the least of which are the monumental bridges that have thrilled rail travellers and inspired many a photographer. Some, like the elegant arched span over Stoney Creek in British Columbia or Alberta's enormous Lethbridge Viaduct, have gained fame not only for their dramatic visual profile, but also for the tales of derring-do associated with their construction and operation. Therefore, it might come as a surprise that it was a relatively insignificant structure, not unlike many others on the railway, that merited the attention of the German High Command in the early days of the First World War.

While studying maps of the North American railway system, one of Kaiser

THE RELUCTANT SABOTEUR
A bridge on the CPR main line between Maine and New Brunswick, which looked much like hundreds of others on the system, was targeted for destruction.
A.1557

Wilhelm's agents, the master spy Franz von Papen, concluded that the Vanceboro Bridge, which crossed the St. Croix River between Maine and New Brunswick on the former CPR Mattawamkeag subdivision, was of great strategic value to the Allied forces.

Assuming correctly that large amounts of supplies and many fully loaded troop trains had to funnel across this short span, von Papen was determined to destroy it. To this end, he enlisted the aid of an underling, Oberleutenant Werner Horn, to carry out the task, assuring him that he would be contributing to the German war effort by taking out the bridge and that no civilian lives need be lost or placed in jeopardy as a result of the operation.

On 30 December 1914, Horn arrived in the quaint little town of Vanceboro, Maine, a short distance from the bridge in question, carrying a nondescript brown suitcase in which he had secured twenty-seven kilograms of explosives. That night, avoiding the CPR's relatively substantial and luxurious McAdam Station and Hotel on the other side of the river where he would risk intense scrutiny, he checked into the more modest Vanceboro Exchange Hotel, where he hoped to avoid the questioning stares of curious locals. After a short rest to steady his already jangled nerves, he set out in the numbing cold to do the deed.

Unfortunately for the hapless Horn, German intelligence was somewhat less than perfect, failing to account for the unscheduled trains that frequently ferried soldiers, civilians, and supplies back and forth across the bridge. Twice while attempting to place the explosive charge, Horn was forced to hang over the edge of the bridge to avoid troop trains, risking life and limb on the deck or a chilly bath in the icy waters of the St. Croix River.

At this point, Horn, being a man of conscience, if not competence, decided he did not want to risk blowing up the bridge while innocent victims might be on it. So he shortened the fuse to get the job done before another train arrived, greatly reducing his own escape time from fifty minutes to fifteen. Abandoning his planned overland escape from the area, he instead quickly returned to the hotel. Just as he arrived, a loud explosion sent the manager scurrying out to the lobby to find out what all the commotion was about.

"Guten morgen," spat the now clearly flustered Horn, in a vain attempt to appear nonchalant. Moments later he broke down and spilled the entire story, imploring the startled manager to immediately inform the railway of the damage to its bridge before any lives could be lost.

While the authorities were being notified, the unfortunate Horn was allowed to return to his room to rest under the watchful eye of the hotel manager and his staff. He then spent considerable time locked up in the nearby U.S. Immigration detention room, before eventually being taken to Boston to stand trial for sabotage. His ultimate fate is unknown, but presumably he was incarcerated for the remainder of the war.

The explosion turned out to have been more noise than anything else, as nitroglycerine becomes almost inert at temperatures below minus forty degrees Celsius. By noon the same day, trains were running normally, but for the rest of the war, armed guards were posted on twenty-four-hour duty at both ends of the unimposing Vanceboro Bridge.

Chapter Two

Proud Ships and Captains of the CP Fleet

Cruising to the Land of the Pharaohs
You have to give this intrepid cruise passenger full points for scaling one of the great pyramids of Egypt in those shoes.
A.20441

Two Minutes Before Noon
In recognition of the role played by Robinson and the crew, the captain was made a Commander of the British Empire.

Cruising to the Land of the Pharaohs

When CPR's *Empress of Scotland* arrived in Egypt in 1927, the Sphinx looked much as it had centuries earlier, when medieval Moslems had chiselled off its nose. The visitors to the Giza Plain watched a continuous line of young women, baskets on their heads, shuffling toward the sandstone colossus. As the containers were filled with sand, the women turned and walked a considerable distance into the desert, then cast their loads to the wind.

One year later, when the *Empress of Australia* disembarked its full complement of cruise passengers at Port Said, centuries of accumulated sand had been excavated from around the paws of the Sphinx, exposing to view the entire creature with the body of a lion and the head of a pharaoh.

The discovery of King Tutankhamun's tomb, in 1922, had astonished the archaeological world and created a faddish fascination in western society with all things Egyptian. The immediate result was more money for digs such as the Sphinx excavation, sponsored by the Harvard Foundation, more artifacts piling up in the storerooms of Cairo's Egyptian Museum, and more cruise ship passengers opting for shore excursions to visit the Khan el Khalili bazaars, see the five-thousand-year-old pyramids, or explore the mysteries of Karnak, Luxor, Thebes, and the Valley of the Kings.

Arriving at Port Said, *Empress* passengers boarded the shiny white railway coaches of the Egyptian State Railways that would take them to Cairo, the largest and most notable city in Africa, and to the welcoming comforts of the Shepheard's and Continental Hotels. From there, it was a short carriage ride to the Egyptian Museum, which now housed the wondrous gold and lapis lazuli encrusted treasures unearthed from King Tut's burial chamber, as well as to the Citadel, which had been built in the Mokkatam Hills by Saladin in the days of the crusaders, using stones from the smaller pyramids on the opposite bank of the Nile.

For the more adventuresome, there were steamer excursions down the Nile to Bedrechein and back, or to the recently completed Aswan Dam, aboard chartered ships bearing names such as *Lotus* and *Sudan*. One could also travel by train to Luxor, where, among the remains of the ancient royal necropolis on both sides of the river, CPR brochures assured, could be seen "temples beyond compare, magnificence that even now, in ruins, gives us a wholesome feeling of our littleness below that wide, tremendous desert sky." Lacking the self-consciousness of modern world travellers, and perhaps suffering from a touch of ethnocentricity, early tourists treated the ancient sites like amusement parks, carving their initials in the stones and even clambering on top of the giant statues of Rameses II.

Most popular were the side excursions by automobile and tramway to the pyramids of Khufu (Cheops), Khafre, and Menkaure, dominating the skyline on the Giza Plain on the west bank of the Nile. Having been stripped over the years of its smooth outer casing, the Great Pyramid of Cheops, in particular, lured tourists to climb even higher up the giant staircases formed by the underlying blocks. "To do this comfortably," insisted one cruise passenger, "you want four Arabs, two to pull from above and two to boost from below. But even then, it is too strenuous to be attractive." That said, however, some not only managed to get themselves to the summit, but also brought along a few golf balls and a club to drive them from the top. Those who put no stock in myths about pharaohs' curses, or legends of mummies rising from their tombs, could hop aboard a camel, mule, or sand cart for a short ride a few miles south, to experience an exotic and romantic night on the edge of the Libyan desert.

Four days later in Suez, the newly converted amateur Egyptologists would reunite with their floating resort hotel, the *Empress*, which had already passed through the great canal. Laden with hammered brass trays, inlaid furniture, glazed pottery in a variety of colours, fine silks, and Egyptian mats, they bid farewell to their "dragomen," or tourist guides, and slipped them a little "baksheesh," the colourful local term for "tip."

Twenty Knots to Canada

When Canadian Pacific entered the competitive North Atlantic steamship business in 1903, it did so with a vengeance. The CPR had spent an inordinate amount of time and effort convincing the Canadian government and the various steamship companies operating on the St. Lawrence route that the country needed a faster service to Europe. When the opportunity came, the company jumped in with both feet and purchased fifteen ships from the Elder Dempster Company's Canadian arm, known as the Beaver Line.

The CPR could speed passengers, freight, and mail from Montreal to Vancouver in less than five days. The company's *Empress* steamships, plying the Pacific routes at sixteen knots since the 1890s, were making the run from the British Columbia coast to Yokohama, Japan, in about ten and a half days. The weak link in Britain's imperial chain was the North Atlantic service, dominated primarily by the Allan Line and the Beaver Line. Advocates of a fast line knew what a boon it would be to the Canadian economy, not to mention the fortunes of the CPR. Their rallying cry was "Twenty Knots to Canada."

By 1903, president Thomas Shaughnessy and chairman William Van Horne were determined that the CPR would go it alone. "As I have said before," reasoned Van Horne, "Canada has for some years been raising the sides of her hopper without enlarging the spout . . . We are apt to get left chartering vessels when we need them the most, so we propose we have our own."

The eight passenger ships and seven cargo freighters initially acquired from

Elder Dempster were modest vessels with a top speed of twelve or thirteen knots. Used primarily for immigrant traffic, the passenger liners often had their berths removed in Montreal, and were fitted with stalls for shipping cattle, a move clearly not calculated to entice a more upscale clientele to travel aboard them to Canada.

The rival Montreal Ocean Steamship Company, better known as the Allan Line, recognized the threat posed by the CPR's entry in the Atlantic shipping trade and had two eighteen-knot passenger steamships built: the *Victorian* and the *Virginian.* Shaughnessy was determined to go one better and in 1904 CPR placed an order for two new ships of its own. They were to be more luxurious than the Allan Line ships, and they were to be capable of obtaining speeds of a little better than nineteen knots. Overdelivering on the specifications, the first of the ships, the *Empress*

TWENTY KNOTS TO CANADA
With the purchase of the Beaver Line steamers from Elder Dempster, CPR acquired the transatlantic link in the imperial chain from Britain to the Orient.
A.20938

of Britain, proved to be a twenty-knotter and, along with sister ship *Empress of Ireland*, proceeded to set new standards for comfort and speed on the St. Lawrence route.

Although the accommodations for immigrants could not compare with the luxury of the first-class cabins, all passengers were spared the lingering bovine odour so prevalent on the company's Beaver Line ships. "The third-class accommodations of old," said the *Montreal Gazette* on 14 May 1906, "has been revolutionized in the present vessel . . . the old order of discomfort which formerly reigned in the steerage department has been swept away. There is even a roped off sand playground for the little children."

For adults, there were more sophisticated diversions. The *Empress of Britain* was one of the earliest ships, and quite possibly the first, to feature motion picture shows. Using a hand-cranked projector that was operated with one hand and focused with the other, operators entertained passengers with productions such as *From the Old Home to the New* and *A Honeymoon Trip through Canada.*

A serious mishap occurred 27 July 1912, in thick fog off the coast of Cape Magdalen in the St. Lawrence, when the *Empress of Britain* collided with and sank the steamship *Helvetia.*

In August 1914, the *Empress of Britain* was commissioned by the British Admiralty as an armed merchant cruiser and served in that capacity for nearly a year. Soon the Admiralty concluded the ship could best be used for troop transport. She was quickly outfitted with berths and proceeded to carry more than 130,000 Canadian, British, and American soldiers to campaigns in the Dardenelles, Egypt, and India. She was attacked by the enemy on twelve separate occasions without sustaining serious damage.

After the war, a modified *Empress of Britain* was the first oil burner to operate up the St. Lawrence. In 1922, she became the company's pioneer cruise ship, sailing between New York City and the West Indies, the first of six such trips over the next two years. By the mid-1920s, many steamship companies were converting their aging vessels to one-class, or cabin-class ships, as their first-class accommodations could no longer compete with the newer, more luxurious competition. Accordingly, the *Empress of Britain* was converted to cabin-class service and renamed *Montroyal*, in keeping with the CPR's practice of designating cabin-class ships with "M" names such as *Melita, Minnedosa, Missanabie*, and *Metagama.*

The *Empress of Britain* was withdrawn from service when the CPR launched its new *Duchess* steamships in 1928 and 1929. She was sold for scrap in 1930. In a curious postscript to her career, her main lounge was purchased by the owner of the Sola Strand Hotel, in Stavenger, Norway, and reconstructed in its entirety as the "Montroyal Ballroom."

Canada's Challenger

For many, the 1930s was a decade of diminished expectations. The stock market crash of 1929, and the economic depression that followed in its wake, left one in every five Canadians jobless. For others, though, it was an era of rapid change and even adventure. Technological advances enabled more people to make long distance phone calls, ride in new automobiles, and fly on transcontinental airplanes.

Into this tumultuous time, the CPR launched the steamship *Empress of Britain II*, on 11 June 1930. The thirty-eight-thousand-metric-ton behemoth was the largest and fastest passenger ship ever to fly the company's red-and-white checkered flag, and many who sailed on her claimed she was the most luxuriously appointed ship ever built.

Among the many onboard attractions were two stages for theatrical performances, a motion picture theatre, an Olympic-size swimming pool, Turkish baths, beauty parlours, a full-size tennis court on the sports deck, and public rooms designed and decorated by prominent artists from the Royal Academy. Eleven hundred passengers could be handled in first-class, tourist, and third-class accommodations, and few who set foot on her decks were unimpressed with the spaciousness of her rooms and passageways, which set the *Empress* apart from all her rivals on the North Atlantic.

On the maiden voyage from Southampton, a record of five days and thirty minutes was set between Cherbourg, France, and Quebec City, truly reducing the Atlantic to "pond" status when compared with the sixty-six-day voyage of the *Mayflower*, more than 310 years earlier. Among the luminaries on board for the historic crossing were Sir Edward Beatty, CPR president and driving force behind the company's post-First World War shipbuilding program; Lady Mount Stephen, wife of founding president George Stephen, later Lord Mount Stephen; and movie stars Mary Pickford and Douglas Fairbanks. Upon arrival in Quebec, Fairbanks voiced two objections to the ship. "The voyage was too short because of the many attractions the ship offered," he said, and "these same attractions robbed one of the sense of being on an ocean voyage."

The route down the sheltered St. Lawrence River was advertised as "thirty-nine percent less ocean" than the route to New York City sailed by the Cunard Line's *Mauretania* and *Aquitania*, chief rivals to the *Empress of Britain*. The CPR characterized the *Empress* as "Canada's Challenger" and "The World's Wondership."

A new pier was constructed at Wolfe's Cove in Quebec City to handle the oversized steamship, and news of her every arrival was flashed across the country. When the *Empress* docked at Quebec on 1 June 1931, the *Montreal Star* reported that the noise from her whistle caused a team of horses to bolt in Alberta, twenty-one hundred miles away. Apparently the CPR's live radio broadcast of the ship's arrival had given them a fright.

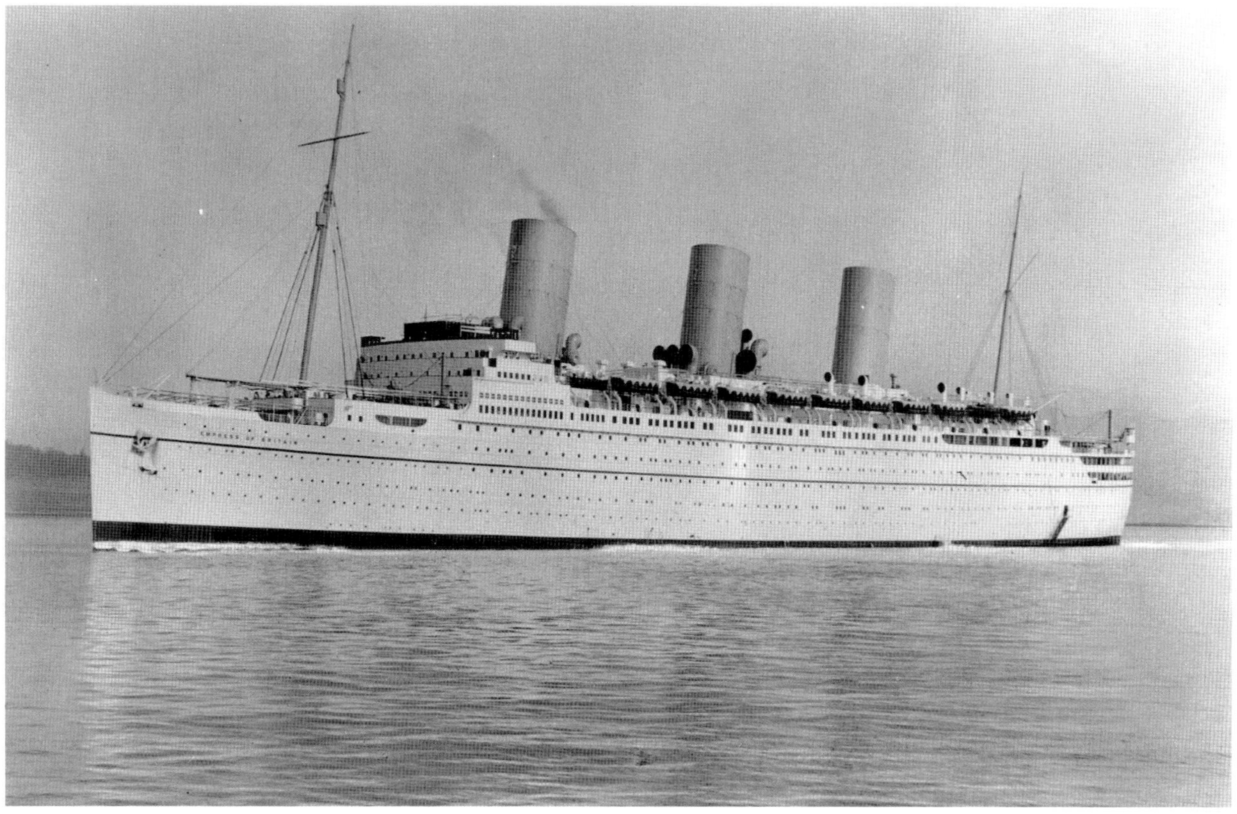

CANADA'S CHALLENGER
The CPR's flagship *Empress of Britain II* was among the most elegant and well-appointed ships ever afloat.
NS.22046

Though the *Empress of Britain* was a worthy competitor in the transatlantic sweepstakes, her starring role was the company's annual world cruise. During the cruise, the *Empress* visited thirty-three foreign ports in twenty-one countries, and her arrival was often accorded front-page status, nudging CPR's reputation to the forefront in transportation circles and making her a favourite with the public.

An onboard, worldwide radio-telephone service made it possible for a businessman in Chicago to reach his family on the *Empress* in less than fifteen minutes on each Sunday during their 130-day voyage. Even the Americans were impressed by her grandeur, when half a metre of her twenty-one-metre masts was lopped off to ensure she would pass under the newly constructed Golden Gate Bridge, in San Francisco, without snagging the safety nets hung below.

In 1939, the *Empress of Britain* was chosen to ferry His Majesty King George VI and Queen Elizabeth home from their tour of Canada. On 3 September, war with Germany was declared, and the ship's bright white paint was replaced with the dull grey of a troopship. In her wartime role, carrying 224 military personnel and their families, she ran out of luck on the northwest coast of Ireland, on 25 October 1940. An enemy bomber rendered the *Empress* all but dead in the water, and the order to abandon ship was given. Two days later, the German submarine U-32 delivered the *coup de grâce*, sending the veteran of one hundred round trips on the North Atlantic and eight round-the-world cruises to the deep.

FROM *KAISERIN* TO *EMPRESS*

It was a day of national pride when the *Kaiserin Auguste Victoria* slid into the sea at the Vulcan Werke, AG, in Stettin, Germany, on 28 August 1905. A great throng had turned out to see Kaiser Wilhelm II, the self-styled Admiral of the Atlantic, whose naval ambitions would ultimately lead to a showdown with the British fleet at Jutland. But the people had also come out to see the German empress, whose name would grace the bow of the biggest and probably the most luxurious ship on the high seas at the time.

Initially the Hamburg-Amerika Line was to have christened the ship *Europa*. Its sister ship, *Amerika*, had just been built by Harland & Wolff of Belfast, Ireland. But to honour the empress, who had agreed to sponsor the ship at the launching, the name had been changed to *Kaiserin Auguste Victoria*.

To a large extent, the ship's design emulated the White Star Line's "Big Four": *Celtic*, *Cedric*, *Baltic*, and *Adriatic*. Her quadruple expansion engines could plow the ship's 1,090 metric tons through the water at better than eighteen knots, rivalling anything on the North Atlantic.

As flagship for the Hamburg-Amerika Line, the *Kaiserin* arrived in New York City in May 1906 to inaugurate service between the Big Apple and Hamburg, Germany, calling frequently at Southampton, in England. Within her spacious confines, she had room for more than five hundred steerage passengers, while the *Kaiserin*'s sumptuous first-class cabins could accommodate four hundred well-heeled travellers in grand fashion. Passengers would sweep down the rococo staircase to the dining room, which extended through two decks under the

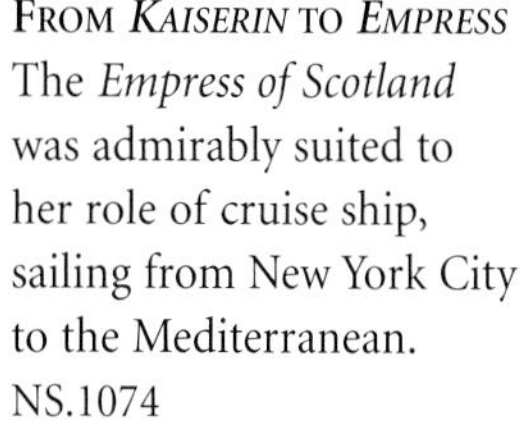

FROM *KAISERIN* TO *EMPRESS*
The *Empress of Scotland* was admirably suited to her role of cruise ship, sailing from New York City to the Mediterranean.
NS.1074

illumination of star-shaped lanterns held by gilded cherubs. Visitors, as the publicity brochures exclaimed, "expressed their admiration for her beautiful appointments in unmeasured terms."

During the First World War, the *Kaiserin Auguste Victoria* remained at Hamburg, where she was cared for and maintained while being laid up. In March 1919, the dormant steamship was allocated by the victorious Allies to the United States, for use in repatriating American troops from Brest, France. At the outset of the war, the Americans had seized many German liners in U.S. ports, including the majestic new symbol of Germany's might, the Hamburg-Amerika Line's forty-nine-thousand-metric-ton *Vaterland*, so the *Kaiserin* was transferred to Britain as part of that country's war reparations.

From late 1919 to 1921, the orphaned liner operated under Cunard's house flag, and in May of that year, when new construction was both slow and expensive due to post-war shortages, she was purchased by the CPR and renamed *Empress of Scotland*. After an extensive six-month retrofit, during which the ship was converted to burn oil, the *Empress* sailed to New York, where she was chartered to the Clark Travel Agency for a seventy-four-day Mediterranean cruise.

In later years, the *Empress of Scotland* was found to be somewhat cumbersome for transatlantic service on the St. Lawrence route, but she was admirably suited to her role as cruise ship, sailing the Mediterranean throughout the 1920s and dropping anchor in many an exotic port on her around-the-world cruises of 1925 and 1926.

In 1925, the *Empress of Scotland* was the largest ship to negotiate the Panama Canal, paying a whopping $17,211 (American dollars) in tolls to clear the locks. One world traveller, Katherine Kinney of Albany, New York, earned a brief spot on newspaper pages around the world when she was recruited to operate the controls to elevate the CPR liner from the Pacific Ocean to Miraflores Lake, sixteen metres above sea level. The task was accomplished in a mere sixty-one minutes. On that particular sailing, the passenger list included seven honeymooning couples. A further twenty-seven globe-trotting couples were reported to have pledged their troth during their adventures afloat.

The enormous popularity and success of the *Empress of Scotland* as a cruise ship was probably a big factor in CPR's decision to build the largest and fastest ship to fly the checkered house flag, the *Empress of Britain II*. Its launch preceded the retirement of the *Empress of Scotland* by only a few months.

After completing seventy-one transatlantic voyages, the *Empress of Scotland* was sold to the Hughes Bolckow Company for scrap. While awaiting the cutter's torch in Blyth, England, the new owners planned a charity ball to give the public one last look at the storied ship. But before the scheduled event, a fire broke out on board and virtually gutted the liner, robbing the owners of the opportunity to sell all of her valuable panelling and fittings. As one writer lamented in a contemporary account: "Aboard the ship were nine pianos in maple, satinwood and oak; settees and easy chairs in French velvet, mauve silk and pink damask; Chinese, Persian and Indian carpets and rugs; and much more. Then came the fire."

THE CROWNING JEWEL

As befitted her standing in the British Empire, India was considered by many at CPR to be the crowning jewel in the company's around-the-world cruises between the two world wars. There was something terribly exciting about arriving in Bombay, dressed in one's finest tropical gear, looking for all the world like someone off the pages of an Abercrombie & Fitch catalogue.

It wasn't just the sight of the gateway to India, a dockside arch that combined elements of east and west, symbolizing British rule in India. Nor was it the exotic mixture of Hindus, Muslims, Parsi, Afghans, Arabs, and Westerners awaiting ships from the world's ports. It was something less tangible—a combination of sights, sounds, and smells that assaulted the senses and conjured up images of Kipling-esque adventure.

From the ports of Bombay and Calcutta, the CPR organized a number of railway excursions throughout the countryside for the benefit of its cruise patrons. Scheduled stops of four or five days in each port allowed the travellers to choose a round-trip tour to Delhi, Agra, Benares (now usually called Varanasi), or Darjeeling, or to opt for an eight-day, cross-India junket completely under the management of Canadian Pacific.

Although Delhi was the official capital of the British Raj and offered wonderful architecture and historical associations, no site witnessed as much "Kodaking" as Agra, home of the Taj Mahal. As they strolled through the luxuriant gardens surrounding this famous landmark, tour guides regaled their charges with tales of Shah Jihan, who had ordered the construction of the milky-white marble mausoleum to house the remains of his beloved wife. The mausoleum had cost three million pounds sterling, and required the labour of twenty thousand workers over a period of seventeen years. Many agreed with the cruise brochure that it was, indeed, "the most beautiful building on the face of the earth."

Along the route of the East India Railway was the ancient city of Benares, where more than one million pilgrims came annually to worship in five thousand temples and shrines and crowd the shores of the Ganges River to pray and bathe in its sacred waters.

From the railway station at British military headquarters, fleets of motor cars were pressed into service for sightseeing and shopping trips. And just as every conductor aboard a CPR train could identify and speak at length about the scenic wonders of the Canadian Rockies, any company attendant who chaperoned a tour group to Darjeeling knew the points of interest among the snow-clad Himalayas, including majestic Mount Everest, unconquered until Sir Edmund Hillary and Tenzing Norgay made their famous ascent in 1953.

Travelling to Darjeeling itself, a hill station at which the British colonial administration escaped the oppressive summer heat on the subcontinent, required a

THE CROWNING JEWEL
In the years between the two world wars, well-heeled travellers had plenty of time to mug for the camera.
A.37256

transfer to a narrow-gauge mountain railway which looped back and forth through tropical and subtropical conditions to the temperate climate above the plain.

The excursion trains were marshalled from the best European-built locomotives and rolling stock in the country and, reflecting their first-class status, were made up exclusively of sleeping and dining cars. Unlike trains in North America, those in India had no inside aisles to allow for movement from one car to another while in motion. Instead, small compartments spanned the width of the cars and were accessible from doorways that opened directly onto station platforms.

Each sleeping car compartment was equipped with its own shower and washroom, frequent stops being required to refill the lavatory tanks that supplied the gravity-fed facilities. However, the open pipes in the roof through which the tanks were filled were exposed to the elements. Consequently, many a weary traveller stepped under the nozzle for a cold shower, only to be doused with a murky mixture that was equal parts water and cinders from the locomotive stack.

In addition, every compartment was outfitted with four berths—two uppers and two lowers—surrounded with curtains for privacy. Small tables and decks of playing cards were provided courtesy of Canadian Pacific, as were the bed linen, pillows, blankets, towels, and soap, all from the cruise ship's stores.

An adventurous passenger from the 1929 world cruise aboard the *Empress of Australia* asked one of the cruise directors about the possibility of seeing a tiger during their tour of India. "Later on the trip," he said, "when entering my compartment one evening, I found sitting in my berth a large toy tiger, made in India, with a long mane, a ferocious expression, sharp teeth and a blood-thirsty tongue, which he stuck out menacingly every time he moved his head. It had been placed there by my good friend, Mr. Irvine, official cruise photographer, with a card saying: 'The policy of the Canadian Pacific is always to please.'"

Tom Bowling's Royal Links

There was never a lack of entertainment on CPR steamship cruises in the 1930s. Whether at sea or in some exotic port of call, the staff on the company's *Empress* liners did its utmost to cater to every whim of the well-to-do passengers.

One such crew member was Tom Bowling, an old navy hand who served as the keeper of the golf gear on the *Empress of Scotland*. Up on "A" deck, a lofty twenty-seven metres above sea level, and situated next to the full-size tennis court, would-be pros could drive golf balls to their hearts' content. Wires were often attached to the balls to keep them on board, or huge nets were strung for the same purpose.

Tom kept everything in order, sweeping the decks, painting the railings, retrieving the balls, maintaining the driving and putting mats, and regaling the eager duffers with tales of prowess in the ancient Scottish pastime. One experience Tom liked to relate was an encounter with His Royal Highness Edward, the Prince of Wales, who was returning to England from a trip to Canada in 1927. Not content to limit himself to stories about "'ow 'e smote the pill and wot 'e said," Tom was always sure to point out that the putting mat on which his clients were playing was the very one on which the prince had tapped a ball or two.

It wasn't too long before he had offers from several of the well-heeled passengers on a particular Mediterranean cruise to purchase the royal mat. Now Tom, of course, was a loyal company man and, recalling the views of the Prince of Wales about British subjects and British possessions not being for sale, declined all representations. So when the *Empress* docked at Alexandria and most of the passengers disembarked for a two-day visit to the pyramids, the Sphinx, and other attractions in and about Cairo, Tom kept one eye fixed on his emerald mat, which by this time had begun to take on legendary significance among the sea-going golf set.

During the stopover, as was the custom, the crew of the *Empress of Scotland* took part in a staff regatta in the harbour, a practice that occupied their time while honing a few of the seldom-used skills of an able-bodied seaman. Tom returned to the ship a winning coxswain for his crew, but he also returned to find "the mat a-missin'." It took only a few short frantic minutes to conclude that the mat was by now securely stashed in the baggage of some nefarious ne'er-do-well and would never again be seen in *this* man's merchant marine.

TOM BOWLING'S ROYAL LINKS
Ol' Tom's golf mat took on near legendary significance for his charges aboard the *Empress of Scotland.* A.26259

Nevertheless, when all of the passengers were back aboard, it was business as usual on "A" deck, one golf mat being pretty much the same as another—on the surface. But ol' Tom now had another story to tell. It seems he had forgotten to mention the wonderful souvenirs Prince Edward had left behind upon leaving the *Empress*: two crisp, new Canadian two-dollar bills. It was only a matter of time before offers to exchange those souvenir bills for well-worn, but still quite good American fives were being made.

They say that by the time the ship arrived back in Canada, Tom had made enough money to cover the decks of the *Empress* from stem to stern with golf mats.

A Ship by Any Other Name

What could be a more fitting designation than "*Empresses*" for the ships that plied the trans-Pacific link in the Imperial Highway from Britain to Asia? For nearly fifty years, CPR's fleet of steamships enjoyed dominance on the ocean route to the Orient. Vessels like the *Empress of Japan* and the *Empress of Asia* were synonymous with speed, comfort, and the lure of the east. The names are so familiar that one could scarcely imagine any other label applied to so majestic a fleet. Yet mere months before the launch of the initial three ships, a final decision on their distinctive and elegant white paint scheme and what they should be christened had yet to be made.

Of course, in 1889, when the order was placed with the Naval Construction & Armaments Company of Barrow, Scotland, Canadian Pacific had no marine image

to uphold. From the beginning, there was a great divergence of opinion within the company on what names the ships should carry. Special representative H. Maitland Kersey, the CPR's chief liaison with the shipbuilders, favoured a series of names ending with "a." He suggested the first three ships be christened *Mongolia*, *Manchuria*, and *Tiara*, while later vessels could be called *Formosa* and *Corea*.

President William Van Horne, however, was of the opinion the ships should bear the names of Chinese dynasties such as *Tai Cho*, *Tai Ming*, and *Tai Ching*.

A Ship by Any Other Name
The bow of the *Empress of India* was graced with a carved figurehead of Queen Victoria, whereas the *Empress of China* and *Empress of Japan* bore dragons.
NS.19498

Kersey was so strongly opposed to this notion that he wrote several letters directly to Van Horne to argue his point, as well as a couple to vice-president Thomas Shaughnessy, pleading that he intercede on Kersey's behalf. Kersey also informed Shaughnessy that three models were to be painted and forwarded to Montreal for inspection. Each was to have a different coloured hull: ivory-white, French grey, and black, so that a decision could be made for the entire fleet.

French grey was the first to be disqualified from the running, partly because several British mercantile marine lines, including the Donald Currie Line and the Harrison Line, used variations of this colour. In a letter to Van Horne, Kersey states quite pragmatically: "Had a long talk with Admiral Morant of the (British) navy, who was in charge of the fleet of the troopers for some years in Hong Kong and other parts of the world, and he informs me that ivory-white is much better than French grey for the reason that French grey is extremely difficult to mix. An ivory hull can always have dabs put here and there to cover any particularly dirty spot, but as it is so difficult to obtain the same shade of French grey, dabs on a ship painted this colour show up badly and look like blotches. He says there is no question whatever but that the ivory-white will be both cleaner and cheaper to keep up. I therefore propose to have the hulls painted this colour."

Another consideration was whether or not the ships should have figureheads. Shaughnessy thought them to be an unnecessary expense, while Kersey, as usual, had his own strong feelings. "I have never seen a steamer or sailing ship with fiddle bows like ours which had not a figurehead and I strongly advise you to have one," he wrote to the vice-president.

By June 1890, two months before the first of the three ships was to be launched, R. B. Angus, a CPR director, broke the impasse on the names. "Angus suggests *Empress of India*, *Empress of China* and *Empress of Japan*," Van Horne informed Shaughnessy. "Think very good. We can use *Empress of Russia*, *Germany* and *Austria* for additional ships." Perhaps Angus had in mind the famous clipper *Empress of China*, which had inaugurated the tea trade between China and New York City more than one hundred years before.

Van Horne was so taken with the names that when Shaughnessy informed him of three small and relatively insignificant vessels already operating with the name *Empress of India* in other parts of the world, he stated simply: "If there are three already, what harm can there be in a fourth."

Kersey, of course, was not about to take the decision quietly. He couldn't resist one last dig in a letter to Shaughnessy: "I'm afraid you will find such long names a terrible nuisance. They take up a lot of room in newspaper columns and it is [a] painful undertaking writing all this on bills-of-lading, documents, etc. I think shorter names would have been much better."

The figurehead issue more or less resolved itself once the names had been chosen. An image of Queen Victoria, the logical choice for the *Empress of India*, was carved at Barrow-in-Furness, close to where the ships had been built. For the *Japan*, a dragon figurehead was crafted in Yokohama, whereas the *China*'s gilded dragon was made in Kowloon.

When the three Pacific steamships arrived on the west coast of Canada in 1891, they established an enduring image with their grand appearance. Resplendent in their ivory-white and buff paint scheme, they also flew, for the first time, the red-and-white checkered house flag designed by Van Horne for the occasion. Never would they be thought of as mere ships plying their trade; they were, indeed, "*Empresses!*"

Two Minutes before Noon

Coloured streamers filled the air as the *Empress of Australia* made ready to pull away from the wharf at Yokohama. Passengers aboard the giant Canadian Pacific liner crowded the decks to wave to the masses gathered for the send-off. It was two minutes before noon on 1 September 1923.

Amid the inevitable turmoil of the ship's impending departure, the first shock waves of a giant earthquake rocked the steamship. Within seconds, the festive mood turned to one of horror, as the world's most destructive natural disaster turned the Yokohama waterfront from the picture of commercial viability to a scene from Dante's *Inferno*. The entire landscape was transformed. The wharf buckled and collapsed, throwing hundreds of people into the bay. Almost every major building was reduced to rubble. Fire and smoke seared flesh and choked lungs, as thousands tried in vain to escape the terror that engulfed the city.

Captain Robinson's report described the catastrophe, as witnessed from the bridge of the *Empress*: "A violent earthquake took place, first a number of very severe shocks, then the land rolled in waves apparently six to eight feet high, like a succession of fast-moving ocean swells—three or four large ones and several small ones. The vessel shook all over in a most terrifying fashion, and also rocked very

Two Minutes before Noon
Captain Robinson (left) looked every bit the man in charge when he posed with his officers and the orphaned dog "Ref," not long after the earthquake.
NS.11245

quickly and violently until it seemed as though the masts and funnels must carry away."

As the waves buffeted the ship, Captain Robinson struggled to regain control. All around, ships bounced like toys in a tub. The *Lyon Maru*—just seconds before lying peacefully at anchor beside the *Empress*—was thrown repeatedly against the CPR liner, endangering both vessels. Huge oil spills, one hundred metres in diameter, shot flames into the sky, threatening to ignite everything on deck. The ship's problems were compounded by a cable fouling the portside propeller blade, making movement within the harbour extremely difficult.

Within minutes of the initial shock, ropes and ladders were thrown over the side of the *Empress*, allowing refugees to climb aboard. Eventually, the captain was able to ease the big ship out into the bay, where relief missions were organized between ship and shore. The following day, Robinson enlisted the aid of a diver from a Japanese battleship to untangle the propeller, allowing the *Empress* to steam closer to shore. As a result of the relief efforts, about four thousand people reached the safety of the ship. Among the survivors was a dog that managed to swim to the ship's rescue boat on the second day after the earthquake. Dubbed "Yokohama Refugee," or "Ref" for short, he soon took to lying under the captain's desk and, before long, was accompanying him on his trips to the bridge.

As a result of the relief efforts, about four thousand people reached the safety of the ship.

In his report, Captain Robinson expressed his admiration for the calmness and conduct of the passengers, "many of whom worked untiringly day and night among the sick and injured refugees of all nationalities. The lower decks and alleyways all over the ship presented a most heart-rending sight, crowded with the hundreds of badly wounded among the rescued, half or partially naked and covered with dirt and blood, groaning and crying bitterly," he related. "Up to the morning of Monday the 3rd, we were entirely without news of the outside world, all telegraphic communication, either by wireless or land, being cut off."

Unknown to the captain, the earthquake had devastated an enormous area known as the Kanto Plain, 160 kilometres of Japan's most densely populated land, including dozens of towns and villages along the Pacific coast. In the villages of Soga and Shimosoga, 90 percent of the buildings had collapsed immediately. Across the countryside, bizarre occurrences amazed and terrified the population. Brick chimneys suddenly and violently sprouted, as well linings were forced up from the earth. Potatoes shot out of the ground as if fired from guns. Huge coal supplies caught fire and were still burning two months later.

More than 250,000 people died, a greater number than would be lost as a result of the atomic bombing of Hiroshima twenty-two years later. The quake torched a larger area than the great fires in San Francisco, Chicago, and London combined.

In recognition of the role played by Robinson and the crew and passengers of the *Empress of Australia*, the captain was made a Commander of the Order of the British Empire. He also was decorated with the Imperial Japanese Medal of Merit with red ribbon, Lloyd's Silver Medal for Meritorious Service at Sea, the Order of St. John of Jerusalem Lifesaving Award, and the Spanish Order of Naval Merit.

The Nine Lives of Captain Poole

Captain Francis Poole swallowed the anchor when he retired from CPR's Pacific steamship service in 1956 after a life at sea filled with romance and adventure. "Those really were the days," he was fond of recalling. "It was a great life on the 'White Empresses', as the CPR vessels were known, and the ports of call were so unspoiled in the 1930s and 1940s. Of course the women were very attractive, too ... Japanese women are the most beautiful in the world, you know."

Reminiscing came easily to Captain Poole, an able raconteur whose energetic and enthusiastic "Stories of Life on the Rolling Seas," for the trade journal *Seaports and the Shipping World*, lured me in, and we became regular luncheon companions. Drinking beer and eating Chinese food, the captain would regale me with his yarns. Though he'd been on dry land for more than thirty years, I never thought of him, nor ever called him, anything but Captain Poole, a rank he earned on his many leaves from the merchant marine to sail with the Royal Navy Reserve.

Francis Poole came to Canadian Pacific from the British India Steam Navigation Company in 1930 to serve as fifth officer on the company's *Empress of Russia*, a low rank for a seaman of his abilities, but he viewed it as steady employment with a good company during hard times. Jobs were scarce in the Dirty Thirties and it was not uncommon for every able seaman on board any particular ship to hold an officer's certificate.

In those exotic climes, the encounters with pirates, smugglers, and stowaways were further enlivened by the vagaries of the weather.

The regimen at sea was disciplined and rigorous, and sailors were granted no more than two months leave a year, but Poole regarded every voyage as an adventure, and rightfully so, judging by the hundreds of anecdotes that he would readily relate.

Anything could happen at sea. The task of securing the *Empress of Russia*—as was the case with all ships in the CPR fleet—was entirely in the hands of the ship's captain and senior officers. Off the coast of Hong Kong and Shanghai the threat from pirates was so immediate, and the activities of opium smugglers so pervasive, White Russian policemen attached to the Hong Kong police force were hired by the company to escort the *Empresses* between ports in the South China Sea. In those exotic climes, the encounters with pirates, smugglers, and stowaways were further enlivened by the vagaries of the weather. The deep troughs and towering waves of the North Pacific Ocean crossing, which turned faces green, gave way to the typhoon winds that buffeted the ship from one end to the other.

Everyday duties, performed for the most part as a matter of course, could lead to unexpected excitement. Poole remembered, with a fair amount of amusement, the day a sling broke while cargo from his ship was being unloaded onto the wharf at Kowloon, across the harbour from Victoria and the Island of Hong Kong, releasing five thousand angry bees and sending more than one sailor diving into the ocean for cover.

Along with their obligations to keep their ship afloat, secure, and on course, officers were expected to volunteer for such hazardous assignments as dancing with unescorted female passengers, taking afternoon tea with the many celebrities who strolled the decks, and serving as entertainment directors for the duration of the voyage. Poole had the pleasure of meeting Will Rogers, Noel Coward, the King of Siam, and the Aga Khan. On one memorable ocean crossing, Cornelius MacGillicuddy—better known as Connie Mack—came on board at Yokohama with his All-American Baseball Team, including Babe Ruth and Lou Gehrig.

At regular intervals, officers would take leaves of absence to serve with Her Majesty's war ships in the Royal Navy Reserves, and Poole was no exception. Among the ships on which he sailed were the battleships HMS *Ramillies* and HMS *Warspite*, and the aircraft carrier HMS *Hermes*.

As the threat of aggression from Imperial Japan grew through the 1930s, Poole, by now a second officer on the *Empress of Canada*, had a few frightening run-ins with Japanese soldiers, including an interrogation at bayonet point while he stopped to admire a group of horses dockside at Kobe, Japan. He figured his charm, more than his good looks, got him out of that scrape.

Having been in close quarters with soldiers, unexploded bombs, sharks, shipwrecks, and the occasional armed and desperate man, Poole would often say he had cheated death many times over. Once, he recalled, a group of two hundred Filipinos embarked on a homeward voyage on the *Empress of Russia*, after two years working on Hawaiian sugar plantations. The ship had barely set sail when the staff captain rushed to the bridge of the *Empress* and thrust a .45 revolver into

THE NINE LIVES OF CAPTAIN POOLE
When not dealing with the hazards of the South China Sea, Poole would socialize with passengers like Connie Mack, on tour with the All-American Baseball Team. A.19337

Poole's hands, gasping out a warning: "He's already shot and killed the ship's plumber and wounded two of the Chinese deck hands." The perpetrator, a passenger who had run amok, as could happen at any time on the hot and muggy South China Sea, was quickly subdued and turned over to the Hong Kong police, but not without a few tense moments for Francis Poole.

"Ah yes," Captain Poole liked to say. "If the cat has nine lives, I've outdone the cat."

The Sun Sets on the British Empire

In 1997, the British handed control of Hong Kong over to China, ending a century and a half of foreign rule which began with the Chinese Opium Wars and was formalized with the Treaty of Nanking, in 1842. The inevitable post-Second World War emancipation of British colonial possessions finally caught up with its most far-flung outpost, one that was, for many years, an integral link in the extended imperial route of the CPR.

Even as the CPR was being constructed through British Columbia, using Chinese labour mostly recruited from Hong Kong, President George Stephen had vowed to arrange a mail and freight service from Vancouver to Japan and China, completing an "All-Red Route" from Britain to the Orient. When the line opened in 1886, a service employing chartered ships had already been put in place.

By the 1890s, the CPR secured mail contracts from the British and Canadian governments and launched its own regular steamship service on the Pacific. The inclusion of Hong Kong as the final port of call on the westbound leg was fundamental to the deal. On a good run, mail from London could be read on the island colony in twenty-nine days.

For years, the CPR's *Empress* ships could be seen at No. 5 wharf in Kowloon, on the mainland, across the harbour from the island of Hong Kong. Fast ferries whisked passengers back and forth every fifteen minutes. The shipping and trading firm Jardine, Matheson & Company acted as agents for Canadian Pacific. The merchant kingpins of the company, the powerful and influential taipans, controlled much of the activity in and around the Hong Kong waterfront.

Over the years the beautiful deepwater harbour near the mouth of the Canton River became increasingly important to the CPR's Far Eastern strategy. Bigger and faster ships were introduced: the *Empress of Russia* and *Empress of Asia* in 1913, *Empress of Canada* in 1922, and *Empress of Japan* in 1930. Hong Kong became the headquarters for the company's steamship operations in the Orient. While much of the upscale passenger business originated at Shanghai, Hong Kong remained the centre of the lucrative, but highly competitive, steerage business.

Trans-Pacific eastbound traffic aboard the *Empresses* consisted of European and

THE SUN SETS ON THE BRITISH EMPIRE
Hong Kong became the headquarters for the CPR's steamship operations in the Orient.
A.37255

North American residents in the Orient, commercial travellers, officials of various governments, British army officers from India, missionaries, Chinese and Japanese, and Asians travelling in bond to work on projects in the West Indies, Havana, and South Africa.

Westbound there were merchants, missionaries, returning Chinese and Japanese students, and a growing number of a new class of travellers: tourists. The relatively long crossing time—three weeks for the nearly 12,900 kilometres from Vancouver to Hong Kong, compared to one week for the 4,354 kilometres from Montreal to Liverpool—gave the Pacific run more of a cruise atmosphere. Those who strolled the decks in the 1930s might have bumped into Shirley Temple, Babe Ruth, Dr. Norman Bethune, or even the King and Queen of Siam.

Canadian Pacific ships were booked solid for the speedy passage of high-priced merchandise and perishable goods. Asbestos, flour, lead, zinc, nickel, newsprint, agricultural tools, and automobiles from North America were traded for tea, silk, rice, glassware, toys, and cigars from China.

In later years, of course, airliners usurped the "Great Circle Route" over the North Pacific to the Orient. Among the Canadian Pacific Air Lines fleet was the four-engined *Empress of Hong Kong*.

When the sun set on the British Empire, on 1 July 1997, and the last British governor vacated his Hong Kong residence on the slopes of Victoria Mountain, it also set on a little piece of CPR history.

Way, Way off the Beaten Path

If you're looking for the ultimate getaway, I have the destination for you: Tristan da Cunha, the lonely isles. You thought Tahiti was remote? Well, this group of three small islands in the South Atlantic, midway between Cape Horn and the Cape of Good Hope, is more than 1,930 kilometres from the nearest inhabited shore. It can be found on a world map in one of those fuzzy areas of the ocean that at one time typically carried the warning: "Here be dragons." We're talkin' remote.

It seems a Portuguese admiral, Tristan de Cunha, discovered the islands in 1506. (If he was looking for a short route to China, he was definitely "lost at sea.") He named the three rocks Inaccessible, Nightingale, and no surprise, Tristan. The crews of British ships, homeward bound from Cape Colony on the African Horn, used Tristan as a rendezvous point and place of refreshment. During the American War of 1812, the ships were often waylaid by American navy cruisers.

The British government laid claim to the outpost in 1816, just about the time Napoleon was being exiled to St. Helena, the closest island, and also about 1,930 kilometres away. William Glass, a British corporal of artillery, led a small contingent of soldiers and settlers to Tristan in 1816. Though most left the following year,

Way, Way off the Beaten Path
To the isolated folks on the islands of Tristan de Cunha, the arrival of a supply ship meant everything.
A.37247

Corporal Glass, his wife, and a few other hardy colonists stayed on and founded Edinburgh Settlement on a narrow plateau thirty metres above sea level.

Over the years, the colony's numbers were bolstered by shipwrecked sailors and the occasional new settler from Cape Town. The importation of horses, cattle, sheep, pigs, and poultry made things a little more livable. Even though the British government was keen to have Tristan da Cunha as a member of the Commonwealth, it was somewhat of a bother to have ships come by with supplies. The islanders' practice of bringing in potential brides from St. Helena was also frowned upon in the mother country. After many attempts by the British government to persuade the citizens of the lonely isles that they would be more comfortable living in South Africa, they just gave up.

Fortunately for the good people of Tristan, between the two world wars the CPR had entered the business of ferrying folks around the world on marathon cruises. Edinburgh Settlement was easily added to the ports of call. All the ships had to do was hold a straight course from Buenos Aires to Cape Town, and Tristan's distinctive volcanic cone would eventually pop up on the horizon—a volcano that became distinctly dangerous in 1961, when an eruption forced the islanders to evacuate to England for two years.

A typical stopover at the colony would see the transfer of eighteen to twenty-seven metric tons of supplies to the settlement. A shipment might include cigarettes, soap, brooms, clocks, books, paint, boots, shoes, cricket supplies, flags, toys, musical instruments, wallpaper, hardware, cameras, rat traps, crockery, stationery, and literally tons of food. In 1929, Queen Mary sent the colonists a harmonium aboard CPR's *Duchess of Atholl.*

Canadian Pacific Steamships have long since abandoned the world cruise business, but Tristan da Cunha is still thriving. There are now roads and a hospital, as well as sophisticated electricity, water, and sewage facilities. Potatoes are the main crop, fishing is the chief industry, and the sale of postage stamps is the main source of outside revenue. But it's still remote as all get out.

Until We Meet Again

Each year for eighty years, Grace Martyn placed a wreath at a stone monument in Toronto's Mount Pleasant Cemetery on the anniversary of Canada's worst marine disaster. Grace, seven years old at the time of the tragedy, was one of only four children and 213 adult passengers to survive the sinking of the CPR luxury liner *Empress of Ireland.* On the fateful night of 29 May 1914, 1,015 people died in the frigid waters of the St. Lawrence River. Rammed by the Norwegian collier *Storstad,* not too far from the south shore town of Rimouski, Quebec, the pride of CPR's ocean-going fleet vanished beneath the waves in a mere fourteen minutes.

UNTIL WE MEET AGAIN This drawing from the *London Illustrated News* shows the festive nature of the send-off afforded Japanese Prince Fushimi for his crossing aboard the *Empress of Ireland* from Britain to Canada. BR.31

The route up the St. Lawrence was less frequently travelled than the transatlantic route to New York City, and combined with the outbreak of the First World War, this contributed to a lack of general awareness about Canada's worst peacetime catastrophe. However, many Canadians were touched by the loss, and even the exoneration of the crew of the *Empress of Ireland* in a subsequent public inquiry could not remove their terrible remembrance of the great ship's passing.

After the White Star liner *Titanic* had gone down two years earlier, marine regulations were tightened considerably. Passenger liners were required to ensure enough lifeboat space to accommodate everyone on board, passengers and crew alike. As an added precaution, the CPR encouraged its captains to conduct rigorous boat drills at every opportunity, a procedure that the *Ireland*'s Captain Kendall had carried out in Quebec City the day before the doomed liner cast off for Britain.

On the night of their sailing, many of the ship's passengers had turned out on deck to take part in the fanfare that generally accompanied transatlantic departures. As the *Ireland* left the pier, a brass band—part of a 154-piece Salvation Army contingent on its way to an international congress in London—struck up a chorus of "God Be With You, 'Til We Meet Again." It was the last song they would ever play.

Young Grace had settled down for the night in her warm pyjamas, but she was awoken by the impact of the collision. "It was like a firecracker going off," she said in later years. "And I knew, just knew, that we were going to sink." Grace's father, Canadian bandmaster with the Salvation Army, also felt the blow and assumed it to be the river pilot's vessel nudging the liner as it drew alongside. But a friend's insistent knocking at his cabin door soon alerted him to the extent of the danger they faced. Unlike many of the unfortunate passengers whose third-class quarters were deep within the bowels of the ship, Grace and her parents were able to make their way to the open air. "The deck," she recalled, "was quiet and composed. There was no screaming and everyone was trying to help everyone else."

Once in the dark, cold waters of the lower St. Lawrence, Grace slipped in and out of consciousness...

Once in the dark, cold waters of the lower St. Lawrence, Grace slipped in and out of consciousness, sinking below the waves and resurfacing to grasp whatever bit of flotsam came to hand. Picked up by a lifeboat and delivered to the townsfolk of Rimouski, who had turned out in force to aid and comfort the survivors, Grace was frightened, cold, and alone. "I had no clothes on after being rescued and was covered with a blanket," she said. "I was clothed by townspeople and given shoes by a very charming shoe store owner."

Grace later learned that her parents had died and was taken under the wings of her uncle and aunt. Although she had identified her father's body in a Toronto funeral home, it took a full year for reality to penetrate the iron defences her young schoolgirl mind had erected. Grace never saw her mother again.

In the ensuing years, Grace grew up, married, and led a fairly happy life, by her own account. Though she once wrote a composition about the sinking of the *Empress* for a school project, in later years she shied away from the topic altogether. For the rest of her life, she avoided travelling by ship, with the one exception of a cruise from Vancouver, British Columbia, to Juneau, Alaska, on which she barely slept a wink. Grace Martyn died 29 May 1995, the last survivor of the sinking of the *Empress of Ireland.*

Every 29 May, a small group of Salvation Army members still gathers at the sandstone memorial in Mount Pleasant Cemetery. The band plays "Abide with Me," and a wreath is placed at the base of the monument. But it isn't the same any more. Grace is no longer there to place the wreath.

Good News, Bad News

On 7 November 1885, the Last Spike was driven on the CPR at Craigellachie, not far from British Columbia's Eagle Pass. Ironically, on the same day nature's challenges were being met and overcome in the west, the CPR steamship *Algoma* was lost, a victim of wind and ice on Lake Superior.

The *Algoma* was one of three modern steel Great Lakes ships launched in the summer of 1883 to provide passenger service between Owen Sound, Ontario, and

Port Arthur (now part of Thunder Bay) on the north shore of Lake Superior, linking Montreal with Winnipeg and points west as the rail line was under construction through northern Ontario. The ships also provided cargo space for the supplies required by the construction forces stretched out along the route.

Travelling under their own steam from the builder's yard in England, the *Algoma* and her sister ships *Athabasca* and *Alberta* arrived in Montreal in September 1883, where they were cut in half for movement through the St. Lawrence River canal system to Buffalo, New York. There they were rejoined and taken to Port Colborne, Ontario, for the completion of their upperworks. All of the woodwork was cut and shaped in the CPR's new shops in Montreal and shipped to Port Colborne to be installed.

When the ships steamed into Owen Sound in the spring of 1884, they were not only the fastest vessels on the Great Lakes, but among the most attractive as well. "The graceful run of the lines indicates strength, seaworthiness and adaptability for speed, even to the eye unlearned in the science of shipbuilding," noted a local newspaper, "while the passenger accommodations are of the highest class."

The *Algoma* was the first to enter service at Owen Sound. More than one thousand fare-paying customers crowded the dock to take passage on her ample decks. First-class passengers were provided with every amenity, confining themselves to the saloon and the saloon deck, while those in second class were required to furnish their own mattresses and bedding and had the run of the entire main deck.

From the beginning, the new ships found favour with travellers. A full-service train, known simply as the "steamboat express," was operated from Toronto to Owen Sound in connection with the steamship service. The first season, along with the conveyance of passengers, the three sturdy vessels were occupied with delivering rails and bridge iron to construction crews at the rustic Ontario camps of Little Pic, Big Pic, Gravel River, Jack Fish, and Maggot River. Lake shipping closed for the winter and reopened by mid-May of 1885.

In the summer of 1885, the regular operation of the steamers was enlivened by the return to the east of troops sent the previous fall to quell the Northwest Rebellion. Whereas on the earlier move the troops had been compelled to bridge the unfinished sections of track with forced marches across the rugged northern Ontario terrain, the returning soldiers were able to avail themselves of the relative luxury afforded by the opening of navigation.

However, the conditions on Lake Superior can be demanding at the best of times. The lake is prone to sudden storms and the weather near the close of the navigation season can be particularly treacherous. The *Algoma* left Sault Ste. Marie, Ontario, on 6 November, propelled by steam and sail, and a strong, steady tailwind. Overnight, the weather worsened and by early morning, the wind, accompanied by squalls and blowing snow, had reached gale force.

Overnight, the weather worsened and by early morning, the wind, accompanied by squalls and blowing snow, had reached gale force.

The captain, first officer, and chief engineer consulted among themselves. Together they reckoned their position to be some twenty-four kilometres off Isle Royale, when, in fact, they were much farther up the lake. The engines were

GOOD NEWS, BAD NEWS
"... and there, with death flapping his wings over us, we knelt down in the snow and water and the captain prayed for us."
NS.8361

slowed and the ship's course altered to take in sail and run back out, farther into the lake. The *Algoma* immediately struck a reef extending out from Greenstone Island. Battered against the rocks by the surf, the ship broke in half. Nothing could be done to save either ship or cargo, let alone the passengers whose lives were now fully left in the hands of fate.

Men, women, and children were swept away like feathers, and the survivors clung to the wreckage of the stern. One crew member, recalling the courage of the ship's Captain Moore, described that desperate moment: "Hurt as he was, he said, 'Men, let us unite in prayer,' and there, with death flapping his wings over us, we knelt down in the snow and water and the captain prayed for us."

The next morning, the winds moderated and the survivors were able to fashion a raft from ship timbers, and sought shelter on Greenstone Island, not far from the northeast tip of Isle Royale. Fortunately the *Athabasca*, which had left Owen Sound on 7 November, spotted the distress signals of the stranded survivors. After forty-eight hours of terror, they were rescued, and news of the tragedy was soon carried to Port Arthur. Of the fifty-six crew members and passengers on board, only fourteen were saved.

It was the last time the CPR's Great Lakes service lost a life, leaving an unblemished safety record between 1885 and 1965.

Vying for the Cane

There's an old tradition in the ports of Montreal and Quebec City that inspires intense rivalry among ship captains: the quest for the gold-headed cane awarded to the master of the first vessel to arrive at each of the two harbours in the new year. For many of the early years of this time-honoured competition, Canadian Pacific was right there in the thick of things.

The annual rite of recognizing the arrival of the first vessel dates back to the nineteenth century in Montreal, possibly as early as 1830, the year the city's Harbour Trust Commission was formed. However, shipping records reveal that the first official winner was the sailing ship *Great Britain*, which won the first of five awards for her master in 1840. In those days, the ceremony had more than just nominal significance, as it marked the resumption of communications between Montreal and Quebec with the outside world, which were interrupted annually by the freeze-up of the St. Lawrence River.

To qualify, an arriving vessel had to be inbound from a foreign port. When it was necessary to tie up or anchor downriver, below Quebec City, to avoid unfavourable weather or sea conditions, a ship could be disqualified if her crew engaged in any commercial activities while delayed.

Vying for the Cane
Captain J. Bisset Smith, O.B.E., poses with his fellow officers from the CPR liner *Beaverburn* and company officials after capturing the gold-headed cane at the opening of the 1947 navigation season. B.471-3

In the early years, a hat made from beaver felt was bestowed on the winning captain upon arrival in Montreal, whereas Quebec officials presented a variety of tokens including, at various times, silk top hats, umbrellas with gold handles, silver cigarette cases, and oil paintings. However, somewhere along the way, tradition in both cities gelled and the Malacca cane was settled upon as the standard gift. In addition to their gold tops, the canes typically bore the Canadian coat of arms, the name and arrival date of the ship, and the name of her master.

Two of CPR's ancestor steamship lines racked up an impressive list of wins over the years. The Allan Line, controlled by CPR from 1909 and fully absorbed by the company's steamship arm in 1915, was first to Montreal on at least twenty-eight occasions, dating back to the arrival of the *Caledonia* in 1842. The Beaver Line, purchased by CPR in 1903, accepted the honour four times, beginning in 1871, when the *Lake Superior* steamed triumphantly into the upriver port.

By 1923, the *Bolingbroke*, flying the checkered house flag of the Canadian Pacific Steamship service, started a tradition that would see many of the company's vessels in the winner's circle. First in for the 1937 and 1938 seasons were the *Duchess of York* and the *Duchess of Bedford*, respectively, popular sixteen-thousand-metric-ton, cabin-class liners that were the largest ships then docking at Montreal. During the post-war years, the CPR's speedy *Beaver*-class freighters were often in contention.

A fierce contest was waged during the dash for Montreal at the beginning of the 1950 shipping season, with Canadian Pacific's *Beavercove* beating the Swedish motorship *Erland* into the harbour by just over an hour. Not until 1966, when the Soviet vessel *Indigirka* edged out the Danish ship *Tor Dan* by a mere seventeen minutes, was the outcome more in doubt.

Before 1960, when the use of icebreakers and the ability of freighters to plow through a certain amount of ice became commonplace, arrival dates in early April were considered exceptional. As recently as the 1970s, navigating the river all the way to Montreal any earlier was so unthinkable that one experienced city marine official commented: "If anyone had suggested twenty-five years ago that we would one day have an open channel from Montreal to the sea in January, people would have thought him insane."

Gold Rush Sternwheeler

In 1897, the Klondike Gold Rush was in full swing, and it looked as if no end was in sight. An enormous flotilla of vessels, from the most luxurious coastal steamers to a ragtag assortment of working boats, was pressed into service to take advantage of the booming demand for passage to the goldfields of the Yukon.

The CPR's own coastal fleet was taxed to the limit, justifying the expenditure for

GOLD RUSH STERNWHEELER
Too late on the scene for its intended use in the Klondike Gold Rush, the *Moyie* went on to become one of the best-known and best-loved vessels in western Canada.
NS.22206

several more vessels to handle the overflow. Among these was the sternwheeler SS *Moyie*, which would go on to become one of the best-known vessels in western Canada. The *Moyie* was originally intended for service on the Stikine River route to the Klondike and consequently was designed with a steel frame and side plates, allowing for greater strength when encountering ice. Although the various components of the hull were fabricated by Bertram Iron Works of Toronto, they were shipped to the west coast for final assembly.

Unfortunately, the gold rush ended as precipitously as it had begun, and the as-yet-unfinished *Moyie* was trundled off to Nelson, in the British Columbia interior, for use on the Nelson to Kootenay Landing run, in connection with the CPR's new Crowsnest Pass line. On 22 October 1898, it was launched. At 835 gross tons, and a little more than forty-nine metres long, it was an efficient boat, if somewhat less than elegant.

More than fifty years later, when the CPR vessel *Minto* was towed offshore at Galena Bay on the Upper Arrow Lake for a fiery Viking burial, the *Moyie* was the last of the gallant sternwheelers to maintain a regular freight and passenger service on the rivers and lakes of the British Columbia interior.

A victim of a vastly improved road system and North America's infatuation with the automobile, the *Moyie*, too, was withdrawn from active duty, on 27 April

1957. On that day, the townsfolk turned out in droves to pay their last respects to a friend whose familiar silhouette would never again cross the horizon, and whose plaintive whistle would never again echo from the mountain walls. All along the farewell route, people paid tribute. In Lardeau, twenty cars and trucks delivered a twenty-horn salute; in Argenta, a decorated wreath was bestowed upon the *Moyie*'s dedicated crew; and, at Kaslo, the boat landing was gaily festooned in red, white, and blue bunting, around a banner that read: "Better Lo'ed Ye Ne'er Be. Will Ye No Come Back Again." While the local Boy Scouts troop stood at attention, the *Moyie*'s Captain McLeod was presented with a photograph of the valiant sternwheeler, duly signed by the more than one hundred passengers and crew members on board for the occasion.

On 1 May 1957, the *Moyie* was sold to the Kootenay Lake Historical Society for one dollar and beached on the shore of the lake at Kaslo. There it took on a new life as a community museum and repository for a plethora of interesting local artifacts.

A Fine Place for Canada Place

During Vancouver's Expo '86, Canada Place was the site of Canada's spectacular harbour-front pavilion, showcasing the country's finest technological and cultural achievements. The former flagship of Expo 86 houses a cruise ship terminal, the Pan Pacific Hotel, and a world-class trade and convention centre, the largest in western Canada, and is now recognized as a famous landmark and a prominent symbol of the city.

But 1986 was not the first time that the massive pier jutting out in Burrard Inlet, upon which Canada Place unfurled its magnificent sails, had achieved a measure of fame. Officially dedicated on 4 July 1927 as CPR's Pier B-C, the dock had tripled the amount of berthing space then available to the company's expanded fleet of coastal and trans-Pacific steamships.

Built over a period of eight years, at a cost of six million dollars, the pier could not only accommodate Canadian Pacific's large *Empress* liners, including the flagship *Empress of Canada*, but also the ships of the Australasian Mail Line, the Royal Mail Steam Packet Company, and any other large vessels requiring oversize docking facilities. Any five large ships could be serviced simultaneously, and the walkways around the perimeter were often crowded with travellers and well-wishers.

The entire construction of the pier was coordinated by the CPR's engineering department and executed by Junkins Engineering and Contracting Company, the firm that had remodelled and extended Vancouver's nearby Pier D, and installed a reinforced concrete lining throughout the eight-kilometre length of the railway's Connaught Tunnel, in the Selkirk Mountains. To erect the six thousand piles on which the pier is supported, the world's largest and most powerful pile driver, dubbed Tarzan II, was floated into position.

Every possible safety feature was incorporated into the design. A fender beam skirted the entire structure with massive double-coil compression springs, to absorb any accidental bump. Fifty-seven fire hydrants and more than five thousand sprinkler heads guarded against errant sparks. More than 18,580 square metres of floor space was available for freight handling.

On either side of the pier were travelling gantries. Two lifts, each with a capacity of nine metric tons, carried baggage into the ships' holds, while eight marine hoists loaded and unloaded freight directly between ship and pier. Eight on-deck railway tracks could accommodate two hundred freight cars, or eight twenty-five-car trains.

Among the most important cargo slung onto the wharf were bales of silk from the Orient, destined for the ravenous silk mills of New Jersey. The awaiting trains carried consignments valued in excess of five million dollars. Armed guards accompanied them across the continent.

Because the structure remained busy both day and night, it was well spotlighted, adding colour and dynamism to the Vancouver harbour. As Canada Place, it follows in the same tradition—a unique addition to the Vancouver skyline.

A FINE PLACE FOR CANADA PLACE
The CPR's Pier B-C was once home to the company's west coast and trans-Pacific fleets. NS.21070

314
314

Chapter Three

First Class Hotels and Hospitality

Roots of a Hotel System
When the CPR opened Mount Stephen House in Field, British Columbia, it launched one of the most ambitious and long-running tourist advertising campaigns ever seen. A.192

The Mysterious Professor Buell
With his wonderful photographs, the itinerant cameraman beckoned "all sensible people" to travel by the CPR.

Roots of a Hotel System

Operations on the CPR main line began in several stages, after each section of track was brought up to running standards and the stations and support structures were put in place. A system of dining halls was established at several of the railway's divisional points, including Winnipeg, Manitoba; Broadview, Moose Jaw, and Swift Current in Saskatchewan; and Medicine Hat and Canmore in Alberta. While their trains were being serviced, railway patrons could supplement their own provisions with hot meals of reportedly generous proportions. Dining cars were not carried for long distances in the early 1880s, as they were heavy to pull and could not possibly generate enough revenue to cover their cost, particularly on rail lines where there was a significant grade.

The first hotel to open was Mount Stephen House in Field, at the summit of the railway line through the Rocky Mountains.

On the mountain divisions, three additional dining halls were planned for Field, Glacier, and North Bend, all in British Columbia. But the need to accommodate dining room staff in these remote locations, combined with the CPR's desire to exploit the exceptional scenery, led to a rethink of their original, modest design. Inevitably, the company reached the conclusion that only small hotels would do.

William Van Horne, the railway's dynamic general manager and the driving force behind the building of the CPR, engaged the services of Thomas Sorby, a British architect already in the employ of the railway, to draw up plans for a structure appropriate to all three locations. The result was a picturesque Swiss chalet design that consisted of a three-storey central structure, with a two-storey wing to one side and a single-storey wing on the other. The hotels at Glacier and North Bend were nearly identical, whereas the one at Field was a mirror image.

While the mountain hotels were under construction, dining cars were placed on sidings adjacent to the main line to provide meals for the patrons of the CPR's *Pacific Express* and *Atlantic Express* who could afford such extras.

The first hotel to open was Mount Stephen House in Field, at the summit of the railway line through the Rocky Mountains. It took its name from the imposing mountain named for first CPR president George Stephen, later Lord Mount Stephen, which loomed up just behind it. On 23 October 1886, the doors swung open to admit the first patrons. The dining car *Marlborough* and its staff were sent back east to other assignments.

At the beginning the intention was to operate the hotels under the auspices of the railway's sleeping, dining, and parlour car department, but it was soon found to be expedient to turn the day-to-day operations over to a private contractor. The hotel managers were expected, of course, to maintain the premises and furnishings to CPR standards.

Mount Stephen House soon became a favourite with railway travellers and was frequented by diverse groups of tourists, hunters, alpinists, and fishermen, not to mention the hungry passengers who descended upon the dining room with the arrival of every train. Among the early luminaries to cross the threshold were the Duke and Duchess of Cornwall and York, later King George V and Queen Mary, during their tour through the British Empire, in 1901.

One unexpected attraction, which drew the attention of the scientific community worldwide, was the abundance of fossil beds on the slopes of Mount Stephen. These deposits were so rich that one could pluck perfect specimens from the surface without ever resorting to pick and shovel.

The hotel was such a resounding success that a massive extension was added, providing many more bedrooms and improved plumbing. Designed by Francis Mawson Rattenbury, who would go on to complete the British Columbia legislative buildings and the CPR's Empress Hotel in Victoria, the addition included a large and impressive hall and billiard room with heavy beams and wood panelled walls and ceilings. A new smoking room and drawing room with commanding views of the Kicking Horse Valley added to the comforts of the house, as did the enormous open fireplace, in which whole logs could be burned.

One unexpected attraction, which drew the attention of the scientific community worldwide, was the abundance of fossil beds on the slopes of Mount Stephen.

Sadly, by the end of the First World War, economic conditions forced the railway to reassess the viability of the hotel. Tourists had begun to favour automobiles as a convenient means of exploring the mountains, thinning the numbers of casual railway users. The wooden construction of Mount Stephen House also made it difficult and expensive to maintain first-class standards. Accordingly, the entire hotel structure was turned over to the recently established railway YMCA organization, and placed at the disposal of the many itinerant railway workers looking for accommodation between shifts. It continued in this capacity until 1953, when it was torn down to make way for a modest railway bunkhouse.

A Splendid Setting for a War Conference

Confrontation was in the air. Not even the spit and polish of the highest-ranking British and American officers could conceal the underlying tension at the Quebec Conference, held at the CPR's Chateau Frontenac in August 1943.

In recent months, the Second World War had taken a turn for the better. Mussolini was under house arrest in Italy, the Germans were in retreat at the Russian front, and the protracted and costly war on the North Atlantic had finally swept the shipping lanes of German U-boats. But Hitler's Nazi regime was still firmly entrenched in Europe, and earlier conferences in Casablanca and Washington that same year had failed to resolve the most fundamental difference between British and American strategists: whether to launch a full-scale strike against Fortress Europe, or to continue a piecemeal campaign of deception, sabotage, subversion, night bombing, and political warfare.

The British high command under General Sir Alan Brooke, chief of the Imperial General Staff (the supreme military post in the British Empire), favoured the latter approach. He was mindful of the lessons learned on the beaches of France during the disastrous assault a year earlier at Dieppe, where an invasion force consisting primarily of green Canadian troops had been crushed by battle-hardened German Panzer divisions.

The Americans, on the other hand, wanted to stage an overwhelming strike against the Nazis on the north coast of France, to confront the might of the German army head-on and destroy the Nazi war machine in one final, bloody, apocalyptic struggle. The U.S. joint chiefs of staff were also of the opinion that the British strategy of forcing the Germans to divert troops to new fronts in the Mediterranean was more politically motivated than calculated to bring the war to a swift conclusion. This was the posture assumed by General George C. Marshall, chief of staff of the U.S. Army, in the opening salvoes of the three-week conference.

In the weeks leading up to the conference, there were many logistical problems to overcome. Security being paramount, more than eight hundred hotel guests had to be relocated, including Maurice Duplessis, leader of the opposition in the Quebec government. A further two thousand hotel reservations were cancelled. By the time anti-aircraft guns had been installed on the terrace of the Chateau, as well as along the boardwalk and even across the river in Levis, Quebec, it was apparent that something big was in the works.

A Splendid Setting for a War Conference While Churchill, Roosevelt, and Mackenzie King planned the invasion of Nazi Germany's "Fortress Europe," they were comfortably ensconced in the CPR's fortresslike Chateau Frontenac, in Quebec City. War.96.0

Though British prime minister Winston Churchill and U.S. president Franklin Delano Roosevelt, along with their host, Canadian prime minister Mackenzie King, would come to dominate media coverage at the conference, their military counterparts handled the preliminary "donkeywork," while they holed up at Roosevelt's estate on the banks of the Hudson River.

D'Alton C. Coleman had just ascended to the presidency of the CPR, following the lengthy illness and subsequent death of Sir Edward Beatty earlier that year. By a quirky twist of fate, his brother, Dr. E. H. Coleman, was serving as Canada's under-secretary of state, charged with the task of coordinating the military planning session.

While hotel manager B. A. Neale fretted, the CPR prepared for the onslaught. The entire third floor of the Chateau—all 101 rooms—was stripped of its furnishings and converted to office space and war planning rooms. The hotel's billiard room and enclosed terrace were used to store beds, couches, chairs, lamps, and carpets, while the military engineers and electricians dutifully knocked holes in the walls for the communications apparatus.

Both the British and Americans arrived in Quebec with large contingents of delegates, advisers, typists, and clerks, armed with the latest position papers and reports. Subjected to rigorous security checks, the hotel staff spent long hours at the beck and call of the largest group of Allied officers yet assembled during the war. Sharing the policing duties were the ever-present RCMP officers in full dress uniform, FBI agents, and British Royal Marines, who had accompanied Churchill to Canada aboard the *Queen Mary.*

To prepare the thousands of meals required, master chefs were recruited from CPR hotels across the country, under the supervision of culinary wizard Leonard Rhode. Before many days had passed, both Roosevelt and Churchill—the latter of whom routinely consumed prodigious quantities of food and drink—had both taken to Rhode in a big way, referring to him affectionately and simply as "chef." His reward was an invitation to accompany the pair on fishing trips to Lac à l'Epaule and Lac des Neiges, in Laurentide Park, not far from Quebec City.

Every night at the Frontenac, after yet another round of ponderous discussion, the tedium would give way to lively dances and movie showings, to which all of the conference attendees were invited. The hotel ballrooms easily accommodated those with a hankering to trip the light fantastic, and the nearby Capitol Theatre offered nightly screenings of Irving Berlin's *This is the Army.*

By the end of the conference, a consensus had been reached, and the British had given their endorsement to "Overlord," the plan that called for the invasion of Europe to be launched on the beaches of Normandy less than a year later. In return, the British commanders had received assurances from the Americans that the once-formidable German air force, the Luftwaffe, would be neutralized, and that the Italian front would not suffer any setbacks as a result of the new offensive.

Ironically, neither General Brooke nor General Marshall would be named as supreme commander of the Allied forces in Europe. That honour would fall to

U.S. general Dwight D. Eisenhower at yet another conference later that year in Teheran.

In a public broadcast to Canadians, Churchill did the CPR proud by declaring that "no more fitting and splendid a setting could have been chosen than we have here in the Plains of Abraham, in the Chateau Frontenac and ramparts of the Citadel of Quebec." Proving that actions speak louder than words, the Allies staged a repeat performance at the Chateau over a ten-day period the following September, albeit on a much smaller scale.

As Allied troops slowly but surely converged on Berlin, the Pacific war theatre rose to the top of the military agenda. Whereas the 1943 conference had allowed precious little time for frivolities, now tensions had eased to the point where Roosevelt and Churchill could take time out to accept honorary doctorates from Montreal's McGill University.

As for Maurice Duplessis, who had been unceremoniously turfed from the Chateau the year before, he was now premier of Quebec and was front and centre at all of the conference's official functions.

BANFF'S PERFECT MOMENTS

> In the perfumed indolence of a tropical setting, with a fountain faintly splashing, and the gorgeous views peeping over the brim of a tea cup, that's another way to enjoy Banff! The Conservatory, poised between murmuring falls and soaring peaks, is almost a glass sphere, except where it opens into the Ball Room. At night, with the lanterns glowing, the dance music floating on the scented air, and the great stars trembling over moon-silvered peaks . . . oh well, that's just another of Banff's perfect moments.
>
> – BANFF SPRINGS HOTEL PUBLICITY BROCHURE, CIRCA 1930

More than any other destination along the lines of the Canadian Pacific Railway, "Banff the Beautiful" has attracted the attention of photographer and writer alike. There is a mystic allure that has compelled both tourists and publicists to lavish praises on the birthplace of Canada's national park system. From modest beginnings as the location of siding 29 on the CPR main line, the railway's presence, and particularly its decision to build a spectacular resort hotel there, have helped Banff achieve a reputation as a tourist destination of near-legendary proportions.

According to tradition, the site of the Banff Springs Hotel was chosen by Tom Wilson, the renowned Canadian outdoorsman and discoverer of Lake Louise. Escorting the CPR's William Van Horne to the foot of Sulphur Mountain, at the confluence of the Spray and Bow Rivers, he pointed out the "million-dollar view" that has enchanted a century of visitors to "Canada's Mountain Playground."

Banff's Perfect Moments
The mystic allure of Banff has compelled tourists and publicists alike to lavish praise on the birthplace of Canada's national park system.
A.11384

With characteristic fervour, Van Horne pronounced the two-hundred-room mountain retreat, opened 5 June 1888, as "the finest hotel on the North American continent." The railway's publicity department described Banff Springs as "a large and handsome structure, with every convenience that modern ingenuity can suggest, and costing over a quarter of a million dollars."

Visitors fairly gushed with enthusiasm. An old railwayman, Morley Roberts, waxed eloquent: "The truth is I could not take beautiful Banff seriously. I dreamed it, and like so many dreams it was at once absurd and beautiful. On a pine-covered bank or bluff above the crystal foam of the Bow, I came to a giant castle. It had no business being there, for when I was thereabouts so long ago, no one could have thought it."

Another early arrival on the scene, F. J. Proctor, recorded his impressions at the end of a long, winding road cut through the forest: "Perched above us, the hotel came into view, a three-storied picturesque building with a broad veranda. At the door, a group of bright-faced, willing bellboys greeted us and took our wraps, and we entered the spacious hall with polished floor and two large fireplaces at either end, where in the chilly evenings log fires burned cheerily."

It was high praise for the hotel's staff and ambience, but nothing the local newspaper *The Crag* (now the *Crag & Canyon*) couldn't better in later years: "On the female side of the staff, there were blondes, brunettes and intermediates – all pretty as pictures – so alluring that no mere man could look them straight in the eye and deny them anything their hearts desired, and the best of it is that the prettiest of them are the most accomplished and talented. On the male side, form and sprightliness predominated, but then nobody is interested in the men these days."

Hundreds of definitive descriptions have been penned over the years, and some are as dated as *The Crag*'s quaint prose, from "a place where men play golf and women change their clothes" to "one of the places in the world where, if you sit long enough, all of your friends, in due course, will pass by."

As one visitor from New York City put it: "I feel the urge to rave. There is sentimental music in the background and such a gorgeous view that I cannot keep my eyes on the paper. Anyone who wants to say, 'See Naples and die,' is welcome to it. But this place makes me want to live to come back."

A Distinctive Look

A Distinctive Look Structures like Price's Place Viger Hotel and Station in Montreal firmly established the railway-chateau style of architecture in Canada. A.12737

One of Canada's hallmarks is the railway chateau, but it was a prominent American architect who introduced the style north of the border. After 1886, with the new transcontinental in full operation, CPR's top priority was to upgrade its station buildings and other ancillary structures. To project an image in keeping with the company's growing stature, CPR president William Van Horne chose to award many of the high-profile contracts to well-known New York architect Bruce Price. Born in Cumberland, Maryland, in 1845, Price had established an excellent reputation based on his work in the United States and several of his friends and

clients were among the most wealthy and prominent members of New York society.

The first project he undertook in Canada was the Banff Springs Hotel, the CPR's showpiece mountain hotel, which opened in 1888. While the work was still in progress, Price was also given the task of preparing the drawings for a new CPR terminal station and headquarters building on Windsor Street in Montreal. The first wing of Windsor Station—later expanded to become one of Montreal's best loved and most widely recognized landmarks—opened its heavy oak doors for business in 1889.

Banff Springs Hotel and Windsor Station incorporated many construction materials native to the areas in which they were built. Hemlock, pine, spruce, and ash woods graced the rich confines of the Banff Springs, whereas Windsor Station benefitted from a nearby supply of Montreal limestone, and slate for the expansive roofline.

While the construction noise echoed through the architectural establishment, Price negotiated additional contracts for a combined station and hotel at Sicamous and an annex to the mountain chalet at Glacier, both in British Columbia. Van Horne shared Price's enthusiasm for distinctive architectural designs and the two would often get together on Sundays to discuss the image that CPR structures should project.

In 1891, a select group of CPR officials formed a syndicate to build a hotel in Quebec City, on the site of the old Chateau St. Louis. The familiar castlelike Chateau Frontenac, which opened there in 1893, is perhaps Price's best known and most loved creation. During construction, Price and Van Horne rowed out into the St. Lawrence River to satisfy themselves that the view of the hotel as seen from the shipping lanes along the river would be sufficiently imposing.

The public certainly found the results to be satisfactory. A reporter for *Century* magazine remarked, in comments directed at Price, that "it is so seldom in this age that one sees a building which depends on its perfect proportions for its beauty, that it gives me a great pleasure to tell you how much I appreciate this structure and admire your taste and genius which has left, in this nineteenth century, a record of strength and beauty for ages to come."

Another significant project designed by Price for the CPR was the Place Viger Hotel and Station building in Montreal, which opened in 1898. The multi-turreted structure, faced with the same orange brick of Quebec's Chateau Frontenac, is reminiscent of the distinctive castles grouped along the banks of the Loire River in France. Alas, the structure's usefulness diminished with the shift of the city's business district to the northwest, and it was later annexed by city hall.

Firmly ensconced as CPR's premier architect, Price was recruited by Lord Strathcona, a prominent member of the railway's board of directors, to design a women's college—to be known as the Victoria Institute—on the campus of Montreal's McGill University.

Price's last work in Canada was a residence for James Ross on Peel Street, in

Montreal. Ross was one of Canada's most successful railway contractors and financiers, and a member of the board of directors of the Chateau Frontenac Company. Although it has been expanded and renovated over the years, the house still stands as a functional part of McGill University.

Even though CPR contracts occupied a large chunk of Price's professional time during the 1890s, most of his work was executed in the United States. Among his many achievements there are two buildings at Yale University, the Wesson House (of gunmakers Smith and Wesson) in Springfield, Massachusetts, some early office towers, and the first fireproof apartment building in New York City. Throughout his career, he occupied many important seats in his profession, including that of president of the Architectural League of New York.

Price died from a disease of the stomach on 29 May 1903. By great good fortune—and the merits of his designs—many of his best-known works remain to commemorate his standing as one of the pre-eminent North American architects of the nineteenth century.

A Good First Impression

When the first guests signed the register at the Chateau Frontenac on 14 December 1893, they were three days early for the opening ceremonies, but the ceremonies themselves were about seven months late. The previous summer Chicago had hosted the world at a spectacular world's fair. CPR management, wanting a piece of the action that such exhibitions were sure to generate, had set the opening date for the Chateau accordingly, on 1 May. Regrettably, construction delays and cost overruns were as much a feature of the nineteenth century as they are today so, after stepping off a ship from Europe, fair goers had to content themselves with one of Quebec City's other fine hostelries.

They say in the real estate industry that the three most important ingredients for making a sale are location, location, and location, and certainly the Frontenac

A Good First Impression
For many newcomers to Canada, this view would come to symbolize the strength of the nation and the strength of the CPR.
NS.21216

has one of the most impressive locations, not only in Quebec City, but also in Canada.

From the time William Van Horne, then president of the CPR, decided the railway would build and operate its own chain of hotels, he had envisioned large impressive structures for the two strategic points where the rail lines met the sea lanes: Vancouver and Quebec City. Of particular importance was the first impression that would-be immigrants and thrill-seeking tourists would get as they floated up the sheltered St. Lawrence route on a Canadian Pacific steamship. There on the bluff at Quebec City, where once stood the French governor's chateau and Fort St. Louis, would rise a castlelike hotel that would convey strength—the strength of the country and the strength of the Canadian Pacific Railway.

Even as late as February 1892, the final location had not been secured. Some consideration was still being given to other sites: the site of the Old Parliament House, and the cape, where Lord Mount Stephen, CPR director and founding president, had purchased a property. A number of proposals for similar schemes had come and gone in the decade preceding the formation of the Chateau Frontenac Company, the most serious of which was formulated by an outfit known as the Fortress Hotel Company, before it ran into a financial dead end. The partners in that company had coveted the spot on the brow of the cliff, but concluded, and rightly so as later events would show, that a structure the size of their proposed hotel would require the removal of the Chateau Haldimand, which, at the time, occupied part of the site.

Though the Fortress Hotel Company was unable to raise the necessary capital, it did rouse the interest of a group of entrepreneurs, including several with close ties to the CPR, in seeing the project through to completion. Thus was formed the Chateau Frontenac Company, at first not directly owned by the CPR, but destined inevitably to come under the railway's control.

Eleven hundred and thirty cubic metres of solid rock were excavated to build the foundation for the hotel, but what arose on the site was more solid still. When the Chateau Frontenac blossomed upon Dufferin Terrace, it instantly became synonymous with Canada, a symbol that has grown and strengthened over the years. Quebec City and the CPR wanted a hotel worthy of their ambitions, one that would capture the imagination of the world. With the Chateau Frontenac, they got it.

The Hotel What?

It's difficult to imagine a CPR hotel named Swastika. Yet in 1912, when the railway's newest hostelry was under construction in Calgary, that symbol—an ancient Eastern good luck charm, forever sullied by the Nazis—might have been applied over its front door. Swastika was one of a dozen names suggested to management

THE HOTEL WHAT? Ironically, the CPR's Palliser Hotel was named for the man who condemned the route chosen for the transcontinental railroad.
NS.2689

for the hotel that, along with the CPR station and adjoining gardens, would serve as the focal point for Calgary's social life for decades to come.

Other more obvious suggestions were Adanac (a brand name of CPR bottled mineral water, as well as Canada spelled backwards), Great Western, Golden West, Pride of the West, and Royal Northwestern. Another rather awkward sounding suggestion, which also sprang in part from CPR involvement in settlement and land development, was Shaughden, a combination of "Shaughnessy" for CPR president Thomas Shaughnessy, and "Dennis" for Colonel J. S. Dennis, assistant to the president in charge of land matters.

Of course, royal names were always in contention; the Duke of Connaught was considered, along with the Royal Mary, after the reigning British monarch. Later royal connections to the hotel included the patronage of the Prince of Wales, eventually Edward VIII, who not only frequented the hotel, but would also "borrow" his favourite staff members to help out on his nearby EP Ranch. In due time, the hotel was also a stopover point on the royal tours of Queen Elizabeth II and Prince Philip.

More interesting still was the proposal to name the hotel after Crowfoot, chief of the Blackfoot Indians and a moderating voice among Northwest First Nations during the CPR's construction period.

Eventually the choice was narrowed down and "Piedmont" came to the forefront. In the year preceding its opening, the hotel was listed as such in several industry and trade publications; however, at the last minute, Shaughnessy is said to have had a change of heart, deciding that "Palliser" would be more appropriate.

So ironically, the CPR's Calgary hotel was named for a man, John Palliser, who condemned the route chosen for the transcontinental railway in an 1863 report to the British House of Commons. Although enthusiastic about the agricultural possibilities of the Red Deer and Saskatchewan River valleys, Palliser was extremely pessimistic about the prospects for an arid section of the southern plains, later dubbed "Palliser's Triangle." He was later proven to be quite right, and the area was subjected to an extensive irrigation program to improve its suitability for settlement.

The Palliser immediately became Calgary's social centre when it opened for business, in 1914, hosting virtually all of the important local events of the 1920s and 1930s. The Old Time Range Men's Club, Calgary Petroleum Club, and Rocky Mountain Gas & Oil Association all held regular meetings there.

On one memorable occasion, the Calgary Flying Club removed the wings from a Tiger Moth biplane and moved it into their party room, nose-down on the top of a hotel elevator. It must have made quite the impressive centrepiece for their festivities, especially when club president Fred McCall fired it up, spewing black smoke throughout the room. With events like these, it's no wonder the locals referred to the Palliser as the "Paralyser."

Welcome to the Hotel Vancouver

When the first Hotel Vancouver opened on 19 May 1888, it was the subject of much idle chatter among the locals. The Canadian government, backed by the demands of the townsfolk, had insisted that the CPR invest half a million dollars on a luxury hotel as a condition of the land grant it received to extend the main line from Port Moody to the new Pacific terminal on Coal Harbour. But as the building stood ready for business at the corner of Granville and Georgia, nobody was quite sure what to make of it.

"An exceedingly ugly workhouse or asylum-looking structure," ruled one critic. "A solid, rather plain structure, a sort of glorified farmhouse, to which a number of extra storeys have been added," suggested another. Indeed, it was a modest structure, in keeping with the frugality of the times, which would soon be overshadowed by the grand railway hotels that were constructed in later years.

There is an amusing tale told about the hotel's opening, in which Van Horne, the railway boss who supervised construction of the CPR, comes to Vancouver on one of his many inspection trips. On this occasion, the story goes, when he was introduced to the hotel's architect, he looked the gentleman up and down, gave a sniff, and remarked: "So you're the damned old fool who has been filling this town up with small windows."

In truth, Van Horne had known said architect, Thomas Sorby, for several years, as he had already completed a number of commissions for the railway, including Dalhousie Square Station in Montreal, and the three chalet-style mountain hotels at Glacier, Field, and North Bend, in British Columbia. Sorby was a great admirer of the Queen Anne style of architecture, from which he had drawn inspiration for the Hotel Vancouver. The plans had been completed in Montreal, as early as 1886, and had been fully approved by Van Horne himself.

During construction, the bricks in the first storey, purchased at a bargain price from a brickyard in Victoria, were pitted so badly by frost the first winter that the entire surface had to be cemented over to secure a decent façade.

Despite its faults, it really wasn't such a bad old place and eventually won over the town with its well-appointed public rooms, in which great receptions were held. It did, after all, bring extra business and prestige to the town.

The rapid growth in the railway's western terminus precluded a long life for the building, which soon became inadequate for the burgeoning community, and a new wing was added as early as 1893. Another addition was completed in 1905 by the renowned Francis Mawson Rattenbury, architect of the British Columbia legislative buildings and the CPR's Empress Hotel, in Victoria. This was planned as a prelude to the construction of an entirely new building, but that project was never completed. Instead Francis S. Swales was engaged to design a six-hundred-bedroom hotel, incorporating some of the public rooms from the existing buildings, but giving the entire site a new, integrated look—and an attractive one at that. Completed in 1917 despite the austerity caused by the war in Europe, the new Hotel Vancouver was the object of much oohing and aahing in the local press and

WELCOME TO THE HOTEL VANCOUVER When the first CPR hotel in Vancouver opened its doors, it was deemed by the locals to be not only plain, but also exceedingly ugly. A.11535

was described in one story as "one of the finest on the North American continent."

But once again the passage of time was quick to catch up. A little more than two decades after its opening, on 17 May 1939, a farewell luncheon was hosted by the Vancouver Board of Trade for the aging hostel, while down the block, a new structure was usurping its name. Under construction since 1929, a third Hotel Vancouver—this one jointly owned by CPR and Canadian National—was the heir apparent. It's still a vibrant component in the Fairmont Hotel chain.

Having a Winnipeg Beach Party

When Sir William Whyte climbed into a small motorboat on the shore of Lake Winnipeg in Selkirk, Manitoba, he had exploration on his mind. The year was 1901, and Sir William, CPR vice-president of western lines, was looking for a beach. However, Whyte had more in mind that day than a refreshing dip. Accompanied by Selkirk merchant Captain William Robinson and CPR officer Charles Rolland, he wasn't just looking for a beach—he was out to buy one.

Winnipeggers were jubilant when they heard the CPR intended to develop a resort on the west shore of Lake Winnipeg. Jubilation soon turned into speculation, as the locals scrambled for real estate around the chosen site, a beautiful crescent of sand beside which the townsite of Winnipeg Beach would arise.

Within two years, the rail line had arrived and a depot stood complete. On Saturday, 6 June 1903, five hundred anxious beach goers piled on board the first scheduled train from Winnipeg destined for the new holiday mecca. The line experienced a few teething pains that morning; the train took a full four hours to haul its eleven coaches over the eighty-kilometre route. One passenger complained that a horse-drawn rig on the road parallel to the railway was able to pass the train four

Having a Winnipeg Beach Party
The oversize platform and awning at Winnipeg Beach station wait for the weekend throngs.
A.3548

times over the course of the trip. But the combination of sand, sun, and water soon won over the malcontents. While the adults socialized, the youngsters headed straight for the main attraction. As the *Winnipeg Free Press* reported: "The children of the party took a very short time to get their boots and stockings off, and soon little tots, holding their parents' hands, were wading in the refreshing water."

The resort was an instant success. Within the next few years, CPR built a power house, a large dance pavilion, a spacious hotel, an amusement park, bathhouses, and boardwalks running the length of the beach and out onto the company's T-shaped pier. Other enterprises were soon attracted to the area. Stores and hotels sprang up to cater to the burgeoning number of settlers and weekend revellers. One Winnipeg contractor, S. B. Ritchie, surveyed lots, cut down trees, built roads and sidewalks, and erected more than three hundred cottages at Winnipeg Beach.

The CPR's own three-storey Empress Hotel held a liquor licence until Prohibition and was renowned for its lavish bar. Thirsty beach goers could supplement their picnic lunches with four and a half litres of beer from the hotel for twenty-five cents. For residents and visitors alike, the Sunday concert at the Empress was the social event of the week. It was invariably followed by a huge bonfire on the beach, around which those out for a stroll on the beach or coming ashore from their boats would gather to sing to the accompaniment of banjos and mandolins. In later years, the beachside entertainment was augmented by a variety of amusements, including a giant roller coaster, merry-go-round, bowling alley, Ferris wheel, theatre, and the expected assortment of penny arcade games and rides.

The dance pavilion was one of the main attractions. It was often overcrowded and was replaced in 1924 by an impressive new structure with more than nine hundred square metres of maple dance floor. Reputed to be one of the largest in western Canada, the hall often required ten broom-wielding handymen to sweep away the evidence of an evening's festivities. Often, thousands danced into the wee hours of the morning.

One of the first Winnipeg Beach cottage owners, a gentleman named C. B. Plant, formed a local dance band. By day a chief clerk in the CPR Manitoba district superintendent's office, Plant took up his violin in the evenings and wowed audiences as a member of the pavilion orchestra for more than twenty years.

Regular train service was vital for accessing the area, and was virtually the only means of transport there for many years. The "Daddy train" left the beachside town early in the mornings, arriving in Winnipeg before the shops and offices opened at 9:00 AM. The 5:20 brought the workers back to the beach in time for dinner. The *Moonlight Special* ran every summer evening except Sunday, transporting Winnipeg amusement seekers to Winnipeg Beach for the cheap excursion return fare of fifty cents. On Saturday night, three trains, hauling seventeen or eighteen coaches each, often were required.

Alas, the arrival of the area's first automobile, in 1913, was a harbinger of things to come: it struck and killed the police magistrate's dog. With the coming of the car, a decline in railway traffic was inevitable. The beach facilities began to deteriorate.

Between the two world wars, the Empress Hotel burned to the ground, and most of the waterfront amusements went into receivership. Road construction increased automobile access to the area, and the trains stopped altogether in 1961.

Now the crowds are gone, but the town continues to prosper, and there are still those who can remember the excitement when the *Moonlight* steamed down to the beach.

The Forgotten Architect

Just a kilometre or two from CPR's old Windsor Station headquarters building in Montreal, one block south of the old east end terminal at Place Viger, is an interesting little greystone building with more than a little historical significance. A large assembly of people gathered there on 28 June 1886, as the train inaugurating regular CPR transcontinental service got underway. No photographs of the event have surfaced, and a small bronze plaque that once commemorated the occasion has fallen off an outside wall and disappeared.

THE FORGOTTEN ARCHITECT
Thomas Sorby's architectural contribution was small but significant, much like CPR's first Montreal terminal at Dalhousie Square Station, which he designed.
A.106

The building was CPR's first Montreal terminal, variously known as Quebec Gate Barracks Station and Dalhousie Square Station. Its rapid slide into obscurity paralleled the fate of its architect, Thomas Sorby. Most of Sorby's creations either never made the leap from drawing board to reality, or have been replaced over the years by loftier structures. However, Sorby did have an interesting career in Canada, which began in 1883 when he arrived in Montreal from London, England, and set up shop on St. James Street. His portfolio of architectural projects must have made an impression on CPR general manager William Van Horne, because within the year he was at work on the company's Montreal terminal building, as well as designing station buildings for Peterborough, Yorkville, and Port Arthur, all in Ontario.

By 1886, Sorby had been sent to British Columbia to supervise the construction of three CPR "mountain chalets" at Field, North Bend, and Glacier. The same year, he was commissioned to design the CPR's Hotel Vancouver and the company's Pacific terminus. Cost control measures forced the elimination of most of the elaboration in Sorby's proposed designs, resulting in an uninteresting, utilitarian station and a hotel described by a local journalist as "a sort of glorified farm-house." The completed architectural plans for the Hotel Vancouver had to be redrawn from scratch before the project was even off the ground, after most of the townsite went up in a huge conflagration on 13 June 1886. When told that the town was afire, Sorby rushed down to the CPR offices to collect as much of the paperwork as could be saved. It was only after fleeing the smoke and heat that he realized his drawings had perished in the flames.

Considerable bad feeling was generated when the CPR used its own bridge and building forces to oversee the construction of most of Sorby's creations, and the architect had a serious falling out with Van Horne and CPR president George Stephen. Sorby subsequently relocated his practice to Victoria, where he was intimately involved in the design and construction of the provincial capital's Inner Harbour.

The Mysterious Professor Buell

During the CPR's construction period, from 1881 to 1885, and the subsequent decade of pioneer operations and upgrading, the railway was approached by numerous photographers eager to be among the first to record the now accessible magnificence of the western Canadian landscape. Among the prominent practitioners who were offered travel assistance by the CPR were William Notman and Alexander Henderson, both of whom were given the use of a special railway car, outfitted as a photography lab with living quarters. A more enigmatic entrepreneur, however, was Oliver Buell, or Professor Buell as he styled himself, who was interested in obtaining photographic views along the line for use in his "entertainments."

Although the presence of photographers was sufficiently distracting that CPR superintendent John Egan referred to them as "photograph fiends," the pictures that resulted from the company-sponsored tours were invaluable tools for publicity and often the source from which engravings were produced for CPR brochures and advertisements. Only a small body of images have been positively identified as Buell's, most photographed during his westward trip on the CPR in 1886.

Born in Henry County, Illinois, in 1844, Buell was a shadowy figure for the first three decades of his life, eventually emerging as the operator of a travelling "stereopticon," or "lantern slide show," in the vicinity of Detroit. During the 1880s, Buell travelled to Canada several times, in the company of his wife Alice, plying his trade and adding to his expanding collection of slides. Some of his most unusual photographs were taken during the Northwest Rebellion and the subsequent trial of Louis Riel, including several that vividly portray the critical role played by the CPR in transporting troops to and from the west.

The professor also turned his attention toward the many attractions, both natural and man-made, that the newly constructed railway afforded. By 1886, CPR vice-president William Van Horne held Buell in sufficient esteem to offer him the use of the photographer's car, admitting the professor to the exclusive inner circle of CPR-sponsored shutterbugs. Company officers were instructed to provide "every facility" for Professor and Alice Buell. Van Horne attested to the results: "The

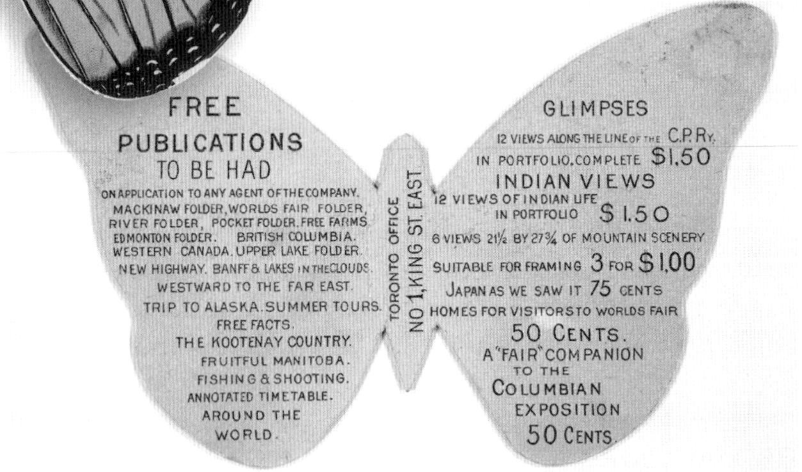

The Mysterious Professor Buell
The professor's photographs were sold in portfolios of "glimpses" along the line.
A.18111, A.18112

pictures, which in themselves are of a very high order of merit, are admired by everyone who has seen them, and I take much pride in showing them on every possible occasion as they are a more faithful portrayal of our magnificent scenery than anything I have yet seen."

Oliver Buell died of a heart attack on 4 April 1910, at the age of sixty-six. He was buried in Montreal, and to a large extent, his body of work was buried with him.

The Alpinist's Antics

Over the years, the Rocky Mountains have attracted their fair share of eccentrics, more than a few of whom have been associated with the CPR. But nobody was ready for Edward Whymper when he arrived at the company's Mount Stephen House hotel at Field, British Columbia, in the summer of 1901.

Whymper was a highly respected alpinist in Europe. There he was known as the conqueror of the Matterhorn, having been the first to make a successful ascent of that formidable peak in the Swiss Alps. But four men had died on that expedition, and though he had achieved further successes in his climbing career, Whymper had never been able to completely rid himself of rumours that he was somehow responsible for their tragic demise.

For the CPR, however, Whymper presented an ideal figure to promote the notion of the Canadian Rockies as the tourist's paradise—"Fifty Switzerlands in One." Whymper's arrival in Canada, along with four Swiss mountain guides, was heralded with much publicity and public attention. When his destination was disclosed, there was speculation that he might try for the first ascent of Mount Assiniboine, often referred to as the Matterhorn of the Rockies, partly because of the resemblance it bore to that peak. The reality, as it turns out, was somewhat less spectacular.

Although several first ascents were made by Whymper and his guides (Stanley Peak, Mount Whymper, and Storm Mountain, to name a few), all were rather tame and not viewed in climbing circles as great achievements. One guide, Christian Klucker, concluded that Whymper's only useful purpose was as a propaganda instrument. The self-deprecating Klucker recalled that, for his own part, "my greatest feat was to climb a tree in the primeval forest to see where we were."

Whymper, in fact, had considerable difficulty getting along with his guides, local outfitters, staff on the trains and in the hotels, and just about everybody else with whom he came in contact. One Banff outfitter, Robert E. Campbell, quoted Whymper's daily allowance on the trail as "one bottle of Scotch and ten pints of ale," which possibly contributed to his cantankerous nature.

Despite Whymper's enormous intake of alcohol, and the fact that he was already fifty-three years old when he first came to Canada, he appears to have had an

THE ALPINIST'S ANTICS
Whymper was ready with camera in hand to record the passing of the Royal Train of the Duke and Duchess of Cornwall and York, in 1901.
NS.1934

amazing constitution, judging from one report to the CPR. "Although remaining in the mountains until winter had set in, and experiencing in the heart of the Rocky Mountains so low a temperature as 15.5 below zero, or 47.5 below the freezing point of Fahrenheit," he wrote, "I have not found it even desirable to employ special dress, and have used from first to last only such ordinary summer clothing as I habitually wear in England."

Throughout the 1901 climbing season, and again during his return as a consultant for the CPR in 1903, 1904, and 1905, Whymper set up his headquarters at Mount Stephen House. Though he often heaped abuse on the hotel staff and his fellow hotel patrons, in his more lucid moments he actually seems to have had a soft spot for the place, as he related in his diaries: "No intimation was given to me that I should find Field a charming place, and it has been a pleasant surprise to discover in the heart of the Rocky Mountains a hotel which is all that a reasonable person can desire, in the midst of attractive scenery."

Sometimes long spells of bad weather confined Whymper to his room, where he found solace in recording lengthy lists of complaints in his ever-present journals. He even subjected the days of the week to his scorn, renaming them Stormday, Rainday, Mistday, Hailday, Thunderday, Snowday, and Sleetday.

Whymper's interest in, and collection of, the region's flora and fauna was the most positive aspect of his Canadian sojourns. He returned to Europe after his first season with an impressive array of fossils, botanical specimens, birds, insects, and animal skins. He also gave a young eagle to the aviary in Vancouver. Arriving at the CPR station in Banff with the bird in a cage, he attempted to persuade the station agent to transport the eagle for free, as company regulations stated that infants under age five were to be conveyed without charge. A six-dollar express fee was eventually settled upon.

The remaining seasons brought little work from the railway, although some new exploration did occur in the Crowsnest Pass area and Whymper undertook a walking tour along the railway tracks between Kananaskis and Yale, a distance of about eight hundred kilometres.

The value of Whymper's various reports to the CPR are hard to assess, as only one (from 1901, the most productive year) has survived in the company's archives. However, it is certain that he was involved in discovering several new mountain passes, putting names to some prominent peaks, and suggesting ways to make a number of local attractions more accessible to tourists and sportsmen. As a business venture, Edward Whymper's endeavours in the employ of the railway didn't amount to much, but he always left the locals with something to talk about.

An Elaborate Deception

In the summer of 1923, guests at the CPR's Banff Springs Hotel were surprised to encounter an impressive figure fully decked out in Plains Indian regalia. Even more astonishing was the ease with which this fearsome warrior could transform himself into a dashing tuxedo-clad gentleman, cutting a graceful swath across the dance floor amid the hotel's most wealthy and influential patrons. Yet not only did Buffalo Child Long Lance suddenly appear in the public rooms of the Banff Springs, he did so at the behest of the CPR, employed as assistant press representative and charged with entertaining the railway's guests in ways that only this singular man could do.

How such a man, in an era noted for racial intolerance, was able to elevate himself into the circles of high society is a unique story. Sylvester Long was born in 1890 in Winston, North Carolina. Although his parents were of mixed white, black, and North American Indian ancestry, they were perceived by the community as being black and, accordingly, were expected to defer to their white neighbours. Sylvester's parents instructed him to never talk back to white folk, to remove his hat in their presence, and to step off the sidewalk whenever they wanted to pass.

From his earliest memories, these indignities had grated upon the young boy, and he resolved to escape his "black prison" in Winston-Salem by any means that might present itself. Contact with a travelling Wild West show gave him an opportunity, and he managed to work his way into the show's Indian contingent. Soon Sylvester was presenting himself as half-Cherokee and, through this deception, was able to enrol at the Carlisle Indian Residential School in Pennsylvania, an

An Elaborate Deception
Sylvester Long held a pose for most of his adventurous and ultimately tragic life.
Glenbow Archives NA.1498-1

academy established for the advancement of the American Indian living in a white man's world. By graduation he had not only climbed to the top of his class, but had also adopted the name Long Lance. He began to weave an accompanying mythology that would both help and haunt him throughout his life.

Long Lance came to Canada in 1916, to enlist in the Canadian Army. He turned down a presidential appointment to West Point Military Academy because he was anxious to fight the war in Europe, a conflict to which the United States had not yet committed. In Europe, he distinguished himself in combat with the Princess Patricia's Canadian Light Infantry and, after being wounded twice, was discharged to the regiment's home base in Calgary.

In the west, he became fascinated by the Plains Indians and often visited with them on one or another of their reservations. The Blood Indians of Alberta gave him the name Buffalo Child, in memory of a respected warrior and in honour of Long Lance's courage during the First World War. Again, Long Lance reinvented his past, this time as a young Blackfoot Indian on the plains of Montana, in the days before the advent of the white man.

Such was his fame, as a result of the stories that began to appear under his byline in various publications, that the CPR hired him during the summer to accompany trail riders in the vicinity of its hotels at Banff and Lake Louise, and to socialize with important guests. During the winter of 1923–24, he was also engaged to prepare a series of menu covers for use on the company's trains. Topics such as "The Indian Scout" and "Indian Medicine Practices" were outlined and illustrated.

Regrettably, Long Lance's association with the CPR was severed after several seasons following a rather nasty incident involving a wealthy socialite and her family's butler. The butler, resentful of Long Lance's growing intimacy with his employer's wife, attacked him one night with a razor. In the ensuing struggle, Long Lance dented the man's skull with a poker, putting him in the hospital. Fortunately, the butler recovered, but the CPR, ever fearful of involving the company in anything that hinted of scandal, dispensed with Long Lance's services.

Buffalo Child Long Lance went on to become a reporter for a number of newspapers and magazines in Canada and the United States. A man of great ambition and talent, he dabbled as an aviator, a movie star, a sparring partner to Jack Dempsey, and a training companion for the famous Indian athlete Jim Thorpe. Although his true roots were nearly exposed on several occasions, he managed to preserve his Indian persona in much the same way as did Englishman Archie Belaney. Belaney, too, had adopted a Native lifestyle and identity, and became a respected conservationist and author under the name Grey Owl.

Eventually cracks began to appear in Long Lance's many fabrications. He was compelled to maintain his fictitious background to even his closest friends, and the strain of totally abandoning his family became more than he could bear. On 20 March 1932, at the age of forty-one, Long Lance was found in a Hollywood mansion, dead from a self-inflicted bullet wound to the head.

596
25376

CHAPTER FOUR

NEW OPPORTUNITY AROUND EVERY CORNER

NOTHING BUT A PILE OF BONES
The railway's capacity to load and move buffalo bones to market to be used as fertilizer was often surpassed by the ability of the wily plainsmen to gather the bleached remnants of the once-plentiful beasts. NS.6679

READY-MADE FOR WESTERN SETTLEMENT
The railway facilitated immigration along its main line to develop a high density of traffic.

Nothing but a Pile of Bones

By the time the CPR rolled across the Canadian prairies in the early 1880s, the vast herds of buffalo were all but decimated. Once these magnificent, woolly beasts had carpeted the vast western plains, but now all that was left were skeletal remains—a virtual sea of bones.

The same scenario had been played out twenty years earlier in the American west. After the Civil War, the buffalo had been hunted to near extinction, thanks in part to the advent of the repeating rifle and the stirrup, which enabled a rider on horseback to shoot at full gallop. The Americans, however, being inveterate entrepreneurs, had been quick to discover that the bleached remnants of these creatures were in great demand in Detroit, Chicago, and St. Louis. Once the bones were reduced to powder, they made excellent fertilizer.

With supplies quickly drying up south of the border, it was only a matter of time before bone hunting became a major industry in Saskatchewan and Manitoba. The grasslands between the Qu'Appelle Valley and the South Saskatchewan River proved to be particularly fertile ground for collecting buffalo bones. Where the Plains Indians had corralled and slaughtered tens of thousands of the beasts for their meat and hides, the earth was literally white with bones.

On occasion, the Sioux—a people in exile from their homeland in the Dakotas, and desperate to make ends meet—would gather the bones. But for the most part, religious beliefs and the sacred status bestowed upon the buffalo kept the indigenous peoples at arm's length from the trade. The Métis, however, had no such qualms about their role in the lucrative business and collected great quantities of buffalo bone from 1884 to 1893, the peak period of the bone trade.

The usual procedure was to load the bones onto Red River carts, which were specially outfitted with racks to add to their capacity, and then leave them along the CPR right-of-way in boxcar-size piles, approximately 2.4 metres high, 2.4 metres wide, and 9 metres long.

The first Canadian shipment was 43.6 metric tons of buffalo bone, enough to fill four boxcars on a siding at Regina and earn the dealer about three hundred dollars for his troubles. Generally speaking, the bone hunters could get from five to eight dollars in merchandise in exchange for a ton of raw product. The dealer, in turn, could ask for double that amount from fertilizer manufacturers in the United States.

Soon the hunters had to forage farther and farther away from the CPR main line and each new railway branch was eagerly anticipated as an access route to unharvested bone fields. With the opening of new horizons, Saskatoon became the epicentre of the bone trade. As supplies grew scarce, gatherers resorted to setting the prairie on fire to expose bone caches to view. Bleached white by the sun, the bones stood in stark contrast to the scorched earth. Often the CPR was blamed for those fires, as sparks from locomotive smokestacks were a constant hazard. Bone hunters took full advantage of this fact to obscure their activities whenever they could.

In one season, Métis gatherers were reputed to have brought in fifty thousand skulls to Saskatoon. Up to fifteen carloads of bones a day might be shipped south by one dealer alone. Volumes grew so large, they often exceeded the railway's capacity to move them, and piles lingered beside the tracks. During the winter of 1891, the temperature dropped so low that bones were frozen in huge stacks, sometimes several hundred metres long.

By the mid-1890s, supplies were completely exhausted and the bone trade faded from the prairie landscape as quickly as it had arrived. Now hardly anyone remembers that Regina was once known as "Pile of Bones."

A Fantastic Dream from the Arabian Nights

With the construction of the CPR through western Canada, many organizations and government departments, not to mention cities and towns, got their start. One discovery made along the CPR main line led to the creation of a government agency near and dear to many Canadians: Parks Canada.

The railway's siding 29, later to be renamed Banff, was laid on 27 October 1883, one of the last tasks before construction work ended for the season. While many of the men on the track gangs had heard tales of mysterious vapours rising

A Fantastic Dream from the Arabian Nights
The federal government improved accessibility and built Swiss-style bathhouses at Banff on the site of what became known as the Cave and Basin.
NS.17450

through the forest on the far side of the Bow River, it was left to section foreman Frank McCabe and one of his men, William McCardell, to investigate.

Taking advantage of a day off in early November, the two men came up the newly laid line to Padmore, Alberta, by handcar. Constructing a crude raft, they crossed the Bow River to the foot of Terrace (now Sulphur) Mountain. There they discovered what McCardell was to describe as "some fantastic dream from a tale of the *Arabian Nights*." They had stumbled upon a basin pool and adjoining cavern fed by hot springs whose sulphurous waters held to a constant temperature of about thirty-two degrees Celsius, or nearly ninety degrees Fahrenheit.

Although McCabe and McCardell did not have the necessary capital to exploit the discovery, the men were acknowledged in 1885 by the Canadian government as the founders of the hot springs, and a sixteen-square-kilometre area was set aside on the northern slope of Sulphur Mountain for future park use.

Shortly after this reserve was established, the Canadian government sent work crews to improve accessibility to the springs and to build Swiss-style bathhouses on the site. In 1887, Rocky Mountains Park was created, which incorporated the original reserve plus many surrounding scenic attractions. Following the example of Yellowstone National Park in the United States, established in 1872, this was Canada's first national park.

The same year the park was founded, CPR began construction of a grand resort hotel within the park limits, at the confluence of the Bow and Spray Rivers. Opened in 1888, the Banff Springs Hotel became one of the park's feature attractions and was the forerunner of today's much larger hotel of the same name. For the next twenty-five years, the CPR provided the only access to the area that would eventually be known as Banff National Park.

Excitement at the Empire Exhibition

The CPR was a prominent participant at the 1924 British Empire Exhibition. A forerunner of modern world's fairs, this ambitious trade show, held in the London suburb of Wembley, was intended to foster trade and focus the attention of the British public on the illimitable possibilities of the great dominions overseas, as well as on Britain's lesser colonies and dependencies.

It was only right that Canada and the CPR should occupy prime real estate at the fair; the country showed great promise and the railway performed a pre-eminent role as the operator of the Empire's "All-Red Route" to the Orient, linking the steamship docks of the mother country to her far-flung outposts in the South China Sea.

The idea for this commercial showcase had sprung from the mind of Lord

Strathcona, a founding director of the CPR, the man who drove the Last Spike, and a noted British imperialist. The First World War put the idea temporarily on hold; but in the years immediately after, the world situation was ripe for Britain to reassert herself as a dominant force in world trade.

The exhibition covered eighty-nine hectares, including twenty-four kilometres of streets named in grand fashion by Rudyard Kipling. Over the course of the fair's 150 days, twenty-seven million people, more than half the population of Great Britain, strolled up and down Drake's Way and Dominion Way. Along the route, crowds gathered at the palaces of industry and engineering. The great stadium dominated the skyline, epitomizing the grand scale of the Empire with all its allusions to sportsmanship and fair play.

The British Navy presented model ships and dioramas of decisive naval battles. Civil aviation was also given its due, and the Royal Air Force showed off the latest in military flying machines. Publicists for the exhibition stated with confidence that any attraction the British Empire had to offer, from Niagara Falls to King Tut's tomb, could be previewed in its displays.

At the very crossroads of the fair grounds, in front of an artificial lake on Empire Way, stood the Canadian government pavilion and that of the CPR. Though the Canadian pavilion was proud to provide information on more than sixteen thousand industries from the great dominion, it was the full-size statue of the Prince of Wales, carved from Canadian butter, that people came to see.

Next door was the showpiece of the fair, the CPR pavilion, built to harmonize with the Canadian pavilion. Constructed under the supervision of E. R. Bruce,

EXCITEMENT AT THE EMPIRE EXHIBITION
At the Wembley Exhibition, the miniature CPR train vied for attention with the statue of the Prince of Wales carved from butter.
A.30587

CPR director of exhibits, the two-storey pavilion featured almost 560 square metres of display area on the main floor alone. Upstairs, a three-hundred-seat lecture hall lured the public to continuous showings of films, enlivened by distinguished lecturers. Giant bronze sculptures of buffalo topped pedestals on either side of the recessed entrance. Similar representations of huge bull moose stood like sentinels at the four corners of the building. Inside were displays that sang the praises of the company's rail, steamship, hotel, colonization, telegraph, express, and other services.

Many of the exhibition's pavilions and other amusements remained on the site after 1924, and the fair grounds continued to operate as a major attraction. A wonderful feature was added in 1925, when the CPR installed a miniature train ride around the newly constructed "Treasure Island." Not even King George V and Queen Mary could resist boarding CPR's *Imperial Limited* at Banff Station for a ride through the Connaught Tunnel, on the way to see such characters as Jim Hawkins and Long John Silver.

Efficiency, Dignity, and Style

Edward Wentworth Beatty was born on 16 October 1877, at Thorold, Ontario. His father, Henry Beatty, was a partner in the pioneer Great Lakes steamship company Northwest Transportation Company and went on to become the CPR's first manager of lake traffic during the railway's formative years. Edward Beatty came to the CPR in 1901 as an assistant to A. R. Creelman in the Montreal law department. Showing the same capacity for hard work that had characterized his father, young Beatty was appointed assistant solicitor of the company in 1905. It would not be long before he caught the attention of the CPR president, Sir Thomas Shaughnessy.

Recognizing Beatty's desire to get ahead, and learning that he was considering other opportunities outside the railway, Shaughnessy paid him the ultimate compliment with the query: "Beatty, do you want to be an ordinary lawyer all your life, or do you want to be president of the CPR?" And so the ambitious young man stayed and soon made a reputation for himself defending the company's position in the official inquiry that followed the tragic sinking of the Canadian Pacific liner *Empress of Ireland*, on 29 May 1914.

In December 1914, he was elected vice-president, followed by appointments to the board of directors in January 1916, and to the executive committee in October 1916. When Sir Thomas resigned the presidency on 11 October 1918, he nominated Beatty as his successor, installing the youngest man ever in the pilot's seat of the self-styled "World's Greatest Transportation System." Shaughnessy's esteem for the energetic Beatty was reflected in his parting address: "When the time came when the future welfare of the company demanded that a younger and more active man should be charged with the duties of chief executive, it was a most fortunate circumstance that the board of directors had at hand a man of such paramount ability, and such unquestioned integrity and such great vision as possessed by our new president, Mr. E. W. Beatty."

The handsome and athletic Beatty had achieved his goal by age forty-one, but he was not about to rest on his laurels. Through the Great Depression of the 1930s and the government's attempts to nationalize parts of the successful, worldwide enterprise that he controlled, he kept the CPR intact, while introducing such innovative services as the elegant transcontinental first-class passenger train, the *Trans-Canada Limited*, and the mammoth new transatlantic company flagship, *Empress of Britain II*.

Outside regular business hours, Beatty was more than ready to give up his leisure time to benefit others. He was soon immersed in a plethora of community involvements, among them serving as chancellor of Queen's and McGill Universities and president of the Shawbridge Farm School, the Canadian Boy Scouts' Association, and the Royal Victoria Hospital. On 23 June 1935, King George V made him a Knight Grand Cross of the Most Excellent Order of the British Empire.

When war broke out in 1939, Sir Edward placed the full resources of the CPR at the disposal of the country and the Empire. Under Beatty's direction, Canadian Pacific Air Services was organized to initiate the transatlantic ferrying of newly built bombers from Canada to Great Britain. Canadian Pacific Air Lines took flight 1 May 1942.

Sadly the gruelling regime that Beatty imposed on himself took a toll on his health, forcing him to resign the CPR presidency in 1942 in favour of D. C. Coleman. Sir Edward died in his home on Montreal's Pine Avenue, on 23 March 1943. Tributes from people who had known and loved him poured in from all over the Commonwealth. Hundreds of people lined the streets for the funeral procession that wound through Montreal to Windsor Station. There a special seven-car train, powered by a stalwart CPR locomotive, number 2824, waited to transport Sir Edward to the family plot near St. Catharines, Ontario.

For twenty-four years, Beatty had dominated the affairs of the world's largest privately owned transportation company, moving the CPR forward with efficiency, dignity, and style.

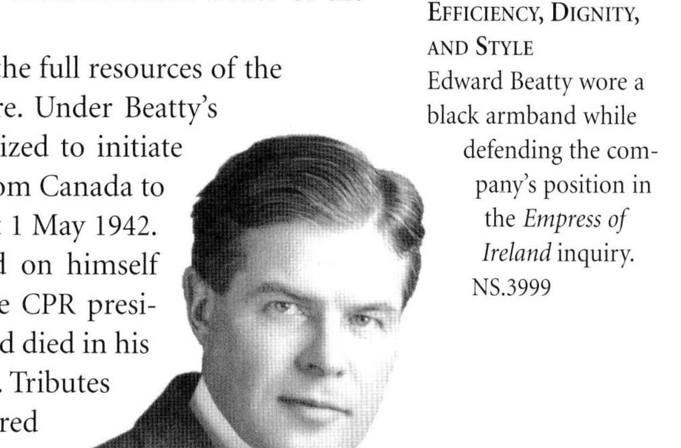

EFFICIENCY, DIGNITY, AND STYLE
Edward Beatty wore a black armband while defending the company's position in the *Empress of Ireland* inquiry.
NS.3999

The Last Best West

The news was alarming: "Police were needed outside 67 King William Street to control the crowds looking through the large window panes to catch sight of squashes (one weighing 322 pounds), maize, carrots, mangels, etc., brought over from Canada." It was the morning of 1 October 1901 and the *Canadian Gazette* had just hit the streets of London, England. But why all the fuss over vegetables?

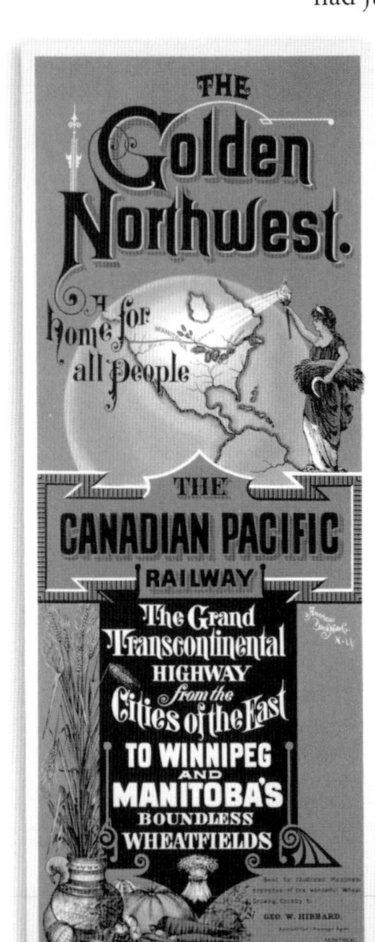

The Last Best West
Posters offered boundless opportunity in a home for all people.
A.6418

Blame William Van Horne. The irrepressible railwayman, who had by now risen to the chairmanship of the CPR, had a flair for advertising and liked nothing better than to turn a few heads in the direction of Canada and the corporation that he commanded. Among his directives had been an insistence on making a splash when it came to touting the virtues of the Canadian northwest. And the CPR's office windows—in this instance those of European traffic manager Archer Baker—were looked upon as prime space for this endeavour.

The CPR, with the large grants of land it received in partial payment for building the transcontinental link, was for some time the largest landowner in the Canadian northwest. As a result, the attention of management was often focused on immigration and colonization as a means of increasing the revenue base that would be the lifeblood of the enterprise. Advertising pamphlets typically included large-format maps upon which the country, stretching from Winnipeg to the Rocky Mountains, was shown to be all but uninhabited. A red index finger pointed to Winnipeg as the gateway to "The Last Best West."

Even before the line was completed around the north shore of Lake Superior, immigrants were being actively pursued, and once enticed, were transported to the west by way of Detroit and Chicago, and on to Winnipeg.

Though potential emigrants from eastern Canada and the United States were eagerly sought, many of the early campaigns centred on Britain and the countries of northern Europe. As early as 1882, the CPR's offices on London's Cannon Street were lavishly decorated. At one point, Van Horne received complaints that the quarters provided for the CPR's traffic department did not look respectable with placards and bills posted in front of the building, to which he replied: "If we can get more traffic by displaying placards, etc., in front of the present building, they must be so displayed, and if we can earn a dollar extra by painting the building yellow and spotting it with blue, it should be so painted." The displays exhibited in the windows of this office, which were changed from month to month, were said to have been "a never ceasing attraction to the throngs of passersby, estimated as three-quarters of a million a day."

Trucks laden with packing cases labelled "General Emigration Agent, Canadian Pacific Railway, London, England" delivered folders and brochures in French, German, Dutch, Norwegian, Swedish, Finnish, Gaelic, Welsh, Russian, Arabic, Icelandic, and Yiddish. In one year alone, more than three million pamphlets were distributed. A London printing firm boasted that their presses had been kept running day and night for six months to turn them out.

In addition, the CPR participated in a great number of agricultural and industrial fairs across Europe, displaying all manner of Canadian grains, grasses, fruits, roots, and seeds. Glass tubes filled with dirt collected at intervals along the CPR route drew appreciative comments from a public all too eager to learn about the wonders of the New World.

In 1904, when the railway's grand new quarters were opened on Trafalgar Square, two large panels were erected on the roof, upon which pictures of scenery along the CPR route could be projected using the magic of the new lantern slide projector.

In the years before the First World War, a travelling van was added to the advertising arsenal, criss-crossing the British Isles to districts remote from railways and manufacturing centres. The van, described as a veritable Canada on wheels, visited 513 places during 1893 alone, travelling more than twenty-nine hundred kilometres of road. Among its contents were wheat and grain samples, artwork, photographs, models and—always sure to draw a crowd—the occasional giant vegetable.

Ready-made for Western Settlement

In the early 1900s, a large part of CPR's attention was focused on settlement in the southern Alberta irrigation block, which was located east of Calgary, between the Red Deer and Bow Rivers. The railway nurtured the area to promote intensive colonization along its main line and develop it for the highest possible density of traffic.

At the time, various assisted settlement programs were underway in Britain, calling for the railway to establish small colonies, complete with house, barn, fencing, and plowed acreage, so that prospective colonists could immediately be settled. This ready-made farm program had the additional appeal for the CPR of discouraging the purchase of railway lands for speculative rather than productive purposes.

These farms were sold to married men only and consisted of from 64 to 128 hectares each, located on lands with easy access to schools, churches, and telephones. On each farm, a very modest but comfortable house and barn were erected, the land fenced, a well dug, a pump installed, and an area from twenty to forty hectares cultivated. Settlers could take possession immediately and were

READY-MADE FOR WESTERN SETTLEMENT Emigrants from the Old Country signed on for a "ready-made" life in Canada. A.6204

given ten years to pay back CPR's initial investment, in equal annual instalments ranging from thirteen hundred dollars to twenty-five hundred dollars.

The first colony of twenty-four farms was developed at Nightingale, in 1909. Populated with British settlers who were not familiar with farming irrigated land, the colony struggled for the first couple of years, despite periodic visits from company specialists offering advice and assistance.

By 1911 the success of the CPR's London office in finding settlers, and of the Calgary office in preparing the ready-made farms, resulted in a shortage of large sections within the irrigation block. Consequently, one hundred families were settled on the CPR line from Wetaskiwin, Alberta, to Saskatoon, Saskatchewan, outside the irrigated area. Eventually, this became one of the most prominent and prosperous group regions.

Other colonies varying in size from 5 to 122 farms were rapidly developed at Coaldale, Namaka, Cluny, Rosemary, Bassano, and Duchess. With each group of settlers, the CPR sent a man with farming experience in both Canada and Britain to act as chairman of the colony. A number of demonstration farms that offered free information were also established for those with no particular knowledge of farming.

One danger awaiting immigrants was the presence of unscrupulous merchants who sought to victimize those unfamiliar with prevailing values and cultural norms in Canada. To counter their advances, CPR literature often included a suggested list of necessities required by prospective settlers. In those days, one could obtain four good horses, a harness, a breaking plow, a set of harrows, a wagon, a seeder, a mower, a rake, two cows, forty or fifty hens, and two hundred dollars' worth of provisions for about thirteen hundred dollars.

Most of the ready-made farms were established in colonies as originally planned, but there was some departure from this policy in later years. The outbreak of the First World War slowed the program somewhat, but in 1916 a plan was developed to settle veterans in ready-made farm colonies in Anzac, St. Julien, and Van Horne.

Between the years 1909 and 1919, more than 760 ready-made farms, in twenty-four colonies, were developed, some of which thrived and became the hub of present-day communities in these locations.

Fairly Stinking with Blossoms

The CPR's contract with the Canadian government provided the company with twenty-five million dollars and 10,120,000 hectares of land in exchange for undertaking to build the main line to the Pacific Ocean. For the most part, CPR received alternate sections of land, in a checkerboard pattern along a forty-kilometre belt on either side of the rail line from the Lake of the Woods, in Ontario, to the Rocky Mountains.

The agreement stipulated that the land be "fairly fit for settlement," a condition that presented a problem: there was not enough land in the railway belt for the government to fulfill its obligation. Most of the land in Ontario and Manitoba was already spoken for, and all of the land between Moose Jaw, Saskatchewan, and the Rockies was rejected by the CPR as too arid for agricultural development. The government had established experimental farms in the early 1880s to encourage settlement in the southern prairies, and during several years of above average rainfall,

FAIRLY STINKING WITH BLOSSOMS Irrigation made southern Alberta "fairly fit for settlement." A.495

they had initially shown great promise. However, a return to the dry conditions that were generally characteristic of the area had ultimately led to the abandonment of the plan.

For two decades the land issue remained unresolved, until the Canadian prime minister, Sir Wilfrid Laurier, anxious to settle the matter with the railway, imposed a deadline on the CPR for the selection of the lands remaining to be granted. William Pearce, a long-time promoter of irrigation on the southern prairies, and a senior official with the federal department of the interior, suggested that, in lieu of lands in the established checkerboard pattern, the railway accept a solid 1.2 million hectares in a huge block between Medicine Hat and Calgary, and the remaining 323,880 hectares in the northern prairies. At last, the two parties had arrived at a mutually acceptable agreement.

In the twenty years that had elapsed, a number of factors had caused the area to be viewed in a more favourable light. Hardy strains of wheat had been developed that required a shorter growing season; new markets for grain had been established and prices were on the rise; and the high cost of land in the United States had encouraged promoters to advertise the Canadian prairies as "The Last Best West." Most promising, several studies had pointed to the feasibility of successfully irrigating the area. The CPR chairman, Sir William Van Horne, was so enthusiastic about the prospect, he predicted the area would soon "fairly stink with blossoms through irrigation."

Since Pearce could not be lured away from the government to manage the CPR's irrigation scheme, another able man, with years of experience as a government surveyor, was found in John S. Dennis. Under his guidance, the irrigation block was divided into three sections, each suggested by topographical characteristics. The central section was deemed unsuited to irrigation and was set aside as ranch land. Irrigating the western section was relatively easy, requiring a simple diversion of the Bow River into a natural hollow that served as a reservoir for the system. It was fully operational by 1910. The eastern section, however, required one of the most extensive projects of its kind to complete the irrigation network. Central to the plan was the Bassano Dam, built across a horseshoe bend in the Bow River at Bassano, Alberta.

To construct a reservoir to feed water through the proposed system of canals, 84,900 cubic metres of dirt were used to construct a 2,130-metre-long embankment. By 26 April 1914, when CPR president Sir Thomas Shaughnessy officially opened the Bassano Dam, more than 850,000 litres of water per second was passing through the sluice gates and over the concrete spillway, bringing prosperity to the region.

Since then, the seasons have taken their toll and some of the old systems and canals have been completely abandoned for new irrigation works. But the Bassano Dam is still performing its life-giving function, and has been upgraded in recent years. An official reopening of the landmark dam, in 1987, marked the beginning of many more years of active service.

A Concrete Curiosity

It's a startling site when it comes into view. But as sure as you're on the CPR main line in southern Alberta, there it is, towering above the prairie and stretching across the horizon, looking for all the world like an ancient aqueduct transported from the glory days of the Roman Empire. In fact, the reality is not so far removed from the illusion, because this imposing structure is indeed a modern-day version of those Roman engineering wonders. It's the Brooks Aqueduct.

A tribute to the ingenuity and vision of the CPR men who developed the irrigation system in southeastern Alberta, the Brooks Aqueduct was one of the most impressive engineering projects of the early twentieth century. It is also one of the least known outside Alberta.

For sixty-five years the giant flume fed water to a desertlike section of CPR lands where irrigation was essential to farming and, therefore, a vital component in the railway's land sale strategy. Productive settlers were potential users of the railway and it was clear that produce from this section of track would not be bulging the doors of CPR boxcars, unless nature received a helping hand.

It took three hundred men the better part of three years to transform more than 1,545 metric tons of reinforced steel and 16,790 cubic metres of concrete into this 3.2-kilometre-long wonder, just a few kilometres southeast of Brooks, Alberta. When it went into operation in 1915, it was the longest concrete structure in the world. But, for the most part, there was nothing impressive about the mechanics of the aqueduct. It was merely a U-shaped flume on a series of stilts, along which water was gravity-fed from Lake Newell Reservoir to a system of canals at a rate of hundreds of cubic metres per second.

Although a stroll along the edge of the flume could be a terrifying experience when irrigation was in full swing, in the off-season, when the flume was as dry as a bone, it provided some thrills for the region's youth. What farm boy could resist the lure of, and maybe just a little bragging to his friends about, an impetuous bicycle ride down the ol' chute? "Yahoo! I bet them old Romans never did this."

A Concrete Curiosity
Like a scene from the days of the Roman Empire, the Brooks Aqueduct spans the horizon.
A.32163

Needless to say, it was not a practice that was condoned by the CPR, and certainly not by the boys' parents who, no doubt, assumed that the young daredevils were engaged in more tranquil pursuits.

There was one obstacle in the way of the aqueduct's course: the CPR main line between Medicine Hat and Calgary. Here the height of the aqueduct did not allow sufficient clearance for the railway, calling for a siphon under the tracks. Where the track bisected the aqueduct, a breach was made in the flume. The siphon joined the two ends on either side of the track with a tube, by means of two pipes angled at forty-five degrees and a section that joined them under the railway roadbed. The sheer force of the water propelled it down the tube on one side, and up the other in a manner that appeared to defy gravity.

Although more than a decade was spent contemplating a fitting tribute to what is now just a curiosity, few wanted to see the aqueduct removed from the landscape.

In 1935, the CPR turned over all the operations of the irrigation system in southeastern Alberta to a group of farmers who formed the Eastern Irrigation District (EID), an organization that continued to use the aging viaduct until 1979. By that time, the annual cost of maintaining the concrete behemoth, and the ever-increasing need for higher volumes of water in the irrigation ditches, necessitated the construction of a more conventional earthen canal to perform the duties once taken up by the aqueduct. Before the canal could be dug, of course, an earth-filled embankment 180 metres wide at the base had to be built the length of the viaduct. Whereas the original system had cost in the neighbourhood of seven hundred thousand dollars to build, its replacement depleted the EID coffers by a whopping ten million dollars.

Although more than a decade was spent contemplating a fitting tribute to what is now just a curiosity, few wanted to see the aqueduct removed from the landscape. Consequently, an interpretive centre was established on the site in a co-operative effort by Alberta Culture and Multiculturalism, Environment Canada's Canadian Parks Service, the Eastern Irrigation District, and the Prairie Farm Rehabilitation Administration. The Brooks Aqueduct was declared a National Historic Site in 1989, guaranteeing that the structure will continue to fascinate passersby for a long time to come.

Lord Strathcona's Horsemen

When young Robert Percy Rooke rode into town, he wondered what all the excitement was about. Tired and cold, the surveyor had come to Winnipeg to escape the rigours of life in the bush, where he had been locating the route for a branch line of the CPR up the west shore of Lake Winnipeg from Selkirk, Manitoba.

It was January 1900, business was booming in the town known as Canada's Gateway to the Northwest, and the whole place was abuzz with talk of the ongoing war between the Imperial British forces and the South African Boers. The latest of

Queen Victoria's "little wars" had become somewhat of an embarrassment for the defenders of the Empire. The British campaign had suffered serious setbacks at the hands of the wily Boer horsemen, of Dutch descent, who eschewed the face-to-face combat of a bygone era for the hit-and-run guerilla tactics of the twentieth century.

The British press was questioning the competence of the expeditionary forces in South Africa, the legitimacy of the struggle against the Boers, and even the desirability of adding another far-flung colony to the administrative and military checkerboard that was the turn of the century British Empire. At this controversial time in British history, one man turned his gaze to the Canadian northwest for answers.

At this controversial time in British history, one man turned his gaze to the Canadian northwest for answers.

Lord Strathcona, Canadian high commissioner to London, was of the opinion that fire should be fought with fire. Strathcona had done much to open up the Canadian northwest, both as a fur trader and governor of the Hudson's Bay Company, as a key figure with the CPR who had the honour of driving the Last Spike, and as a government representative for Selkirk. He knew the courage and tenacity of the men who led the way for settlement in the region and was sure that their marksmanship and facility with horses would equal that of the notorious roughriders of the African veldt. "In a war of this kind," he said, "fighters of the Mounted Police of the Canadian Prairies would be more [of] a match for the Boers than the sedulously drilled infantrymen of the British patterns."

Determined to make a contribution to the war effort, the high commissioner personally had offered to recruit, equip, and send off to battle a regiment of fully trained, hard-riding mounted troops, drawn not only from the North West (later Royal Canadian) Mounted Police, but also from among the hardened frontiersmen and born-to-the-saddle cowboys who populated the Canadian west.

It was in the midst of this recruitment drive that twenty-year-old Robert Rooke caught the fever. He was among the thousands of enthusiastic volunteers who stepped forward to join the regiment, already referred to in the press as "Strathcona's Horse," which would be sent to the front under British command. The new regiment aroused much interest. Some proposals even came from outside the country, including one from a group of six hundred Arizona cowboys who offered to show up in Winnipeg for duty, complete with rifles, side arms, and battle-worthy horseflesh.

Candidates were expected to be good horsemen, good shots, unmarried, and "in other respects qualified." They were to be of "standard height," about 1.7 metres tall, from twenty-two to forty years old, with a chest measurement of at least eighty-six centimetres. Horses, too, were subjected to stringent examinations; a height of 14½ to 15½ hands was specified for the five- to ten-year-old mounts, which were expected to be in all respects "practically sound."

When young Rooke stepped up to the recruitment desk, he took liberties with the calendar, boosting his age by four months to what he thought would be a more acceptable twenty-one. "Better make that twenty-two," said the recruitment

Lord Strathcona's Horsemen
Officers of the regiment were wined and dined by Lord Strathcona, in London, on their way home from the Boer War.
A.37248

doctor, conscious of the strict lower age limit that had been imposed on the regiment by the newly appointed commanding officer, Samuel Benefield Steele.

Already a larger-than-life figure, Steele had made a name for himself during the Northwest Rebellion as the military commander of Steele's Scouts. An officer of the North West Mounted Police, he had been instrumental in maintaining order in the rowdy construction camps of the CPR and had only just returned from the goldfields of the Klondike, where he had done much to keep the peace among the steady stream of rough-and-tumble fortune seekers.

New recruits for Strathcona's Horse were issued Sam Brown belts, Colt .44 revolvers, and Lee-Enfield rifles. Trooper Rooke surely must have cut a dashing figure in his "rifle green" serge uniform, worn under an ankle-length greatcoat and topped by the now-familiar, flat-brimmed mounted police Stetson, which was selected by Steele to be the official headgear of the fledgling force.

As fate would have it, Rooke was the last man to sign up. By virtue of his minor deception in the recruitment office, he also was the youngest, with the exception of a fifteen-year-old bugle boy who accompanied the regiment to South Africa.

Within a few short weeks, CPR trains were steaming into Winnipeg with men, horses, and baggage from every major centre to the west. The railway had provided "Palace Horse Cars" for the force's spirited mounts, whereas the erstwhile volunteer troopers had set up house in CPR tourist cars, now liberally festooned with streamers and banners reading: "After Kruger's Head," referring to Paul Kruger, the president of the Boer republic, Transvaal, north of the Vaal River in South Africa; and "Off to Pretoria," the capital of Transvaal.

From Winnipeg, it was on to Ottawa for drill and basic training on the exhibition grounds at Lansdowne Park. By early March, the regiment was in fighting form, armed, trained, and anxious to set sail for South Africa and a dust-up with the enemy. Parading down to the Parliament buildings, the regiment was presented with full-colour guidons, or regimental banners, from the Ottawa Ladies Guild, and honoured by an address from Prime Minister Sir Wilfrid Laurier, who wished the troops "Godspeed." A final gala dinner and ceremonial send-off was organized in Montreal, where Lord Strathcona was one of the leading citizens, long prominent in business and government circles.

Back aboard CPR coaches for the run to Halifax over the Intercolonial Railway, Rooke took his turn guarding the horses overnight. It was bitterly cold, he later recalled, and "we ran about outside each time the train stopped to keep warm."

In a letter to Strathcona, Commander Steele praised the CPR for its service and deemed the Palace Horse Cars excellent. "In every way, the Canadian Pacific people have met our wishes and carried out their part effectively," he exclaimed.

The Strathconas sailed to South Africa on the SS *Monterrey*, a ship that would be sold to Canadian Pacific by the Elder Dempster Line, in 1903, when the CPR extended its reach across the North Atlantic. On board were 537 officers and men, and 599 horses.

Landing at Cape Town in April, the regiment soon made a name for itself, taking part in British commander-in-chief General Redvers Buller's pursuit of the enemy into the Transvaal. Strathconas were scouts for the advancing army, suffering numerous casualties, but reputedly taking six or seven Boers out of action for every loss to their ranks. The South Africans named the Strathconas "Big Stirrups," because of the large foot stirrups that allowed riders to fire rifles at full gallop, which helped to build their reputation as formidable fighters. "Of all the regiments, British or colonial, regular or irregular," wrote one *London Daily Express* correspondent, "Strathcona's Horse among the Boers were the most dreaded, and strange to say, the most respected."

On 5 June, at Wolver Spruit, about 160 kilometres southeast of Johannesburg, a party of Strathcona's Horse, thirty-eight in number, engaged an enemy force of eighty at close quarters. When the order came to fall back, Sergeant Arthur Herbert Richardson rode through heavy crossfire to rescue fellow trooper Corporal Alex McArthur, whose horse had been shot and who was himself wounded in two places. For his gallantry, Richardson was awarded the Victoria Cross.

On its way back to Canada, the regiment was routed via London at Queen Victoria's request. She died while the Strathconas were at sea, however, and the members of the celebrated force were presented with the South African War medal by King Edward VII, who had acceded to the throne. Steele himself was made a member of the Victoria Order, Fourth Class, and the regiment received its royal colours, a singular honour for mounted units in the British Empire. Officers of the regiment were wined and dined by their patron, Lord Strathcona, who had arrived dockside to meet his troops for the first time.

Lord Strathcona chartered the Elder Dempster ship SS *Erie* to return the troops to Canada. Upon arrival in Montreal, the CPR's luxurious *Imperial Limited* boarded an older and wiser Trooper Robert Rooke on his way back home to Winnipeg, where he promptly enlisted with the Second Canadian Mounted Regiment for another tour of duty in South Africa. At war's end, he stayed there to help rebuild the country's railway network, before marrying a South African and bringing her home to Winnipeg, in 1908. He spent the latter part of his career as a clerk in the CPR's purchasing department. Rooke died in February 1958 at age seventy-eight. He was thought to be the last of the original Strathcona's Horse troopers.

LEST WE FORGET
The company patriarch, R. B. Angus, would not allow himself to miss an opportunity to honour the CPR people who never returned from war.
NS.1701

Lest We Forget

From his seat in the Windsor Station waiting room, R. B. Angus had a perfect view of the ceremony. Angus had been with the CPR since the construction era, serving on the board of directors for years, and was now the company's distinguished patriarch. Though frail of limb in his ninety-first year, and now needing assistance to get around, he had not wanted to miss the chance to pay tribute to the thousands of Canadian Pacific employees who had fought and died in the Great War.

Their contribution had been massive. More than 11,000 fighting men recruited from the company's workforce had sailed for the battlefields of Europe, and 1,115 had never returned. In the midst of the horrors, 2 Victoria Crosses (VCs), 6 Orders of the British Empire (OBEs), 17 Distinguished Service Orders (DSOs), and 327 other military decorations had been awarded to company men.

From his well-positioned bench, just inside the waiting room door, Angus could see His Excellency the Governor General Lord Byng of Vimy approach the draped statue looming large at the southern end of the station concourse. He could see the honour guard of CPR war veterans led by Lieutenant-Colonel F. A. Gascoigne, secretary of Canadian Pacific Steamships and holder of the DSO.

It was the morning of 28 April 1922, and an expectant crowd had gathered at the foot of the monument that had been nearly three years in the making. CPR president Edward Beatty stood with the Right Reverend George Gauthier of the diocese of Montreal, and the Right Reverend John C. Farthing, bishop of Montreal, who would say the benediction. Invitations had been extended to local MPs, senators, and consuls general. The presidents of the Board of Trade, the Chamber of Commerce, and the Men's and Women's Canadian Clubs mingled with members of the Great War Veterans Association, the Montreal Ex-fighting Men's Association, and the Victorian Order of Nurses.

The Montreal sculptor, Coeur de Lion MacCarthy, had fashioned, in heroic proportions, an intricate plaster figure of a soldier "borne heavenwards by a winged and laurel-wreathed Angel of Victory." Now, three bronze castings stood shrouded and waiting, one in Windsor Station, the others in the CPR stations in Vancouver and Winnipeg, where simultaneous ceremonies were about to begin. The band would play "God Save the King," "O Canada," "The Last Post," and "Praise God From Whom All Blessings Flow." All thoughts would turn to the senseless sacrifice of brave men to human folly.

As the appointed hour arrived, all three statues were exposed to view. At the same time, twenty-three bronze memorial tablets were unveiled at CPR offices and agencies around the world. And in the Windsor Station waiting room, an elderly but still proud man pulled himself to his feet with the aid of his cane and stood erect in silent tribute.

Death of a Grey Wolf

Once, it had been feared and hated. With Germany's capitulation, it had been reduced to a mere curiosity. Now, four years after Armistice day and the end of the Great War, it was nothing more than a large hunk of scrap metal, abandoned and ignored, in the cavernous sheds at Angus Shops—a U-boat out of water.

When war had been declared on 4 August 1914, it was widely assumed that the conflict would be a short one, terrible perhaps in its violence and destruction, but ultimately little more than a brief interlude in the twentieth century's march of progress. But the nature of war had changed. Whereas once continental armies had tipped the balance of power in close-quartered combat, total war was now the norm, and with it came a new set of ethics that did not exclude economic infrastructures and civilian populations from its list of legitimate targets. Death could come day or night, from the sky or from under the sea.

It was clear to Germany that Britain, with nearly one half of the world's shipping tonnage, did indeed rule the waves. But, on 22 September 1914, when three proud British battle cruisers were sent to the bottom, just off the Dutch coast, a collective shudder shook the British Admiralty from stem to stern. Below the

DEATH OF A GREY WOLF
Twelve steamships from CPR's fleet were lost to enemy action during the course of the war, ten of which were torpedoed by U-boats.
A.6015

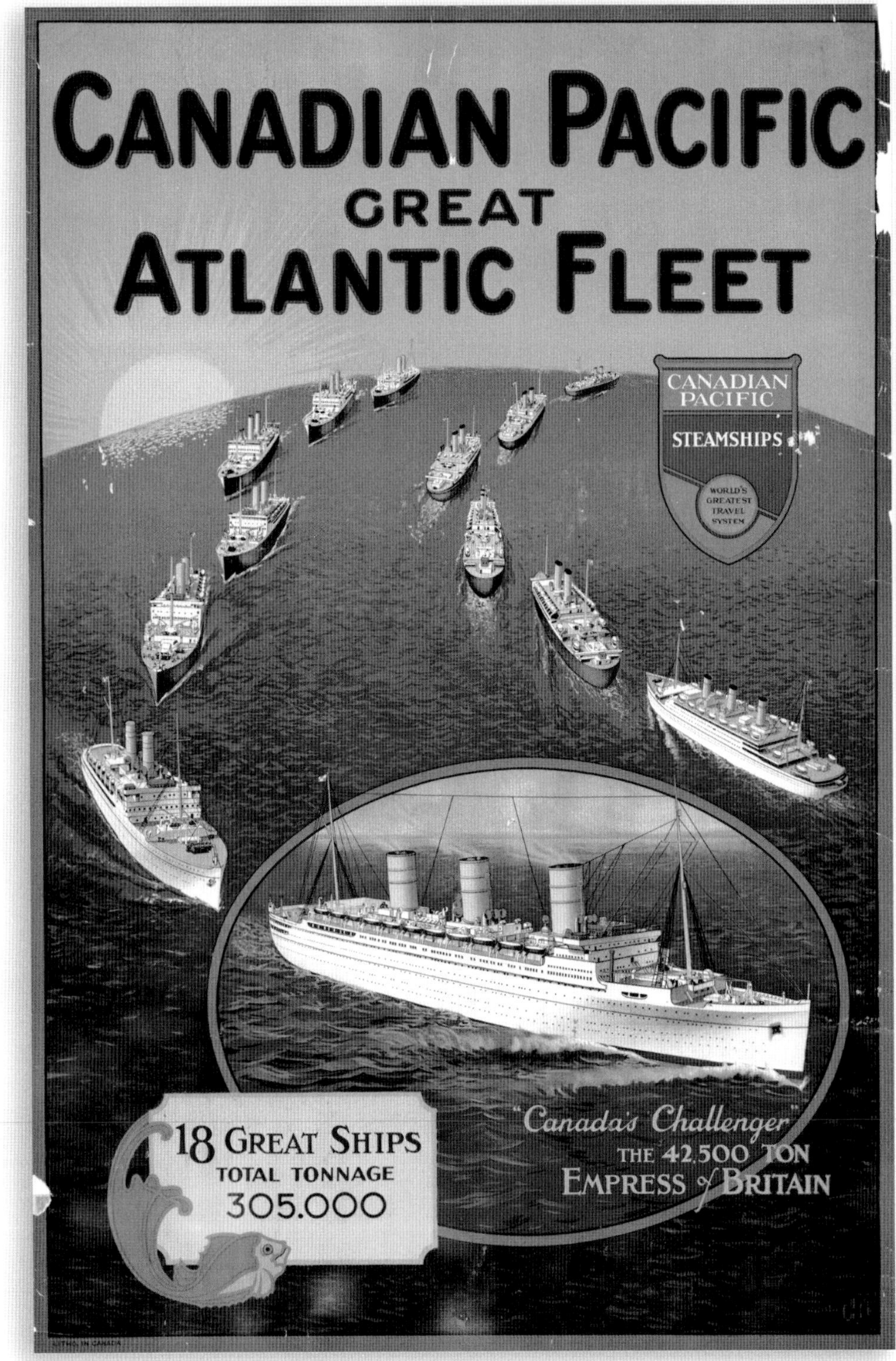

waves, Germany ruled. The submarine had made the leap from marginal defensive weapon to deadly instrument of attack, striking swiftly and silently and then turning tail to dissolve into the vast expanses of the world's waterways.

The Germans were in the forefront of submarine development. Known as *unterseebootes*, or U-boats, their underwater vessels were sleeker, faster, and more deadly than those in the Allied fleets. To the Allies, the submarines were "grey wolves," roaming the shipping lanes and engaging in a type of warfare that was somehow "not quite cricket"; but, to the German propaganda machine, the U-boat crewmen were Teutonic knights, engaged in a glorious struggle for the Fatherland. When German submarine U-9 proved the mettle of submarine warfare by dispatching three heavy cruisers in a single engagement, its commander, Lieutenant Otto Weddingen, not only received the Iron Cross First Class, but also the Pour Le Merite, Germany's highest award for valour.

More than five thousand ships, carrying ten million metric tons of cargo, were sent to the ocean floor during the course of the war. The CPR, alone, saw twelve of its vessels lost to enemy action, ten of which were torpedoed by U-boats. Though the tide was turned against Germany by the combined economic might of the Allies, especially after the United States entered the war, the U-boats held their own and were still inflicting damages far and wide when the ceasefire came.

In one of the last engagements of the war, Lieutenant Karl Donitz was captured when he was forced to scuttle his U-boat in the Mediterranean. Donitz, on the strength of his knowledge and experience with submarine warfare, would go on to become the chief of the German Navy in the Second World War and, ultimately, Hitler's successor as head of the German Reich.

One hundred and seventy-six U-boats fell into Allied hands. Most were scrapped immediately, but some were paraded in front of a cheering public, eager to witness the final humiliation of the most deadly naval weapons ever to ply the seas.

It was one of these U-boats, all but forgotten and slowly rusting in a corner at Angus Shops, which drew the attention of C. H. Temple, soon-to-be-chief of motive power and rolling stock for the CPR. The U-boat at Angus had been billed as the first to be captured by the British and, as such, had been a useful war prize to display during a post-war Liberty Loan campaign in New York and a subsequent Victory Loan campaign in Montreal. Somehow, through a series of bureaucratic manoeuvrings, it had been shipped from the Canadian Vickers Dock to Angus Shops, where it quietly faded from the limelight.

In December 1922, the CPR received permission to scrap the vessel and keep the proceeds as some small compensation for storage costs. The scrap value turned out to be little more than one thousand dollars, and the cost of cutting up the submarine, nine hundred dollars. One hundred and fifty-nine dollars and twenty cents was left for the CPR. Small compensation for the damage the U-boats had inflicted on the company's fleet.

Ogden Shops Gear for War

The CPR's western shops, built in 1913, were named for the company's first auditor, Isaac Gouverneur Ogden. Equipped for repairing passenger and freight cars, as well as rebuilding steam locomotives, the shops rising on the prairie in southeast Calgary assured the city of prosperity. A thriving community populated by railway workers grew on the adjoining flats.

Among the reminiscences in a local Ogden-area history, *Ogden Whistle*, is a description of life in the small railway settlement, reflecting the strong camaraderie that has always been an important part of railway life: "We had our own railway station—our mail came addressed to Ogden, Alberta. It was by far the most progressive subdivision of Calgary. Ogden was a blessing to the workers. Here they found a new way of life and a chance to own their own homes. It was more than a CPR small town; it was a family town."

Ogden Shops Gear for War
Guns like those turned out from Calgary's Ogden Shops would rid the skies of the feared German Luftwaffe.
A.15492

Many Ogden workers were soon on their way to Europe to fight in the First World War. Their wives and daughters took their places in the shops to relieve the shortage of men. However, it was not until two decades later, with war clouds again on the horizon, that a remarkable transition would place this peaceful enterprise on a full wartime footing. When war was declared in 1939, CPR president Edward Beatty telegraphed a message to Prime Minister Mackenzie King that would reverberate through the community: "In the grave situation now developing—which must be a source of extreme anxiety to you and your colleagues—I wish to assure you that, in the event of hostilities breaking out, the resources of my Company are entirely at the disposal of the Dominion; and I trust you will not hesitate to advise me the extent to which we can be of assistance."

Within weeks the call came. By March 1941, Ogden's huge 2.4-hectare locomotive shop was converted to the manufacture of armaments. At more than 975 metres above sea level, and four thousand kilometres from the Atlantic by rail, the site of the company's western shops was considered ideal. Barring the remote possibility of sabotage, there was very little danger of an enemy attack on the plant.

Where powerful, freshly painted steam locomotives once had rolled out in increasing numbers, a different kind of power was now manufactured on the 350 new machines installed for war production. More than eighteen hundred workers raced to produce the weapons of destruction that would fuel the first fully mechanized war. Field artillery pieces were badly needed by the Allied troops struggling against Hitler's war machine. Anti-aircraft guns, in particular, were required to neutralize the German Luftwaffe's submarine killers patrolling the skies over the North Atlantic in search of prey.

All of the engineering and mechanical skill of the company's workforce was needed to meet the exacting specifications of the thousands of gun barrels, housings, mountings, and sights that came off the assembly lines at Ogden. Many accolades were lavished on the workers for their significant contribution to the successful conclusion of the war. The speed and quality of production were singled out for particular praise.

In September 1945, the federal department of munitions and supplies relinquished the plant. Renovations were immediately undertaken to resume peacetime operations. The locomotive pits were uncovered, tracks were run into the shops once again, and machines relocated. Everything was brought up to modern standards, once more placing Ogden Shops at the forefront of the CPR's western operations.

On 23 October 1945, locomotive number 607 rolled out of the shops to the lusty cheers of the railway workers.

Destination Camp X

Little Ile Ste. Hélène played a starring role when Montreal hosted the World's Fair in Canada's centennial year. Expanded to three or four times its original size with hundreds of thousands of truckloads of earth, the quaint island park in the middle of the St. Lawrence River was magically transformed by the fantastic pavilions that arose on the site of Expo 67. It has been visited by millions of people since that landmark cultural event and is now a pleasant, mid-city green space and recreation area. Few, however, remember it as the site of an internment camp used to house Nazi prisoners of war during the Second World War.

It was one of twenty-six similar camps, the larger ones being at Medicine Hat and Lethbridge, in Alberta, and Gravenhurst, Kingston, Bowmanville, and Angler, in Ontario. In 1939, under the threat of an impending invasion by the German army, Britain had begun a systematic evacuation of prisoners to Canada. The British feared that if these men were liberated, they would swell the ranks of the invading force. Not surprisingly, given the vast extent of the CPR's transportation infrastructure and services at the time, the company became involved both officially and unofficially in the movement of these prisoners of war.

Among the ships used to transport the prisoners was the Canadian Pacific liner *Duchess of Atholl*, requisitioned by the British Admiralty early in the war. The curious crowded the dock in Halifax, Nova Scotia, to catch a glimpse of the ones they had come to hate and fear: men of the Afrika Corps, Luftwaffe pilots, and U-boat and merchant navy sailors. From the steamships, the prisoners were led to waiting CPR trains, to be moved to their final destinations at the internment camps.

The first director of internment operations for the Canadian government was Brigadier-General Edouard de Bellefeuille Panet, a decorated officer from the First World War, and the head of CPR's department of investigation. When he was appointed, shortly after war was declared, he didn't know that his wartime responsibilities would overlap so extensively with his civilian position with the railway.

DESTINATION CAMP X
As head of CPR's department of investigation, Brigadier-General Edouard de Bellefeuille Panet directed the internment of German prisoners in Canada.
NS.2794

All German officers were duty bound to do their best to escape captivity, so the attempts were many. Once while a prison train was travelling from Montreal to Smiths Falls, Ontario, two German flyers, Franz von Werra and Otto Hollman, jumped through a window as the train slowed through a local railyard. Hollman was recaptured through the vigilance of an alert railway employee, but von Werra managed to flee to the still-neutral United States and, eventually, made his way back to Germany in time to see further war action.

Perhaps the greatest escape occurred when twenty-eight prisoners tunnelled out of the camp at Angler, known to the Allies as "Camp X." On the lam and miles from shelter on the unforgiving northern shores of Lake Superior, two of the men saw the nearby CPR main line as the best bet for quickly exiting the area. Waiting for a heavy and ponderous freight train to slow as it struggled up a grade, the pair were most unfortunate to force their way into a refrigerator car, where they spent many uncomfortable hours before arriving at Kenora, on Lake of the Woods, close to the Manitoba border. There they were able to secure a warmer ride in an empty boxcar on another train, but their luck ran out when they reached the bustling little Alberta railway town of Medicine Hat. Quickly apprehended by CPR police, they were soon back in Angler renewing acquaintance with their fellow internees.

Another three escapees surrendered to a CPR sectionman, Mike Gopek of Peninsula, Ontario, shortly after the hapless trio wandered onto his trackside property. Armed with nothing more than his maintenance-of-way shovel, he approached the men for questioning, and in their weakened state, the prisoners offered no resistance to his citizen's arrest.

Meanwhile Erik Thorsen, the quick-minded, nine-year-old son of the manager in the CPR station restaurant at Ignace, Ontario, was doing his bit for the war effort. As two escapees inquired about train times at the depot, Erik recognized them from police descriptions and alerted provincial police, who soon swooped in to recapture the German airman and his companion, a wireless operator.

Yet another escaped prisoner was discovered tied under a train in Montreal's Windsor Station by plainclothesman George Gravel and a Constable Smith, both from CPR's investigation department. Baggageman René Audette spotted a pair of feet dangling under a passenger coach, five minutes before the train was due to depart for New York City. The prisoner, who had escaped from Bowmanville, had used a piece of clothesline and a wool scarf to secure himself to the air pipes running under the rail car, between the battery boxes. The observant Mr. Audette, a fifteen-year veteran with the CPR, was quite overcome by his encounter. "I was only trying to do my duty to the company," he explained modestly. "I thought for sure it was a hobo and I was afraid he would fall beneath the wheels. I sure never thought he was a damn Nazi."

When hostilities ended in 1945, CPR trains and steamships were once again employed to repatriate the POWs to Germany. Under the wraps of wartime security, few Canadians realized how many enemy soldiers, airmen, and sailors had sat out the war in Canada.

The World's Greatest Travel System

In the years between the two world wars, the CPR became very adept at moving people and freight by a number of conveyances. It was so adept, in fact, that the company's trademark slogan, "The World's Greatest Travel System," was accepted by the public as self-evident, rather than just a slick piece of advertising copy.

Several generations had grown up with the company and had come to expect a quality of service that didn't neglect the niceties that made a trip not just comfortable, but memorable. But the expertise of Canadian Pacific's cruise department was taxed to the limit in providing world-cruise passengers with the necessary transportation arrangements to make an off-ship tour a thing to write home about.

In many of the ports of call, sea-going tenders, not unlike the landing crafts used for military invasions, were required to transport passengers from a ship's offshore anchorage to the shallow waters of a waterfront docking. At Bombay, these ferries would leave a visiting CPR *Empress* ship every half-hour for sightseeing excursions on the Indian mainland. The Yangtze River was often so crowded that the company's ships were obliged to anchor downstream at Woosung, shuttling passengers up to Shanghai through a veritable flotilla of vessels, including

Chinese junks and armed cruisers of the British and Russian navies. Occasionally the CPR chartered river steamers. On the Nile River, the renowned travel agency Thomas Cook & Sons operated charming vessels topped with decorative awnings to protect passengers from the intense glare of the desert sun.

Railway excursions, of course, were an absolute must for inland journeys to India's Taj Mahal, at Agra, or to Peiping (now Beijing) in China. The best equipment was sought out in each country, an activity that sometimes resulted in bizarre configurations of mismatched coaches not seen in Canadian railway service. In 1934, a twenty-car train assembled in China for the use of passengers from CPR's flagship, *Empress of Britain II*, was the longest to have operated in the country at the time. In Madeira, a mountain railway was used to climb the more than

THE WORLD'S GREATEST TRAVEL SYSTEM
Arranging touring bicycles for eager cruise passengers was always on the agenda for CPR's shore staff in Bermuda.
A.20334

nine hundred metres to picturesque Terreiro da Lucta; the trip back down could be negotiated on wicker sledges equipped with wooden runners, guided along by native attendants with the aid of a rope on either side.

From Hong Kong to Canton, passengers could avail themselves of a cross-country train ride, if they so chose, and catch up with their steamship accommodations in the later port. The Orient, in particular, provided many opportunities to employ a number of novel forms of conveyance. For the ladies, a lift in a sedan chair up the mountain in Hong Kong could be arranged by a CPR representative. In Ceylon, rickshaws were hired to give rides along the ubiquitous rice paddies, and in Peking and Singapore, the demand for the two-wheeled, man-powered carts was so great, often as many as five hundred would be readied for the arrival of one of the *Empresses*. Passengers were so intrigued by the vehicles, they often switched places with the men pulling them, much to the astonishment of the young entrepreneurs.

For the adventuresome travellers who desired to get out and explore on their own, fleets of cars awaited at Monte Carlo and on the quay at Algiers, each vehicle numbered and carrying a small Canadian Pacific house flag. In Bermuda, bicycles were available and were usually in great demand from the time the gangplanks were lowered until the ships pulled anchor. And not to be forgotten were the trips from Cairo to the pyramids, by camel for the men and by sand cart or donkey for the women. Even the demanding climb up the giant stone sides of the Great Pyramid of Cheops was aided by several strong guides provided by the company.

Small wonder that the company's claim to be the best travel system in the world received so little argument. Where else could one find so many modes of transportation available to the public under one management?

On the Job

The hiss of steam filled the cavernous expanse. Overhead a hulking, streamlined Royal Hudson locomotive glided through the air like a looming thundercloud, to be placed gently on a shop track over a work pit in the CPR's Ogden Shops.

When word came, it spread like a virus. The Nazis had invaded Poland. Canada was at war and all of the nation's resources would be needed. Half-repaired locomotives soon would be sidetracked to make way for the armaments assembly lines that would equip the Allied armies for a modern, mechanized conflict.

But Ogden was awake. The CPR's industrial capacity was second to none, its electrically driven air compressors providing high-pressure air to the latest generation of power tools. When war struck in 1939, the railway was ready and involved at once. More than 273 million metric tons of freight were moved, 86 million passengers were hauled on its trains, and twenty-two of its ships were requisitioned by the British Admiralty for war service. As had occurred more than two decades before, the mechanical department's industrial might was turned to the manufacture of munitions, anti-aircraft guns, marine engines, and tanks.

The massive war effort helped to bring Alberta out of recession, but also foreshadowed an end to the railway's domination of the economy. The post-war era ushered in a massive expansion of trucking services, the development of intermodal services, and a joint effort by CN and CP Telecommunications to communicate across the country through Telex, a system of direct printout transmission that soon revolutionized communications in Canada.

Oil, first discovered in Alberta's Turner Valley in 1914, generated an industry that grew to symbolize the province as surely as the railway had. Things moved into high gear for the Alberta oil business when the Leduc field proved to be a winner in 1947. By 1952, CPR was collecting royalties on more than four hundred oil wells in the province. In 1958, Canadian Pacific Oil and Gas was incorporated to look after all of the company's energy resources and mineral rights. By 1971, the name had been changed to PanCanadian Petroleum Limited, and with the amalgamation of Central-Del Rio Oils Limited, CPR became Canada's largest player in the petroleum business.

ON THE JOB
Despite its massive contribution to the war effort, the railway was no longer dominant in the post-Second World War era.
A.6786

Another significant move in 1958 was the acquisition of Smith Transport. A year later, CPR was operating 3,860 tractors, trailers, and many other road vehicles.

While CPR president Norris "Buck" Crump was modernizing the motive power fleet, replacing steam locomotives with diesels, the company was racking up annual losses in the neighbourhood of $25 million on passenger, mail, and express services. Despite a $500-million investment in new, stainless-steel equipment for the transcontinental route in 1955, and the introduction of some fifty diesel dayliners on secondary routes such as the Calgary to Edmonton run, the ascendancy of the automobile and the increasing viability of the airplane for long distance movement of people and goods continued to play havoc with the CPR's bottom line.

In the 1960s, Crump brought further diversification to the company, along with the desire to establish each entity within CPR as a profit centre. In 1962, Canadian Pacific Investments, headquartered in Calgary, was established to manage all of the company's non-rail assets. Two new subsidiaries were formed: CP Hotels Limited and Marathon Realty. One of Marathon's first big redevelopment projects replaced Calgary's CPR station and gardens with a complex of commercial and shopping facilities, an office tower, and an apartment building, over which rose a 190-metre communications and observation tower, complete with a revolving restaurant, which would define the city's skyline.

By 1968, the company had adopted a new symbol called the "multi-mark" to identify its various components: CP Rail, CP Ships, CP Air, and so on. The name Canadian Pacific Railway Company no longer reflected the diversity of the company's many operations, and in 1971, the parent company's name was changed to Canadian Pacific Limited.

In 1977, the federal government moved to fully subsidize intercity rail passenger services in Canada. A new Crown corporation, Via Rail Canada, was created to take over and manage the combined passenger business of Canadian National and Canadian Pacific.

Although the 1970s proved to be trying times for passenger rail service, the freight business was booming. By 1971, upgrading programs at Alyth Yard had transformed the facility into the ultra-modern Alyth Diesel Shop, where minor repairs are undertaken even now on the latest generation of AC (alternating current)-traction locomotives. The huge Alyth classification yard was the largest fully automated operation of its kind on the continent. In addition, an ambitious double-tracking project between Calgary and Vancouver would culminate in the $500-million Rogers Pass Project the following decade, the largest railway engineering endeavour since the construction of the CPR main line.

With more people on the move for both business and pleasure, the hotel industry experienced somewhat of a renaissance. By 1988, with the absorption of CN's hotel operations, CP Hotels owned eight properties in Alberta: Hotel Macdonald in Edmonton, The Palliser and Chateau Airport in Calgary, The Lodge at Kananaskis and Hotel Kananaskis, Jasper Park Lodge, Chateau Lake Louise, and the Banff Springs Hotel.

By now the CPR was employing about three thousand men and women in Alberta, with a total annual payroll of $148 million. Expenditures in the province in 1993 alone, for employment, purchases, capital spending, and taxes, were about $288 million.

In 1996, CPR uprooted its entire headquarters structure, now more than one hundred years old, and moved it to Calgary. Much like the first arrival of the railway, in 1883, the moment was festive and brimming with new promise for the fortunes of the CPR.

CP Lighter than Air

The North Atlantic crossing had been accomplished twice from Canada by conventional aircraft: once in May 1919, by a U.S. Navy flying boat from Newfoundland to Portugal, with a fuel stop in the Azores; and again in June 1919, by former RAF fliers Alcock and Brown, when they flew a converted Vickers Vimy bomber non-stop from Newfoundland to a nose-first landing in an Irish bog.

More remarkable than the feats of the winged aircraft, however, was the potential of rigid airships, or zeppelins. In July that same summer, the British airship R34 had demonstrated its ability to buck strong headwinds on the east-to-west transatlantic crossing, something its heavier-than-air rivals were incapable of doing at that time, opening the possibility of transoceanic, intercontinental passenger flight.

Seeing the writing on the wall, CPR president Thomas Shaughnessy moved quickly to have the Canadian government alter the company's charter to read, in part: "The Canadian Pacific Railway may establish, equip, maintain and operate services of aircraft of all kinds, for the carriage for hire of passengers, mails, express and freight between such points and places, within or without the Dominion of Canada, as may from time to time be determined upon by the Company."

In the post-First World War era, conventional wisdom was that the airplane, although it might play a limited role in the intercity carriage of mail and passengers, was no threat to the steamship as an intercontinental mode of transport. However, the zeppelin or dirigible, developed and modified since the turn of the century, was a different story. The transatlantic flight of the R34 had graphically

CP LIGHTER THAN AIR When the great airships began to make the transatlantic crossing from Europe, CPR president Thomas Shaughnessy made his move to change the CPR charter.
A.767

illustrated the great cruising range of rigid airships. Not only could their speed and navigability be used to avoid most abnormal weather conditions, but their steadiness when bad weather *was* encountered was also incomparably better than that of the best of the steamships, sparing passengers the stomach-wrenching side effects of a rough crossing, and at comparable rates.

Whereas the CPR fast mail steamers sailed from Liverpool to Quebec City in about six days, the R34 had flown from its home base in East Fortune, Scotland, to New York City in 108 hours, 12 minutes. This took seven times longer than the Alcock and Brown crossing, but was fast enough to beat the steamships handily. Mail contracts were the bread and butter of the Atlantic shipping companies, and the airships seemed poised to inherit the steamships' mantle of speed and reliability. Of course, it didn't work out that way.

Most of the countries that were in the airship business were so because they had been awarded various and sundry zeppelins from Germany as war reparations.

Most of the countries that were in the airship business were so because they had been awarded various and sundry zeppelins from Germany as war reparations. They often paid the price for their pioneering passenger service efforts with mishaps, many of them tragic and some catastrophic, usually caused by the ignition of the hydrogen used to fill the airships' gas bags. At the time, the United States was the only country with access to non-flammable and prohibitively expensive helium. The post-war austerity programs in virtually all of the Allied countries had also caused a general downturn in airship development.

Efforts to perfect the zeppelin's design continued, however, and in Germany, the resurgence of the fortunes of the Zeppelin Company, named for Count Ferdinand von Zeppelin, the father of the rigid airship, heralded a whole new era that seemed to originate in the pages of a Jules Verne novel. In 1928, the Deutsche Zeppelin Reederei's *Graf Zeppelin* was launched. It was the most sophisticated and luxurious airship of its day and went on to circle the earth, touching down on five continents, exploring the Arctic, and operating a viable and regular passenger service between Europe and South America.

Canada's only visit from a great intercontinental zeppelin resulted from British efforts to establish commercial service between Great Britain and Europe, as well as to explore the possibility of flights to South America, the United States, Australasia, and the Far East. On 29 July 1930, the R100 flew from Cardington, near Bedford, to Montreal, with forty-four persons on board, covering the more than 6,115 kilometres in seventy-eight hours and fifty-two minutes. Three years earlier, the Canadian government had purchased a suitable site for a mooring mast at St. Hubert, south of Montreal, where the R100 docked, to the wonderment of all who looked up to see its hulking silhouette, accompanied by the low, eerie drone of its six Rolls Royce Condor engines.

By then, the giant airships were not only touting their speed, but also their luxurious accommodations and services. One of the R100's designers, the author Nevil Shute, raved that the comfort on board his creation was "almost staggering." He went on to note in his diary that one could "sleep all night in bed, get up, shave in hot water, dress and eat a normal breakfast served in a Christian way."

Edward Beatty, Shaughnessy's successor as president of the CPR, was kept well informed of incidents and developments in the field, including a close encounter between the R100 and a CPR freighter, in mid-ocean, when the zeppelin descended to check its position with the ship's navigators. The president may even have discovered that on board the airship was a representative of the French language press named, ironically, Jacques Cartier.

Beatty's interests were really the same as Shaughnessy's had been, readying the CPR to take best advantage of the changing face of global transportation. If the best of the company's steamers could neither compete for speed with the airships, nor maintain their monopoly as the only civilized way to go, the CPR was certainly well positioned to participate in the airships' success as the primary Canadian agent, if the opportunity arose.

On a few occasions, it did look like that time might be at hand, despite the loss of the R101, sister ship to the R100, at Beauvais, about sixty kilometres northwest of Paris, not even three months after the latter's successful transatlantic flight. By 1936, the Deutsche Zeppelin Reederei's flagship *Hindenburg*—and flagship it was, bearing the swastika of Nazi Germany on its tail fins—was making twenty Atlantic crossings annually, carrying twelve hundred passengers in complete safety that year alone. By then, the CPR's *Empress of Britain II* was cutting a speedy three-day swath across the North Atlantic sea lanes, but the *Hindenburg* was holding to an average schedule of only sixty-five hours from Germany to the United States, and a mere fifty-two hours on the homeward leg.

The death of the airship dream came on 6 May 1937, at Lakehurst, New Jersey, when the Hindenburg *exploded in a ball of fire.*

At the same time, Beatty's attention was drawn to developments in the heavier-than-air arena. Whereas the airships had the potential to erode the traffic base of the company's steamships, airplanes were beginning to chip away at the railway business. When he failed to obtain a 50-percent interest in the Canadian government-controlled Trans-Canada Air Lines (now Air Canada), Beatty decided the CPR would go it alone. He was appointed president of Canadian Airways in 1939 and, in the following two years, purchased that company along with nine other small bush operations.

The death of the airship dream came on 6 May 1937, at Lakehurst, New Jersey, when the *Hindenburg* exploded in a ball of fire. The dramatic on-site media coverage ensured that the demise of the greatest of the rigid airships would stay in the public consciousness for all time.

The outbreak of the Second World War, and the swift development of every type of aircraft other than the militarily useless zeppelin, ensured the ascendancy of the heavier-than-air modes. Before the CPR went on to establish Canadian Pacific Air Lines Limited in 1942, the company would play a vital role in ferrying bombers across the ocean to Britain to aid in the war effort. But that's another story.

ACROSS THE PACIFIC TO THE ORIENT

When the Second World War ended, the CPR once again reached out to the Orient and Australasia. Its pre-war infrastructure of steamship offices, agencies, and personnel had survived the conflict intact. But this time there would be no ocean-going behemoths plying the vast expanses of the Pacific Ocean and South China Sea; this time, the service was launched on a wing and a prayer.

Grant McConachie, president of Canadian Pacific Air Lines, CPR's fledgling air division, had mesmerized the railway's board of directors with his unbridled enthusiasm for an airline service that would chop sixteen hundred kilometres off the steamship lanes from Vancouver to Asia. Canadian Pacific Air Lines would take the "Great Circle Route," the shortest distance between Vancouver and Asia, as McConachie loved to demonstrate on his trusty inflatable globe with his ever-present piece of string.

McConachie backed his presentations with a wealth of statistics, many conjured up in his own mind from a mixture of intuition and wishful thinking, that left even the most level-headed listener with no doubt that his proposed transoceanic airliners were the rightful successors to CPR's proud *Empress* steamships.

There were no market studies, no economic projections. The Canadian government's own Trans-Canada Air Lines (TCA) showed nothing but disdain for the route. "We're not in the business of squandering taxpayers' money," sniffed TCA's president, Herbert James Symington. Yet in mid-November of 1948, McConachie began a mission to secure landing rights in Australia, Tokyo, Shanghai, and Hong Kong. He was in a jubilant mood, as his dreams of spreading Canadian Pacific's wings across twenty-four thousand kilometres of ocean were about to become a reality.

What he wasn't ready for was the reception he got in Australia. The socialist government of the day had no problem joining with the British and New Zealand governments to operate British Commonwealth Pacific Air Lines, but it also expected to obtain a similar arrangement with Canada. "It was our understanding that your government service, Trans-Canada Air Lines, would be designated for the Australia route," McConachie was informed by the Australian transport minister. "We don't propose to issue an operating permit to a capitalist corporation like Canadian Pacific."

Fortunately the snub did not preclude a polite luncheon meeting between the CPR delegation and Australian prime minister Ben Chiffley. Sure enough, McConachie worked his persuasive magic, charming his hosts with tales of his rise through the union ranks when, in his youth, he had worked as a railway engine wiper, watchman, hostler, fireman, and locomotive engineer. The very same day,

CPA was issued a "temporary" permit, one it was still putting to good use many years later.

Next stop: Tokyo, January 1949. Japan was occupied by the United States and General Douglas MacArthur ruled over the South Pacific like a feudal lord. "I had no idea there were so many generals in the entire United States army," McConachie later recalled, "but I saw them all during those weird weeks in Tokyo."

"We would need a food permit for staff and passengers. A general looked after that. Fuel for the aircraft; another general to see. Permit to export money, the general in charge of administration; another general for radio permits; yet another for housing and office space, and so on. Every one of those generals gave me the same answer: 'See MacArthur first.'"

Across the Pacific to the Orient
Canadian Pacific Air Lines was launched on the strength of Grant McConachie's unbridled enthusiasm.
A.37249

Toward the end of the month, when McConachie finally got a fifteen-minute audience with MacArthur himself, the general spent the entire session harping on about his need for shipping, and regaling the visibly nervous airline president with stories of his travels from Banff to Lake Louise on board the CPR. "Canadian Pacific—a great corporation," he muttered, while McConachie fairly blurted out his need for permits, all thought now gone from arguments, statistics, and inflatable globes.

By now, however, MacArthur was in a congenial mood, having tamped some tobacco into his signature corncob pipe, and dismissed McConachie with the assurance that the permits could be obtained with no problem in the morning. True to his word, they were cleared the next day, and McConachie turned his attention to mainland China.

In Shanghai, the CPR delegation decided to pursue its objectives on two fronts. While McConachie lobbied for an audience with General Chiang Kai-shek, head of the Nationalist Chinese government, his director of northern development, Wop May, renewed his old acquaintance with General Morris "Two-gun" Cohen, personal bodyguard to Chiang, whom he had once met in Edmonton, Alberta.

Cohen was quite a character. He had been sent to Canada from England by his parents as an incorrigible and worked on a ranch while learning to handle playing cards and a six-gun. In Edmonton he earned a reputation by foiling a robbery in a Chinese restaurant, thus ingratiating himself with the local Chinese community. When the Chinese Nationalist leader, Sun Yat-sen, toured through Canada, in 1911, he was so impressed with Cohen that he hired him on the spot to join his staff.

In the meantime, McConachie was working the diplomatic channels. One evening, at a reception hosted by the Canadian embassy, he met Madame Chiang. It is not clear how much influence Cohen brought to bear on the matter, but there can be no doubt that Madame Chiang was favourably impressed with McConachie. By the end of the reception, the Canadian ambassador was able to report to McConachie that Chiang had approved CPA's application to serve Shanghai on the Pacific route. "It was the easiest permit I ever got, but the least fruitful," McConachie recalled.

When the first CPA flight winged into Shanghai shortly thereafter, the crew could see fires on the city's outskirts. By dusk, when the CPA "North Star" aircraft lifted off for Manila with a load of passengers, the Chinese communists had all but overrun the city. It was the last plane to leave before the occupation.

Hong Kong, by contrast, proved to be a straightforward proposition, with the company employing the influence of the Canadian embassy to obtain operating and traffic rights. But paperwork aside, the airline needed to start bringing in revenues to justify McConachie's bold initiative. Shanghai and the Chinese mainland had vanished behind the Communist curtain. Japanese nationals were not allowed to travel abroad, and the predicted traffic of sun-seekers to and from Hawaii had dried up as a result of Canadian government currency restrictions.

When all seemed lost, McConachie's luck was fuelled by Chinese immigration to Canada and U.S. military logistics. For decades, there had been a slow, but steady influx of labourers to the Chinese restaurants and laundries that flourished in every small community in the Canadian west. In Hong Kong, the compradors, economic middlemen, loaded CPA planes with immigrants, many smuggled from mainland China, but all paying the full first-class price for a seat to Canada. This traffic poured more than $17 million into the airline's coffers during the next five years. By the end of 1949, the Korean War had broken out. Another $16 million were raised ferrying U.S. military personnel to the Korean theatre.

Luck aside, CPA courted its passengers with a champagne service that was unrivalled. Beginning a tradition that would last throughout the many years the airline operated, McConachie developed a philosophy that kept the company a step ahead of TCA in the one area where he knew it could compete—on-board service. "We don't need an expensive staff of commercial missionaries," he said, preaching his word-of-mouth gospel. "Flying CPA should be like getting religion, with every happy customer spreading the good word."

A Pinch of Windsor Salt

Canadians are the largest consumers of salt in the world—about 360 kilograms per person per year. Good thing we have a lot of the stuff. We may take salt for granted, but it is essential to human life. The expression "not worth his salt" comes down to us from ancient Greece, where slaves were traded for the precious commodity. Rations of salt—without enough of which wounds would not heal—were distributed among the Roman legions and were called "salarium argentium," from which the English word "salary" and the French word "salaire" are derived.

But what does all this have to do with the CPR? A fair bit, really. Let's go back more than a century to where the story begins. In the 1890s, salt production was a thriving enterprise on the American side of the Detroit River, and much of

A Pinch of Windsor Salt
In the unique stone station the CPR shared with the Sandwich, Windsor & Amherstburg Electric Railway, the Windsor Salt Company was born.
A.21874

If the CPR could secure its own source of salt, the railway would control its production, move it to market, rake in the profits, and the devil take the competition.

Canada's needs were met by that source. However, CPR president William Van Horne—a one-man think tank, if ever there was one—was a fiercely independent man and ran the railway in the same manner. If the CPR could secure its own source of salt, the railway would control its production, move it to market, rake in the profits, and the devil take the competition.

Although Sir William always seemed to have an intuitive knack for this kind of thing—and there were, of course, large, confirmed deposits of salt at Goderich, Ontario, and along the St. Clair River—he really hit pay dirt this time, securing geological confirmation of one of the world's biggest salt deposits underneath Windsor, Ontario. Moving quickly to exploit this discovery, Van Horne formed the Windsor Salt Company, Ltd., with himself as president and a board of directors recruited from among CPR bigwigs. Ernest G. Henderson, the railway's resident engineer in London, Ontario, was delegated to supervise the drilling of the first salt well at Windsor and the construction of a plant for processing the raw commodity into a marketable product.

In those days, the CPR station in Windsor was a unique stone structure that was jointly occupied by the Sandwich, Windsor & Amherstburg Electric Railway Company. It was in this tower that the Windsor Salt Company held its first board meetings.

Warm, salty water from the Windsor processing plant was released into the Detroit River in the vicinity of the CPR docks, particularly in the evenings when the salt pans were flushed. Old-timers from the area used to say that local boys, as well as some of the older folk who suffered from rheumatic ailments, would remove planks from the dock to sit on the cross beams and dangle their legs in the water.

Today, the Windsor Salt Company is owned by the Canadian Salt Company, a subsidiary of Morton's Salt Company, in Chicago, who still produces its product under the name Windsor Salt. Although the CPR no longer controls the board of directors, it still has a strong connection to the salt company—hundreds of thousands of tons strong.

The Province of Quebec was the first Canadian region to make extensive use of rock salt on its roads to help melt snow and ice during the winter; but most other provinces quickly followed suit, creating a boom in Canada's salt production in the 1960s that has continued to grow by leaps and bounds. During peak periods, normally from January through March, CPR has transported as many as twenty-five to thirty railcars of rock salt a day, seven days a week, to large cities such as Montreal and Toronto. Montreal alone uses more than 113,640 metric tons per season.

A Taste of the American Wild West

Tales about taming the American west are rife with armed desperados terrorizing frontier towns and often staying just out of reach of the long arm of the law. Canadians, on the other hand, take pride in what they like to think of as a more civilized expansion, with the formation of the North West Mounted Police posts and the suppression of the prosperous whisky trade precluding the more rowdy and sometimes murderous behaviour of their neighbours to the south.

In October 1884, Michipicoten was virtually taken over by a small-time gang of hoodlums who styled themselves the "Michipicoten Vigilante Committee."

Regrettably, however, nobody remembered to outline this clichéd scenario to the gang of bootleggers and bandits who set up shop at Michipicoten, Ontario, in 1884, thereby causing considerable agitation to the tender sensibilities of the poor souls in Toronto and Montreal.

Primarily out of self-interest, the railway had been more than diligent in stifling the flow of liquor to work gangs struggling with building the line along the north shore of Lake Superior. The Public Works Act prohibited the sale of spirits within sixteen kilometres of the railway track, and CPR contractors had a vested interest in seeing that it was enforced. Despite precautions, though, an enormous amount of illicit booze poured into the area, disguised as everything from barrels of peas to coal oil. From the distribution point of Sudbury, Ontario, bootleg whisky was transported to the small harbours that dotted the shoreline to supply railway construction crews. Available in Toronto for fifty cents for 4.5 litres, the hootch could fetch up to fifteen dollars on the black market.

The mounted police, in marked contrast from their practice in the northwest, did not patrol the rail line in Ontario. Consequently, matters of law and order were often in the hands of the usually ineffective local constabulary.

In October 1884, Michipicoten was virtually taken over by a small-time gang of hoodlums who styled themselves the "Michipicoten Vigilante Committee." They were led by an American, Charles E. Wallace, otherwise known as Montana Charlie, and the town's former police chief. Among the members of his gang were two Canadians, Gordon Doherty and Arthur Asselin, the latter an escapee from the Stoney Mountain Prison near Winnipeg.

The local magistrate and the CPR agent, Alexander Macdonald, who were opposed to the gang, were frequently threatened. The situation got out of control one night when the two were forced to seek refuge in the railway's construction office, where the walls were soon riddled with hundreds of bullet holes. In response to the depravations, CPR offered the unprecedented reward of twelve hundred dollars for the capture of the gang, and a force of Toronto police set out for the area to restore order. Taking the train to Owen Sound, they boarded the CPR's new lake steamer, the *Alberta*, placed in service that year between Owen

A Taste of the American Wild West
The Toronto police came by rail to Owen Sound, where they boarded the CPR's new lake steamer, *Alberta*, on their way to restore order in Michipicoten.
A.460

Sound and the Lakehead. At Sault Ste. Marie they made the switch to a smaller boat, the SS *Magnet*, operated by the Owen Sound Steamship Company, under contract to deliver supplies to the railway construction crews operating out of Michipicoten.

Unfortunately, by the time the police arrived, the gang had long since disappeared into the bush. The only welcoming party on hand was a jeering citizenry, distrustful of outside intervention and resentful of big city interference. Taking up residence in the community boarding house, the cops had to be content with rounding up a handful of ne'er-do-wells and convincing an itinerant group of gaudily garbed prostitutes to continue their promiscuous odyssey westward. In addition, 545 litres of rye whisky were uncovered and destroyed.

Unable to flush out the Wallace gang, the police hightailed it back to Toronto, allowing Montana Charlie and the boys to reappear in full outlaw regalia, brandishing heavy revolvers, Bowie knives, and Winchester repeating rifles. After a brief show of bravado, the gunmen boarded the steamboat *Steinhoff* and proceeded to fire one last volley in the direction of the CPR office and the hapless agent Macdonald, before setting sail for the United States, via the Sault. No sooner had they landed in Michigan, however, than they were arrested and returned to Sault Ste. Marie to stand trial for their misdeeds. Wallace eventually got an eighteen-month sentence for his part in the nefarious affair, and the Canadians, Doherty and Asselin, got one year each in prison for "rioting." Disrespectful of authority to the end, Asselin entered his occupation in the prison record as "bartender."

The Staff of Life

Moving wheat is so important to the Canadian economy that everyone gets involved. Farmers, trucking companies, wheat pools, federal and provincial governments, and of course, the railways are all part of a complex network that is mostly taken for granted.

There was a time, however, when the CPR shouldered most of the responsibility for getting the crop to the marketplace. At stake was the welfare of the struggling farmer, the prosperity of the fledgling railway, and the reputation of the Canadian northwest as a major player in the world food market.

Although thousands of boxcars were required to move the wheat to port, a system of local grain warehouses and elevators for storage at the main transfer points was equally essential. To encourage private investors, CPR offered a rebate of one half of the tariff rate for moving lumber to be used in the construction of warehouses, elevators, and mills. Depending on the agricultural potential of the surrounding areas, townsites were targeted for elevators of ten, fifteen, or twenty thousand bushels minimum bin capacity. Interested parties wishing to erect an elevator on railway land could do so rent-free for twenty years, provided they agreed to charge market rates for grain storage and not to discriminate between clients.

In most cases, elevators were more desirable than warehouses, as they could easily be equipped with machinery for cleaning grain and generally had separate bins for storing different types and grades. In warehouses, grain was not cleaned and good crops were mixed with bad, resulting in a market value only slightly better than the poorest grade stored. But in areas where there were no elevators, warehouses were allowed as an interim measure, pending the eventual increase in business that would justify a larger facility.

The CPR's bridge and building gangs were also pressed into service, in 1883, to construct a temporary warehouse at Port Arthur, Ontario (now part of Thunder Bay), for handling the flow of wheat over the completed line from Winnipeg. In the meantime, an enormous elevator with a capacity of 320,000 bushels was also being built. The railway contracted steam barges to move grain from the head of Lake Superior, as the CPR main line was not yet completed along the north shore of Lake Superior. The *Erin* was the first boat to pull away from the docks, its hold fully loaded with bags of grain brought aboard in wheelbarrows.

The following year, the elevator at Port Arthur opened for business. Nine boxcars of grain could be unloaded simultaneously. Three new Clyde-built lake steamships—the *Algoma*, *Athabasca*, and *Alberta*—made the transatlantic voyage to Canada, were cut in half to negotiate inland canals and locks, and were rejoined at Owen Sound. The CPR put them into service between Port Arthur and Owen Sound, greatly improving the company's ability to move large volumes of grain.

THE STAFF OF LIFE
In Vulcan, Alberta, as in most prairie towns, everybody got involved in the grain business.
W.69

The first wheat to be shipped overseas by the all-Canadian route was loaded that year. Transported to Port Arthur by rail, to Owen Sound by lake boat, and to Montreal once again by rail, it was loaded aboard an ocean steamship bound for Glasgow, Scotland.

By the end of the 1884 shipping season, a large, new elevator with a capacity of 1.2 million bushels had been constructed on the banks of the Kaministiquia River in Fort William, right next to Port Arthur. Before the elevator could be fully operational, a considerable amount of dredging was required at the mouth of the river to accommodate the CPR's two-thousand-metric-ton steamers.

In the spring of 1885, the schooner *Slige* took the first load of seventeen thousand bushels from the new elevator, followed shortly by the *Algoma* taking on a full load. That season alone, the CPR injected more than 1.5 million bushels of wheat into the now fairly sophisticated supply chain, and the numbers continued to grow apace in succeeding years.

But the real value of Canadian wheat depended on the quality of flour that it yielded, and the reputation it built abroad. Fortunately, baking tests conducted in Britain attested to the high quality of grains from the Canadian northwest, and proclaimed them among the best in the world—perfect fodder for the grain marketing machine back home.

A Game of Golf

Appropriately enough, publicity brochures have often referred to the Banff Springs Hotel as a "Scottish baronial castle." The CPR did have a great Scottish tradition, as evidenced by the names of its founders: Stephen, McIntyre, and Angus. Some say that this Scottish heritage is most apparent in the fiscal policies that have brought the railway through good times and bad, but I think that the real legacy of those bewhiskered and kilted clansmen lies elsewhere.

Do you know how many golf courses are within a stone's throw of the CPR main line? As far back as 1922, a company brochure noted that some sixty new courses had sprung into existence that year alone—an impressive statistic, to be sure.

Take a long, deep breath and read what the same 1922 CPR advertisement had to say about the royal and ancient sport: "Golf is fast becoming the national pastime in Canada, and from the Atlantic to the Pacific a traveling devotee of the 'game of games' on the World's Greatest Highway can have his golf—and good golf too—on two hundred and more seaside and inland courses, many of them of championship caliber, quite up to the best standards of Great Britain and the United States, whilst as regards scenic environment, mountain, lake, river and woodland—there is nothing in the world that compares to them." Clearly, we're on to something here.

Now where is the best place to verify the existence of this "link" between railway and fairway. Why "Banff the Beautiful," of course, named after first CPR president George Stephen's ancestral stomping grounds. When the Banff Springs Hotel was

A Game of Golf
On the CPR travel system, you were never very far from a spectacular golf course. A.1118

constructed on the side of Sulphur Mountain in the late 1880s, its location above the confluence of the Bow and Spray Rivers provided a million-dollar view looking east along the Bow River valley. It was in this valley, surrounded on all sides by massive peaks, that a unique nine-hole golf course was created by the CPR in 1911. It was immediately successful and was often cited by the hotel management as a great calling card for the mountain retreat that prided itself on being a sanctuary from the rigours of city life, while sparing no effort to provide for the comfort of its guests.

Within a decade, the administration of the course was transferred to the Parks branch of the Canadian department of the interior. The grounds were opened to the general public and the course expanded to a fully professional eighteen holes. In 1927, Stanley Thompson, the internationally acclaimed golf course architect from Toronto, redesigned the links with an ingenuity that impressed duffers and pros alike.

The scenic beauty of the course, combined with the challenges of mastering holes with names like the "Cauldron," the "Hoodoo," and the "Jinx," guaranteed a virtual parade of celebrity golfers, among them kings, queens, movie stars, and politicians. The alpine course was even the site of a highly unusual film project called, simply, *A Game of Golf*, shot in 1935 and used as a CPR promotional piece. In an era when off-the-wall publicity was the ticket to marketing success, the cast of Tommy Tweed, Jabob Twoyoungman, and Mary Douglas, clothed respectively in a suit of armour, full Indian regalia, and a bathing suit, certainly fit the bill for wackiness.

In the last few years of the 1960s, the golf course was subjected to an interesting experiment. Heating wires were installed a couple of feet below the surface of the practice green as a method of reducing winter kill and potentially extending the annual golf season by six weeks. However, the novel idea was shelved when a number of technical difficulties, and the overall cost of expanding the installation to all of the greens, threatened to blow the course's budget—no good Scotsman would approve of that.

Patron of the Arts

Among the original CPR directors there was more than a passing interest in Canadian fine art. Along with Sir William Van Horne, a connoisseur and an adequate painter himself, Lord Mount Stephen, R. B. Angus, Lord Strathcona, and other railway officers were ardent collectors. This ready market for artwork, coupled with the company's need for advertising material, led to a unique program of art patronage, which lasted throughout the first two decades of the railway's existence.

Patron of the Arts
Lucius O'Brien was among the first to take advantage of the CPR's appetite for high quality Canadian art.
GR.119

Van Horne took a personal interest in the company's brochures and pamphlets and would not consider anything but the highest quality of illustrative material to use in their production. There were also major exhibits to consider, both in North America and in Europe, for which the company required visually dynamic display pieces. To these ends, Van Horne proposed, and the company agreed, to offer artists free transportation to and from the west coast, with a view to obtaining the appropriate glimpses along the line.

Among the first to take advantage of the arrangement were Lucius O'Brien and John Fraser, both of the newly formed Royal Canadian Academy of Arts. O'Brien was provided with a periodical pass, allowing him stopover privileges in areas of interest, and was given introductory letters to the railway's western superintendents, Harry Abbott and Richard Marpole.

Fraser and Van Horne corresponded frequently and, invariably, Fraser looked to his patron for advice and criticism, which Sir William was more than ready to give. On one occasion, Fraser submitted a sketch of Mount Stephen to which Van Horne took exception. The railway boss wrote: "The black and white sketch will hardly answer our purpose, the mountain not being sufficiently imposing. I made last night a rough sketch in lamp black which will illustrate my idea: it is made mostly from memory and I have taken a great deal of license, but I do not think that anyone going to the spot without the picture in hand to compare, will ever accuse us of exaggeration."

Fraser's subsequent sketch embodied the desired proportions and was eventually used in the company's booklet *The New Highway to the East.* Three of Fraser's large oil paintings were purchased by CPR's first president, George Stephen, and were prominently exhibited at the 1886 Colonial Fair, in London.

The patronage program was extended to include such well-known figures as John Hammond, Frederic Marlett Bell-Smith, William Brymner, Marmaduke Mathews, and Thomas Mower Martin, among others. The arrangements with each artist varied and were often ad hoc, as is clear in a letter from Mathews to the company:

> I now propose another visit to the mountains and coast and should like to accompany Mr. T. M. Martin, R. C. A., who tells me he has asked for a pass this year and, if you can grant one to myself, shall feel grateful and would be happy to give you a choice of one out of all the pictures I may send, or bring, back East in consideration of your kind help.
>
> Last time as well as this though, of course, if I should chance on a commission or sale of any particular subject while out, from wealthy tourists, I should like to be able to accept it.

One artist who had Van Horne's favour was the American landscape painter Albert Bierstadt. Not only did he receive the usual pass privileges, but he also had special reservations made for him at the CPR mountain hotels at Banff and Glacier House.

In later years, the company often requested that the artists stop at specific places on the CPR main line to promote unique landmarks and tourist attractions. A number of these views were eventually compiled into collectors' portfolios and marketed as "Glimpses along the Line, Mountain series A, B and C."

Chief Man-of-Many-Sides

In a tribute to John Murray Gibbon, D'Alton C. Coleman, president of the CPR from 1942 to 1947, described him as a very unusual type of publicity man for a large corporation to employ, "being much closer to the shrinking violet type than to the check-suited, cigar-smoking gentleman sometimes associated with publicity." However, the man known to the Stoney Indians as Chief Man-of-Many-Sides was one of diverse talents and accomplishments.

Gibbon was born in Udewelle, Ceylon, in 1875, the son of a tea plantation owner. An imaginative boy, he had ambitions to be a circus ringmaster, a locomotive engineer, a rootin' tootin' cowboy, or the proprietor of a chain of candy stores. These boyhood dreams dissolved, however, in light of his sojourn to Aberdeen, Scotland, to be formally educated. He eventually graduated from Oxford and pursued studies in both France and Germany. After graduation, Gibbon joined the staff of the *Black & White*, a British literary journal of which he became editor.

Gibbon's first association with Canadian Pacific came in 1907, when he was hired as an advertising agent in the company's London office. As the railway was then co-operating with Britain's Liberal government in an ambitious campaign to promote immigration to Canada, it is not surprising that one of Gibbon's first official assignments was to escort a group of British newspaper editors on a Canadian tour of inspection, together with Colonel George Ham, the CPR's Montreal publicity agent.

Ultimately the trip brought him to the realization that the CPR was not merely a railway company, but an organization dedicated to building a nation. With Colonel Ham's retirement in 1913, CPR president Lord Thomas Shaughnessy offered Gibbon the position of general publicity agent in Montreal. Gibbon accepted on the condition he be allowed to come to Canada via Russia and the recently completed Trans-Siberian Railway. Though the request was freely granted, he tried Shaughnessy's patience by dallying in Japan to the point where the exasperated railway boss felt compelled to cable the errant Gibbon, asking him if he ever intended to report for work.

It was in this post of general publicity agent, where he stayed until retirement in 1945, that he realized his ambitions as author, historian, musician, artist, and event organizer extraordinaire. Among his many literary achievements were five novels: *Hearts and Faces, Drums Afar, Eyes of a Gypsy, Pagan Love*, and *The Conquering Hero*. His work entitled *Canadian Folksongs Old and New* began a vogue for ethnic verse which culminated in the CPR sponsorship of several "Folksong and Handicraft Festivals" at its major hotels during the 1920s. French-Canadian music was featured at the Chateau Frontenac in Quebec City, sea music at the Empress in Victoria and the Hotel Vancouver, English music at the Royal York in Toronto, and Scottish music at the Banff Springs Hotel, while the "new Canadians of the West" got their own festivals in Winnipeg, Regina, and Calgary.

In 1938, Gibbon put together a series of ten radio broadcasts known as "Canadian Mosaic" and when the tunes, tales, and melodies were published in book form, he was honoured with the Governor General's Award.

Gibbon's love of the Canadian Rockies inspired him to establish two societies, the Trail Riders of the Canadian Rockies and the Sky Line Trail Hikers of the Canadian Rockies, in 1924 and 1933, respectively. He also founded and served as the first president of the Canadian Authors Association.

Throughout his career, he remained a man of extreme

CHIEF MAN-OF-MANY-SIDES
Gibbon was described as "the most extraordinary example of reticence and male modesty to be found, perhaps, on the North American continent."
NS.22737

shyness, leading one observer to describe him as "the most extraordinary example of reticence and male modesty to be found, perhaps, on the North American continent."

As for his affection for the CPR, Gibbon said, "I have been thrice fortunate in my connection with a great broad-minded corporation which has always been alive to the romantic and delicate side of life." Reflecting this belief, he penned a lengthy romantic history of the CPR and its connections from the Orient to Europe, entitled *Steel of Empire.*

John Murray Gibbon died in 1952, after a short illness, and was buried in a small cemetery in Banff among the mountains he loved so much. At his gravesite, his friends from the Trail Riders installed a bronze plaque designed by local artist Charles A. Beil, a noted sculptor and long-time friend of Gibbon. His name is commemorated in Gibbon Pass, which lies between Shadow Lake and Twin Lakes, below Ball and Storm Mountains in the valley of the Bow River, midway between Banff and Lake Louise. Gibbon had discovered the pass while scouting a route for the Trail Riders.

Celebrating the Canadian Mosaic

Renowned CPR publicist John Murray Gibbon was among the first to characterize Canada as a mosaic of cultures. Unlike the American melting pot, Canada has been less homogeneous and more appreciative of the rich traditions brought to the country from abroad. This diversity was celebrated by Gibbon in a variety of writings, both descriptive and lyrical.

Works such as *Canadian Folksongs Old and New* and *New World Ballads* were compilations of traditional French-Canadian songs, rewritten in English to promote a better understanding of the "French Canadian character." But Gibbon was not one to pursue his interest from one direction only. Much of the material for his books was assembled as a result of his involvement with British folksong revivalists.

Gibbon's position as general publicity agent for the CPR, under the supportive presidency of Edward Beatty, provided him with the ideal opportunity to promote the ethnic traditions of Canadians, while showcasing the company's facilities across the country. During the years 1927 through 1930, he orchestrated a series of folksong and handicraft festivals at the major CPR hotels, offering programs of entertainment tailored to the settings and the origins of the people in the various regions.

The first of these festivals was held at the Chateau Frontenac in Quebec City, in May 1927. Financed by the CPR, it was co-sponsored by the National Museum of Canada, primarily through the loan of a number of Huron Indian artifacts for the handicraft exhibits. Festival goers were treated to an incredible variety of folklore in laments from the fishermen of Gaspé, singing as they mended nets; religious hymns of the Huron from Ancienne Lorette, taught to their forefathers by Jesuit missionaries; songs of the lumberjacks and rivermen that accompanied a hard day's work; and the little ditties of village wives and daughters who sang as they spun cloth and hooked rugs. Special CPR trains brought in loads of visitors, and the main events, staged in the Chateau's ballroom, were standing-room-only, sold-out events.

At the Banff Springs "Highland Gathering and Scottish Music Festival," the traditional athletic games and highland dances were enlivened with the skrill of the bagpipers from each of the several Highland Regiments in Canada. The first year's program included such exotic fare as an open air church service in Sundance Canyon, and a music program that included "two concerts of Scotch music arranged in historical sequence, commencing with thirteenth century ballads in Gaelic and in Lowland Scottish dialect, followed by a group of songs of the period of Mary Queen of Scots."

CELEBRATING THE CANADIAN MOSAIC The festivals celebrated the diverse ethnic traditions of Canadians, while showcasing the CPR's hotel facilities across the country. A.6187

Soon the popularity of these festivals justified other engagements. The "New Canadian Folk Song and Handicraft Festival" was held at the Royal Alexandra Hotel in Winnipeg; the "Great West Canadian Folk Song, Folkdance and Handicrafts Festival" was organized at the Hotel Saskatchewan in Regina one year, and at Calgary's Palliser Hotel another year. The "Sea Music Festival" and the "Old English Yuletide Festival" were staged at the Hotel Vancouver and the Empress Hotel in Victoria, respectively; and the "English Music Festival" was presented at the Royal York in Toronto.

Supplementing the music programs at the gatherings were demonstrations of crafts presented by the Canadian Handicrafts Guild, which Gibbon had helped to establish. Often a selection of Canadian fine art would be assembled to suit the locale or theme, adding to the scope and attraction of the festivals. The National Gallery of Canada was encouraged to participate in this way and loaned paintings from its collections on more than one occasion.

Although the public invariably gave the festivals a warm reception and, indeed, many lost their restraint in calling for encores during the musical performances, the press was sometimes uncertain what to make of the goings-on. Although the general consensus in Quebec was that the festivals were positive vehicles for promoting the tradition of rural society in that province, the western Canadian newspapers showed much more ambivalence in their coverage.

One interesting review in the *Winnipeg Free Press*, describing the 1928 gathering at the Royal Alex, captured the mood: "Blazing in colours, the hotel rotunda presents a motley scene. Garbed in seemingly grotesque clothes of many bright hues, the European mingles with the conservatively-clad westerner. The new Canadian seems perfectly at home in this setting, for it is that of his native land. But the westerner is bewildered, there are many things that arouse his interest."

The onset of the Great Depression of the 1930s, and the resulting halt to immigration, put an end to the extravaganzas at the CPR hotels. Gibbon, however, stayed very much involved with promoting ethnic cultures through his writings, and through the new medium of railway-sponsored radio shows.

Lights, Camera, Action!

The early railway builders were quick to recognize the advertising potential of still photography, but nothing could capture the public imagination like a good flick or motion picture. As early as the turn of the twentieth century, the CPR was exploring this new and fascinating medium as a means of promoting its interests.

In 1900, the Charles Urban Trading Company of England sent photographers Cliff Denham, F. Guy Bradford, and Joe Rosenthal to Canada to shoot a number of films that would eventually be released as the *Living Canada Series.* The purpose of the films was to promote immigration to Canada. Most of the scenes were shot during the summer months, as the railway did not want to strengthen the popular notion that Canada was a land of perpetual ice and snow. The CPR passenger traffic manager Robert Kerr, publicity man George Ham, and colonization agent L. O. Armstrong were assigned by the railway to liaise with the filmmakers and facilitate their travels across the country.

For the North American market, the attraction of such projects soon became apparent as nickelodeons, early five-cent movie houses, proliferated across the continent. Although there was much debate in railway management circles about the value of courting such an audience, by 1909 CPR's president, Sir Thomas Shaughnessy, had approved an expenditure of five thousand dollars for a film encouraging Canadian tourism and emigration from the United States, to be shown at an Alaska-Yukon Exposition in Seattle.

However, the most ambitious attempt to accomplish this dual purpose was

Lights, Camera, Action!
Actress Wanda Winters watches the action unfold in the Bow River valley beneath the Banff Springs Hotel, as cameramen and signalmen coordinate the shooting of a scene from the Famous Players-Lasky film *The Alaskan.*
A.468

made in the summer of 1910, when the Edison Manufacturing Company of New York created thirteen pictures along the CPR right-of-way between Montreal and Victoria, and on the Soo Line, a CPR subsidiary railway in the United States (now known as the St. Paul and Chicago service areas). For a two-month period, the troop of actors and actresses, stage managers, make-up people, and a whole entourage of support staff had hotels, trains, mountain guides, railway crews, and even an ocean-going steamship weighing 9,090 metric tons at their disposal.

Intended for theatres in the United States, Canada, and Great Britain, the films were mini-dramas and mini-comedies. With titles like *An Unselfish Love*, *The Little Station Agent*, and *The Cowpuncher's Glove*, these movies were meant to be entertaining as well as instructive. As a contemporary journal explained in the quaint idiom of the day: "What does Johnny, the conductor from East Harlem, care about the mining industry in southern British Columbia or the ranching business in Alberta? Not a rap. Not a jot, nor a tittle. He and his girl go to see the show for the fun they'll get out of it."

One of the most successful of the early cinema entrepreneurs in Canada was Ernest Ouimet. His Ouimetoscope Theatre opened in Montreal in 1906. Ouimet was employed by the CPR for several years to make promotional films.

In 1924, the great success of such ventures led to the formation of Associated Screen News, in which CPR had a considerable financial interest. Located in Montreal, the company's original intent was to produce motion picture films for Canadian industry. By the end of the decade, not only did it have nearly every large Canadian corporation as a client, but it had also extended its activities to scenic, travel, and adventure films. In an early industry merger, Associated Screen News eventually became part of the Bellevue-Pathé film empire.

The Rocky Mountains, in particular, were the backdrop for Canadian movies during the 1920s, although the Maritimes and the prairies were also popular. Among the notable movies filmed in whole or in part along CPR lines were *Back to God's Country*, *The Sky Pilot*, *Glengarry Schooldays*, *The Man from Glengarry*, *Frivolous Sal*, *Strongheart*, *The Foreigner*, and *The Alaskan*. Much of *The Alaskan*, a Famous Players-Lasky film, was shot in the vicinity of the Banff Springs Hotel and featured movie stars Thomas Meighan and Wanda Winters.

Literally hundreds of films have been produced since then using CPR facilities in one way or another, but two early ones are of special interest, as they portrayed the construction years of the railway with varying degrees of accuracy. In 1935–36, Gaumont-British Films produced *Silent Barriers*, a fairly serious attempt to show the drama of the construction period. But the story took on a distinct Wild West flavour when Twentieth Century Fox shot *Canadian Pacific* in 1949. The film starred Randolph Scott and Jane Wyatt and featured action-packed scenes of hard-driving, gun-toting surveyors, and aggressive Indians with a penchant for shooting flaming arrows at things—perhaps not the way that the CPR would have told the story, but it did capture the attention of thousands of moviegoers.

Making the News

Dynamic and diverse in the early decades of the twentieth century, the CPR was continually making news, whether improving or adding to its many services. But the railway wasn't content to just make the news; it intended to record and distribute it, as well.

It had already been the CPR's policy to import film producers from England and the United States to make pictures of Canadian attractions and distribute them to various theatre chains around the world. These early efforts at promotion were successful on a small scale, but the company was intent on receiving maximum exposure through newsreels and specially produced motion pictures.

In July 1920, the CPR's advertising committee formed Associated Screen News of New York to create and distribute newsreels to the three or four thousand theatres in the United States, Britain, Australia, and South America. A subsidiary company, Associated Screen News of Canada, was established at the same time to focus on production in Canada. The American company never really got off the ground, but the Canadian branch flourished.

It was said the firm began with two men and a camera, and they could not have

Making the News
This grainy view from the CPR's *Staff Bulletin* shows the beginning of operations at Montreal's Associated Screen News. C.174

been better chosen, both having been in the vanguard of the motion picture industry in Canada. Bernard Esterbrook Norrish had been engaged during the First World War to promote Canada's abundant natural resources to audiences in the United States, where support was needed to secure loans for the British government's war efforts. Still photographs and motion pictures were excellent tools of persuasion, and the pitches brought outstanding results.

After the war, Norrish was responsible for the Dominion Government Motion Picture Bureau in Ottawa. It was there that he met John Murray Gibbon, general publicity agent for the CPR. When Norrish left Ottawa to organize and direct Associated Screen News, his colleague John M. Alexander left with him.

Still photographs and motion pictures were excellent tools of persuasion, and the pitches brought outstanding results.

Alexander was a true pioneer in the field. His first job had been as projectionist in Ottawa's Imperial Theatre, when it opened in 1914. Because of his work with Norrish at the Dominion Government Motion Picture Bureau, he came to Associated Screen News as an experienced cameraman. Together the two men built an organization that eventually employed more than two hundred people.

From the beginning, innovation was the watchword. In 1923, the company was the first to use bilingual titles for silent films. Three days after the idea was proposed, French and English movie patrons were sitting side by side at bilingual screenings in Montreal's Capitol Theatre.

The following year, Associated Screen News sent Alexander on cruises to the West Indies and South America aboard the Canadian Pacific liner *Empress of Britain*. Two years later, with a crew of five assistants, he was on the *Empress of France*, operating a photo darkroom for the passengers on CPR's Mediterranean cruise. Both still shots and moving pictures were produced for publicity purposes on these voyages. The passengers on shore leave in various ports of call were recorded participating in such eclectic pursuits as golfing from the top of the Great Pyramid of Cheops, exploring the recently excavated Roman city at Pompeii, or hiking along the Great Wall of China.

In 1926, a large motion picture laboratory was erected in Montreal at a cost of $150,000. The increasing demand for film, previously imported from the United States, encouraged the Kodak Company to begin manufacturing it in Canada.

During the 1930s, an agreement was signed with Bell and Howell of Chicago, Illinois, for the exclusive Canadian distribution of their photographic products. Arrangements were also made with the J. Arthur Rank organization and Odeon Theatres to share in the distribution of Gaumont-British Instructional Films in Canada. In 1935, Associated Screen News was approached by C. F. Notman, president and managing director of William Notman & Son Ltd., to take control of the family photographic business. As a result, some very valuable resources, including Notman negatives dating back to 1856, were brought under the company's wing. A modern fireproof building was erected by Associated Screen News on Sherbrooke Street in Montreal to house the collection.

Under an agreement with the CPR hotel department, amateur photo finishing services were set up at the Banff Springs Hotel and Chateau Lake Louise, in

Alberta, and at the Empress Hotel, in Victoria, British Columbia. On display in the lobbies were colour photographs and slides of attractions in the vicinity of each hotel. Sixteen-millimetre film shows were organized in the evenings.

Associated Screen News produced educational and promotional films for a number of clients, including the Canadian government, the governments of Quebec, Ontario, Nova Scotia, and New Brunswick, Massey-Harris, the Bell Telephone Company of Canada, and of course, the CPR. Some of these films were mini-dramas, whereas others were simply cinematographic tours through factories or other industrial facilities.

One-reel theatrical films known as the *Canadian Cameo Series*, dealing with various aspects of life in Canada, were Associated Screen News standards. These entertaining films gradually received broader and broader distribution, until they were appearing on movie screens worldwide. The company's feature film, *Kingdom for a Horse*, was showing in Paris when Hitler's troops made their triumphal march into the city. Production of the series was suspended for the remainder of the war, but was quickly revived at the end of the hostilities. A new release was introduced every six weeks. Subjects varied from the stylish *Ornamental Swimming* to the more sophisticated *Music from the Stars*, and the folksy story of an Indian and his beaver friend, *Grey Owl's Little Brother*.

The company's feature film, Kingdom for a Horse, was showing in Paris when Hitler's troops made their triumphal march into the city.

In 1954, CPR sold its controlling interest in Associated Screen News to a Toronto group headed by Paul Nathanson, vice-president of Empire-Universal Films, Ltd. Associated Screen News was then absorbed by the Bellevue-Pathé film organization and ceased to exist as a separate entity.

Something in the Air

In an age of instant satellite communications and personal computers, it is hard to imagine a time when radio broadcasting was the most exciting and innovative form of home entertainment. Yet when the CPR became active in the field in the early 1930s, this was very much the case.

The broadcasting activities of the railway were a natural development of the commercial telegraph system already operated across Canada by the CPR. In the United States, such transmissions could be made over the telephone circuits of the American Telephone & Telegraph Company's wires, but in Canada, the vast distances, combined with a sparse population, compelled telephone companies north of the border to lease the railway's lines. In light of this, more than a million dollars was expended by the CPR on the installation of a new "carrier current" system, capable of transmitting ninety-six messages simultaneously over a single pair of wires.

Originally the CPR sponsored Friday evening radio hours, featuring the dinner orchestra from Toronto's Royal York Hotel, alternating with folk songs or light opera. In early 1930, these programs were so successful that by mid-year they were being broadcast across Canada in all the major cities from Quebec to Vancouver. So highly were they regarded that they were the first programs originating outside the United States to be accepted by Canada's National Broadcasting Company.

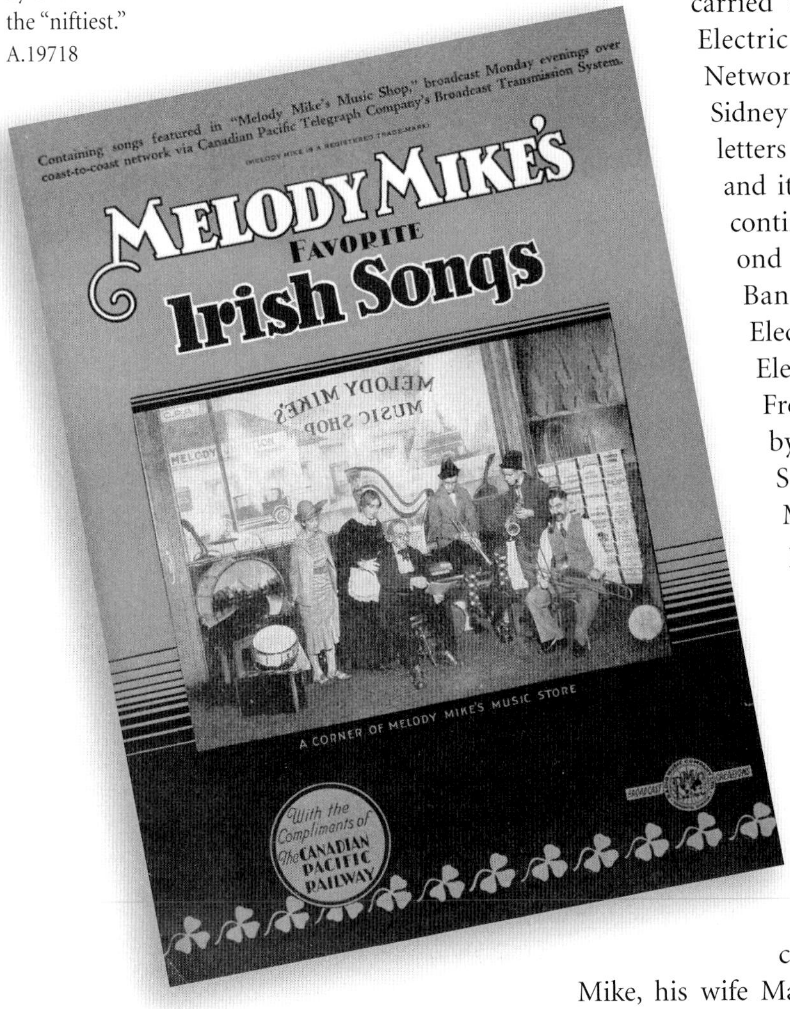

SOMETHING IN THE AIR The radio show with Mike, Mary, and Lack-a-day Liz was deemed by one listener to be the "niftiest." A.19718

By June 1930, the Royal York had established its own radio station on the top floor of its new extension, and the studios were reputed to be among the finest on the continent. The design of the systems was carried out and installed by the Northern Electric Company Limited (now Nortel Networks), and the project engineer was Sidney T. Fisher of Montreal. The station call letters were, appropriately enough, CPRY, and its slogan, "Cheerful and good music," continued to govern the programs. A second set of studios was established at the Banff Springs Hotel, where Northern Electric supplied and installed a Western Electric type 8-B speech input system. From these studios, programs sponsored by CPR were expanded to include Sunday afternoon broadcasts by the Musical Cruisaders, aboard the company's *Empress of Australia* round-the-world cruise, illustrating with song and music the life on board a cruise ship and in the various ports of call.

However, by far the most popular show was Monday night's *Melody Mike's Music Shop*. The shop was located at an imaginary railway divisional point called Melody Junction and was run by the proprietor, Melody Mike. It was the centre of numerous adventures in which Mike, his wife Mary, and their sons Ted and Larry all played roles, along with Scotty Macgregor, an argumentative but friendly neighbour, and Lack-a-day Liz, the most eccentic of the characters. The theme song, featuring locomotive bells and whistles, was called "The Train," and was especially popular with children.

"I think your Monday evening broadcast of the doings of *Melody Mike's Music Shop* is just the niftiest half-hour program we receive," bubbled one listener. Another claimed, "There may be a more loveable or whimsical group of entertainers on the air than Melody Mike's, on yon point I'll no argy wi' ye, but if there is, I have yet to hear it." Hundreds of such kudos were received each week after a broadcast; however, regrettably, the CPR did not stay in the field of broadcasting for long.

When the Canadian government decided to emulate the British Broadcasting Company with the formation of the Canadian Broadcasting Company, in 1936, CPR president Sir Edward Beatty wished to avoid any political complications and decided to get out of broadcasting altogether. The company's telegraph lines continued to be used for radio transmission, and the CPR sponsored a half-hour program of folk music called *Canadian Mosaic*, under the direction of its publicity agent, John Murray Gibbon. Although the program was an effective advertising medium, the company's commitment to broadcasting had ended, a mere six years after it had gained pre-eminence in the field.

Including the Kitchen Sink

For the CPR, the early 1970s was the end of an era. The last CPR passenger trains, including the near legendary *Canadian*, were being phased out; the *Empress of Canada II* was sailing off to bluer seas in the Carribean with the Carnival Cruise Line; and the once elegant Royal Alexandra Hotel, in Winnipeg, was closing, a somewhat seedy ghost of its former self.

That left a heck of a lot of stuff lying around branded with the CPR initials—functional, dirty, exotic, mundane, nostalgic, pedestrian, educational, useless, artistic, and silly stuff. Lamps, lanterns, buttons, badges, timetables, silverware, furniture, china, posters, pamphlets, signs, blankets, uniforms—you name it, it was there. It seemed like such a waste to let all that history be carted away, scrap prices being what they were in the 1970s.

It was then that some sage CPR functionary, whose name has since faded into obscurity, had a brilliant epiphany while standing waist deep in a pile of old sleeping car berth curtains. The travelling public, to a lesser extent, and the North American rail fan population, to a greater extent, had been walking off with this stuff for years, whenever and wherever the opportunity presented itself. Now here was a golden opportunity to give everybody a chance to acquire a bit of CPR's past, at little more than scrap value, and with proof of ownership. This stuff was collectible!

So the great Canadian Pacific Collector's Sales program was born, under the auspices of CPR historian and archivist Omer Lavallée and the railway's department of public relations and advertising. All that was needed was a catchy name, and it would be open for business. A contest was clearly in order.

Through the company newspaper, all Canadian Pacific employees were invited

INCLUDING THE KITCHEN SINK
Two summer employees, a moonlighting Montreal radio announcer, and a pair of hired models contribute to the campy launch of *CP Bygones*.
72-170-20

to submit their suggestions, keeping in mind that this would be a public venture and should, therefore, be given a name worthy of its sponsor. In poured the responses: *CP Nostalgia, CP Articles, CP Vanishing Era, CP Golden Years, CP Railtiques, CP Memoirs, CP Hasbeens.* Clearly people were being influenced by the 1970s corporate names for CPR's various new operating arms: CP Rail, CP Ships, CP Hotels, and so on. But somehow they were missing the mark.

Loco-notions, Leaves from the Railroad Tree, La Belle Epoque. A little better perhaps, but still not on the money. *All the Things I Would Like to Have for Free,* ventured one obvious railway buff, reminding us of the missing silverware. *CP Antiques and Junque, CP memo-rail-bilia, Seepy Sales,* suggested three fanciers of alternative spelling. *Casey's Caboose, Collectors' Paradise, Pioneer Junction, Antiquity Alley, The Passing Past.*

How about *Working Tools of the Railroad?* Nah, too long. *CP Rail McCoys?* Too Corny. *CP Pickings?* Too gross, somehow. *The Van Horne of Plenty?* Sir William began to spin in his grave. *CP Bygones?* (long pause) Hey, now that wasn't half bad, even if some other inspired soul had submitted *Bygone Hall* to the nomenclature sweepstakes. Prizes would be awarded to both contestants; anything to stop the flow of suggestions. *CP Collector's Progress, Heritage Canadian Pacific, Pioneer Railroad Relics, Antique Pacific, CP Adventure, Canadian Past Remembered, CPR Trading Post*—give me a break!

Yes, now we had the necessary ingredients: inventory, business plan, and catchy name. All we had to do was let bygones be *Bygones.*

Further Reading

Berton, Pierre. *The National Dream: The Great Railway 1871–1881.* Toronto, ON: McClelland and Stewart, 1983.

Berton, Pierre. *The Last Spike: The Great Railway 1871–1881.* Toronto, ON: McClelland and Stewart, 1983.

Choko, Marc, and Jones, David. *Canadian Pacific Posters: 1883–1963.* Montreal, PQ: Meridien Press, 1995.

Cruise, David, and Griffiths, Alison. *Lords of the Line.* Markham, ON: Penguin Books, 1988.

Gibbon, John Murray. *Steel of Empire: The Romantic History of the Canadian Pacific Railway, the Northwest Passage of Today.* London, Eng.: Rich & Cowan, 1935.

Ham, George H. *Reminiscences of a Raconteur.* Toronto, ON: The Musson Book Co., 1921.

Hart, E. J. *The Selling of Canada: The CPR and the Beginnings of Canadian Tourism.* Banff, AB: Altitude Publishing, 1983.

Keith, Ronald A. *Bush Pilot with a Briefcase: The Happy-go-lucky Story of Grant McConachie.* Don Mills, ON: Paper Jacks, 1972.

Lamb, W. Kaye. *History of the Canadian Pacific Railway.* New York, NY: MacMillan, 1977.

Lavallée, Omer. *Van Horne's Road: An Illustrated Account of the Construction and First Years of Operation of the Canadian Pacific Transcontinental Railway.* Toronto, ON: A Railfare Book, 1981.

McKee, Bill, and Klassen, Georgeen. *Trail of Iron: The CPR and the Birth of the West, 1880–1930.* Vancouver, BC: Douglas & McIntyre, 1983.

Miller-Barstow, D. H. *Beatty of the CPR: A Biography.* Toronto, ON: McClelland and Stewart, 1951.

Musk, George. *Canadian Pacific: The Story of the Famous Shipping Line.* London, Eng.: David & Charles, 1981.

Smith, Donald B. *Chief Buffalo Child Long Lance: The Glorious Imposter.* Red Deer, AB: Red Deer Press, 1999.

Index

Note: Illustrations are indicated by **bold** *type.*

Author Bio

David Laurence Jones is manager of internal communications at Canadian Pacific Railway. A history graduate from Concordia University, he worked for fourteen years in the railway's corporate archives, researching and collecting stories and anecdotes about the CPR's rich heritage. He has contributed many historical writings to company publications and is co-author of *Canadian Pacific Posters: 1883–1963*. He lives in Calgary with his wife and daughter and continues to delve into the CPR's colourful past.